A NEW HOLIDAY

TRAVEL GUIDE

THE CARIBBEAN
and the
BAHAMAS

THE

CAR

and th

The New Holiday Guide to

...BBEAN

...BAHAMAS

...e New Holiday Travel Guide Series

... Evans and Company   New York

Library of Congress Cataloging-in-Publication Data

The New Holiday guide to the Caribbean and the Bahamas.

 Rev. ed. of: The Holiday guide to the Caribbean and
the Bahamas. Rev. ed. c1976.
 Includes index.
 1. West Indians—Description and travel—1981- —
Guide-books. I. Holiday (Philadelphia, Pa.) II. Holiday
guide to the Caribbean and the Bahamas. III. Title:
Caribbean and the Bahamas.
F1609.N49   1988   917.29′0452   87–5422

ISBN 0-87131-513-0

ISBN 0-87131-513-0
Manufactured in the United States of America
1 2 4 6 8 9 7 5 3
Revised First Edition

General Editor: Theodore Fischer

M. Evans and Company, Inc.
216 East 49 Street
New York, New York 10017

CONTENTS

CHAPTER

1 THIS IS THE CARIBBEAN 7

Seven thousand islands peopled by races from every part of the globe. The world's most beautiful beaches—most luxurious resort hotels—and some of the most colorful of island nations.

2 THE CARIBBEAN PAST AND PRESENT 13

The background. Islands Columbus found and Spain exploited. The pirate wars. Practical information on where to go, climate and clothing, how to get there, money, tipping, food, shopping, and special events.

3 THE ISLANDS 33

History, description, and practical information on hotels, restaurants, sports, and shopping facilities on 50 of the major islands of the Caribbean.

THE BAHAMA ISLANDS 33
HAITI 43
PUERTO RICO 53
THE VIRGIN ISLANDS 66
ST. KITTS, NEVIS, ANGUILLA 83
THE FRENCH WEST INDIES 88
ANTIGUA 98
BRITISH WINDWARDS 103
BARBADOS .114
TRINIDAD AND TOBAGO 120
THE NETHERLANDS ANTILLES 129
JAMAICA 143
CAYMAN ISLANDS 151
SAN ANDRES 153

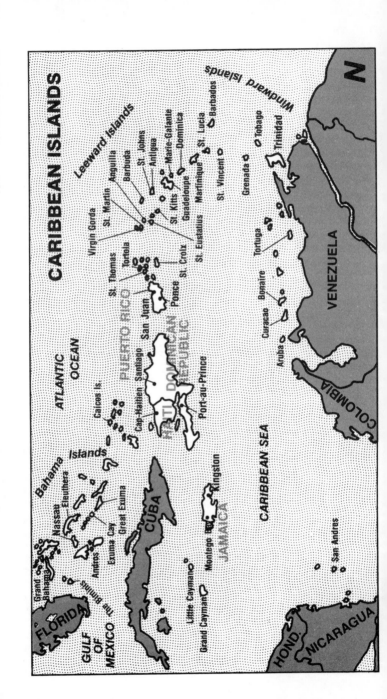

CHAPTER 1

THIS IS THE CARIBBEAN

". . . the best and most fertile and temperate and level and goodly land that there is in the world . . . the most beautiful thing that I have seen, nor can I tire my eyes looking at such verdure . . ."

Is this the prattle of a schoolgirl on her first trip away from home? Sounds like it—but it isn't. It is the entry made in the log of Cristoforo Colombo upon making a landfall in the Caribbean. And Columbus was no novice at travel. He had sailed the length of the Mediterranean to Asia Minor, visited the Gold Coast of Africa, England, and Scotland. As for islands, he was an authority—he knew the islands of the Aegean, Madeira, Cape Verde, the Canary Islands, the Azores. He had been north to the cold rocks off Britain, to the Faroes, and perhaps even to Iceland. But the Caribbeans were almost more than the admiral could find words to describe. "There came so fair and sweet a smell of flowers or trees from the land that it was the sweetest thing in the world."

That was nearly 500 years ago, and ever since then visitors have been echoing Columbus' delight. The islands of the Caribbean have been called many things—The Golden Chain, Islands in the Sun, Paradise Islands, The Golden Caribbees—and always the names run from one extravagance to another.

Until they have seen it, few people realize the size and extent of the Caribbean. If you were to follow the curve of the island chain from Florida to its tip just off Venezuela, you would have traveled nearly 2,500 miles.

The airline distance from Miami to Trinidad, the southernmost island, is almost 1,800 miles. If you were to fly that far west or north of

Aruba Caribbean Hotel in the Netherlands Antilles

Miami, you would be either in El Paso or in Caribou, Maine. Nobody knows how many islands there actually are in this vast area equal to two-thirds of continental United States. One estimate says 7,000—not counting the rocks. Jamaica, Haiti, and Puerto Rico alone have a total population of 11.5 million, nearly as many people as the six New England states combined.

Like islands everywhere, each of these is separate, and each in its own individual way has absorbed and blended the heritage which came with its own masters and slaves, traders and conquerors. Alike only in that they are all dappled with a melange of races, customs, and colors, the islands offer the visitor an infinitely varied experience. You will find staid chips off the Old World block, lively offshoots of the African jungle, physical traces of the aboriginal Indian, here and there exotic touches from Asia. Wherever you go, you will see these diverse elements bubbling up in new forms that often exhibit remarkable social maturity, and sometimes strange and dangerous perversity. You will see every skin tone—gradations of red, yellow, white, brown, and black. And you will discover that there is something new here, something singularly West Indian—a people whose ancestors were Arawak and Carib Indians, willing and unwilling immigrants from Holland, Spain, England, Denmark, France, Africa, and Asia, a people whose future is in an unpredictable Caribbean amalgam.

Your first problem is one of choice, and among these thousands of islands it is not an easy one. Only sixty miles off Palm Beach lie the upper Bahamas, northernmost of a group of 700 islands and more than 2,000 cays scattered over 70,000 square miles of Atlantic. Although they are not actually in the Caribbean chain, they appear on the same charts (entitled "West Indies"), share many of the same characteristics, and are frequently considered, as they are here, to be the nearest of the escapist islands. Cutting across their southern flank are the Greater Antilles—Cuba, which is beginning again to attract North American tourism; Jamaica, another hundred miles south toward the center of the Caribbean; Hispaniola, second in size, divided between Haiti and the Dominican Republic; and Puerto Rico, commonwealth outpost of the United States. Just east of Puerto Rico are the Virgin Islands and the beginning of the great southern curve of the Lesser Antilles, sweeping almost to the coast of South America and dividing the Caribbean Sea from the open Atlantic. Here are more hundreds of islands—some famous for years for their resort facilities, some only now beginning to develop accommodations for tourists, still others so small and remote that they remain undiscovered retreats for escapists. To many people these are the pearls of the West Indies—Anguilla, St. Maarten, Saba, St. Kitts, Nevis, Antigua, and Guadeloupe among the Leewards; and among the Windwards Dominica, Martinique, St. Lucia, St. Vincent, Barbados, the Grenadines, and Grenada. Still closer to the shoulder of South America are Tobago and Trinidad, and 400 miles to the west the enormous chain ends with the Dutch islands of Bonaire, Curaçao, and recently-independent Aruba.

Startlingly different in accent, attitude, and manner, the islands are all cut from the same basic pattern. All of them, geologists tell us, were once part of an unbroken bridge between North and South America. Though a few are low-lying coral formations that grew from the shallow underwater shelf around them, most are volcanic peaks of a great submarine mountain range. The climate ranges from subtropical to tropical, with temperature varying predictably between 70° and 90°F. Days and nights are of almost equal length, and spectacular sunsets are followed by sudden, short twilights that deepen quickly to starlit blue. All the islands are air-conditioned by the trade winds, those steady breezes out of the northeast which provide motor power for the islands' sailing traders.

Since there is little temperature variation, the Caribbean year traditionally has been separated not into winter and summer, but into the dry and the rainy seasons. The division is real but misleading. Rains do come between May and October; but they are not the continuous deluge people who live in the temperate zone associate with the word. Rarely do these trade-wind islands have a gray day. Showers bring water by the bucketfuls, but when they stop—which they do as suddenly as they come—they leave a trail of spectacular rainbows, and the islands sparkle with brilliant washed color that inspires photographers and artists alike.

In winter, the islands become a busy haven for the millions who flee the northern cold. Hotels and guest houses are thronged, and everywhere efforts are made to please and entertain the visitors. In summer it is quieter and the climate—thanks to the trade winds—is no less temperate, the beaches are no less inviting for having fewer people on them. Summer is the favorite time for the locals, a time when all the islands bloom and the trees are heavy with flowers and fruit. In May the mangoes ripen; June brings the avocados; July and August is the time for those essential ingredients of Planters' Punch: limes and sweet lemons. The air in spring is sweet with the heady scent of mimosa. The flamboyant trees, crimson with blossoms, arch the country roads.

Flowering shrubs cover the hills and spill down onto the beaches to mix with the bright patterns of umbrellas and cabanas. The air is warm, the breeze gentle. And always in the background is the lulling sound of the breakers washing in on the windward side of the islands.

Perhaps the timeless rhythm of the waves accounts for the relaxed pace of life on the islands. Perhaps it is only the sun, or the luxuriousness of nature. Whatever the reason, it is difficult to hurry—to rush is nearly impossible. It's the *mañana* mood of the Spaniards of the Western Hemisphere; but the leisurely feeling is a part of all the islands—Spanish, French, Dutch, British, or American. The European languages are spoken more slowly here, the harsh sounds are smoothed out, and the West Indian inflection is less an accent than a musical lilt.

Just as it has made its inherited language somehow its own, so each island, accepting its particular Old World heritage, has quietly translated it into something new, something individual. The pinnacled tower of a Gothic cathedral rises majestically from a grove of mango trees. Gabled Dutch houses maintain their solemn old stateliness—but painted in pastel hues that would dumbfound Amsterdam. Occasionally a mongoose makes a dash across the cricket pitch—and the West Indians, it happens, are among the best cricketers in the British Commonwealth. Other islands enjoy some of the finest baseball in the world.

In this curious and delightful commingling of old and new cultures, you'll come upon apparently unexplainable oddities: sunbonnets of a style that was once familiar on the California Trail are worn by the women of St. Barts; fishermen's hats in Iles des Saintes are identical to those worn by Siamese fishermen; the Caribbean jig will remind you immediately of an acrobatic Russian dance; the Trinidad calypso songs are suggestive of the calls of the old town crier, but here they are set to eastern music with an African rhythm. And how can you account for the illiterate cane cutter who, without knowing its meaning or source, chants *Horatio at the Bridge?*

The overtone of all the islands is African. You feel it in the warmth of the people, their easy laughter, their religion, and their art. It is most evident and wonderful in their music and dance—the backbreaking limbo dance of Trinidad, now spread to all the islands; Jamaica's magnetic reggae beat; the Barbadian "British Quadrille" with its slightly wicked wiggle. Even the swaying beguine of Martinique began in the Congo.

The past lies all about you in layers of history and legend. This was Columbus' western landfall, and almost every island lays claim to at least one visit by the great mariner. Past these islands sailed Spanish galleons carrying the fabulous gold of the Western World—and here many of them ended their voyages, for this was also the Spanish Main where Drake and Hawkins won knighthood in piratical forays. From the hidden coves of these islands Morgan and Kidd and Edward Teach

Caribbean pattern: rugged hills, lush valleys and the sea at St. Kitts

(Blackbeard) descended on their prey. And somewhere on the bottom of the Caribbean lie the skeletons of hundreds of pirate ships, with the greatest and bloodiest booty of all time.

Small wonder that these islands were the locale of the most rousing adventure tales of the past few centuries. The doughty Captain Bligh was in the Pacific to load breadfruit trees for St. Vincent Island when he was set down in an open boat by his mutinous crew—and then navigated almost 4,000 miles of sea to survival and revenge. Robinson Crusoe's adventures, it has often been said, occurred on Tobago. Norman Island in the British Virgins is said to have been the inspiration for Stevenson's *Treasure Island*—and there are those who still think that the treasure-trove is buried there.

Pirate gold is elusive, but there is still booty for the traveler, for today the Caribbean is a shopper's paradise. Most of the islands have free or nearly free ports where products from all over the world are sold at prices often below those of the countries where they are made. The loot that is carried off each year by American visitors would make Blackbeard blanch.

The islands have not forgotten their colonial past, but they are firmly grounded in the 1980's. There are voodoo drums and Rastafarian rhythms, French haute cuisine and down-home creole cooking, British tea shops and gigantic shopping malls. Along the beaches there are mammoth resorts where rooms, meals, water sports, even drinks and cigarettes are all part of the package so you don't have to spend another dime after you arrive; there are also tiny cottages on miles of empty shore where the only sounds are the cries of the gulls and the lapping of the turquoise sea.

Columbus set out to find the East Indies. Instead he discovered the Islands of the Sun. They were something of a disappointment to him —no spices, no silks, no jewels. But everything that he hoped for is there now. The thousands of islands that dot the Caribbean are in themselves jewels, each priceless in its own way, each part of a strand whose fascination is endless.

CHAPTER 2

THE CARIBBEAN, PAST AND PRESENT

The Caribbean Islands may not be remote, but they *are* different from anything that you have known in the United States or Canada. Each in its own way reflects its heritage—French, Spanish, British, Dutch —and out of its past each has created its own personality. There is no need for you to make a study of the area before you go there, but some understanding of what the islands were and what they are today will make your trip more meaningful.

CARIBBEAN PAST

It has been said that the past never dies. In the Caribbean it flourishes. Wherever you go, you will see the fruits of nearly five hundred years of history. Not that you will see many monuments of the past: there are only a few moldering remains of the first centuries. But in the people themselves—in their beliefs, customs, language, and attitudes—history has contrived a blend of cultures as complex and colorful as anything the world has ever known.

The islands that Columbus discovered on that fortunate landfall in 1492 were occupied. When he knelt to give thanks for his deliverance and took possession of San Salvador in the Bahamas in the name of the Spanish sovereigns, he was surrounded by natives whom he described as "gentle, peaceful people of great simplicity." They offered the discoverers gifts of "parrots and cotton thread in skeins and darts and many other things" and "remained so much our friends that it was a marvel." Columbus gave them glass beads and little bells, and noted prophetically that first day, "They ought to be good servants and of good skill . . ."

A schooner approaches Carriacou in the British Windwards

They were Arawaks, these people Columbus found on the outer islands of the Bahamas (now called the Out Islands), but the Great Mariner had set out for the East Indies, and he was not a man to change his mind easily. He called them Indians. A peaceful people, pottery makers and agriculturists, they had been driven out of the major islands by a larger and fiercer tribe, the Caribs. Far less tractable than the Arawaks and often cannibalistic, the Caribs were not unskilled. Their canoes, some large enough to carry a hundred or more people, easily outdistanced Columbus' sailing ships. They cultivated yams and other food plants and knew the uses of tobacco. And they had invented the hammock, a device which Columbus immediately installed in his own ships and which became standard equipment in sailing craft all over the world.

On that first voyage Columbus set the pattern that was to determine the fate not only of the 2,000,000 or more natives of the islands, but also of the great Aztec civilization of Mexico and the Inca empire in Peru. Guided by Indians he had kidnapped, the admiral set out searching through the islands for Cathay and Japan and for the gold and jewels and spices he knew were near at hand. On January 14, 1493, Columbus sailed for home, leaving the 30-man crew of his wrecked flagship in the hastily built settlement called La Navidad in Hispaniola —the first in the New World.

Though he returned with scant evidence of the riches which he said existed in the islands, the story of his discovery of the westward route to the Indies was enough to stir the hopes and avarice of the Spanish rulers. Within a few months of his return Columbus sailed westward again, this time as Admiral of the Ocean Sea, with a fleet of 17 ships and a company of more than 1,200 men—seamen, soldiers, scholars, ecclesiastics, and gentlemen adventurers—all determined to gather the golden harvest that awaited them. But La Navidad had disappeared, and in the new colony of Isabela sickness, death, dissension, and the enmity of the mistreated natives soon destroyed the hopes of the explorers. Twelve ships returned to Spain with disheartening news, and, though Columbus continued his search for a full six months, he too was at last forced to set sail for home with empty holds. In 1498, meagerly outfitted with three ships, he was permitted to try again. On this voyage he finally reached the mainland of South America, but the gold and jewels which would have justified his voyages still eluded him. At Isabela murder, mutiny, and the slaughter of the natives had already begun, and as Governor, Columbus was held responsible for the growing disaster. From the third voyage Columbus returned to Spain in chains. Nevertheless, in 1502 he was given his fourth and final opportunity to bring back the gold and pearls which for 10 years he had been promising. His last voyage was his most disappointing and disastrous. He found no treasure, lost his ships, was marooned and rescued, and, two years after he had sailed, limped home with a few of his men

Simson Bay Lagoon, St. Maarten, with its incredible beaches.

in a leaky rented vessel. In 1506 he died, a scorned old man who had become a bore to the court with his endless petitions demanding titles, rights, and privileges.

Others found the treasure that Columbus had vainly pursued. The Arawaks and the Caribs were quickly reduced to slavery and forced to work the few mines and streams that produced gold. Hundreds of thousands were slaughtered within a few years, and before the end of the 16th century the whole population of the islands—two million or more people—had been destroyed. But the *conquistadores* who followed Columbus filled the coffers of Spain. In the early years of the 16th century Cortés conquered Mexico and Pizarro took Peru. In one of the most brutal conquests of history, Aztecs and Incas were stripped of untold treasure, and through the Caribbean sailed galleon after galleon loaded with gold and jewels in quantities the world had never dreamed of.

Nor was gold the only wealth that flowed from the West Indies. When the Spanish discovered that the sugar cane of the Canary Islands would grow here, vast plantations were slashed out of the forests. Indian slaves were put into the fields, and, when they died of hardship, tougher and more tractable slaves were imported from Africa. By the middle of the 16th century, the Caribbean and the Spanish Main had become the world's richest possessions.

THE BUCCANEERS

The wealth of the Caribbean could not be concealed, nor, as it turned out, defended. The first blows came from privateers sailing in the service of Elizabeth, Protestant Queen of England. John Hawkins began his freebooting career in the 1560's with raids along the African coast to capture slaves which he sold in the West Indies and along the Spanish Main in defiance of the Spaniards, who had restricted the traffic to their own traders. Having accumulated a fortune in the slave trade and in attacks against Portuguese and Spanish shipping, Hawkins entered Parliament, became comptroller of the navy, and was knighted for his part in the destruction of the Spanish Armada in 1588. A young kinsman who had sailed with Hawkins, Francis Drake, improved on his instruction. For 25 years he harried the Spanish in daring raids on their cities and ships all over the world. He sacked settlements throughout the Caribbean, captured three mule trains on the Isthmus loaded with 30 tons of plundered Aztec silver; from one round-the-world foray in the *Golden Hind* he returned to England with treasure said to be valued at 2,500,000 pounds. Knighted by Elizabeth, he sailed into the harbor of Cadiz with 30 ships and destroyed a fleet that the Spanish had assembled there. He later served as vice-admiral in the battle that saw the destruction of the Spanish Armada, but died in the Caribbean in 1596 after a defeat by Spanish forces.

From privateering to piracy was an easy step, and during the late 17th and 18th centuries the Caribbean Islands sheltered as bloodthirsty a group of cutthroats as was ever assembled. Not only were they able to prey on the rich trade of the West Indies, but the islands provided a ready market for their plunder and a maze of hidden coves where they could lay in supplies and refurbish their prizes. In time they banded together and took over the government of whole islands— Tortuga (Ile de la Tortue, off northern Haiti), a notorious rendezvous; New Providence, in the Bahamas; Port Royal, in Jamaica, which was called the wickedest city in the world. Henry Morgan, one of the most brutal of all the corsairs, commanded the pirates of Port Royal. After he had sacked a dozen cities along the Cuban and American coasts and in Panama, he was accused of dividing the spoils unfairly and returned to England charged with piracy. He was convicted and sentenced—and then knighted and sent back to Jamaica as lieutenant governor where, rich and pious, he lived out his life.

Though some of the buccaneers flew the flags of their countries, many of them openly sailed under the skull and bones, and attacked wherever there was promise of ransom or booty. All through the 18th century the Caribbean continued to be the stronghold of such infamous characters as Edward Teach, called Blackbeard, Charles Gibbs, Edward Mansfield, Jacques Nau, Barataris, Jean Lafitte, Esnambuc, Roissey, and many others, equally bloody if less famous, including the lady pirate, Anne Bonny. For more than a century they dominated the history of the Caribbean.

SUGAR AND SLAVES

Spain had within a few years recklessly plundered the New World of the treasure accumulated over centuries. But sugar—the "white gold" of the West Indies—rum, coffee, and cocoa were still the source of enormous and increasing wealth in the Caribbean. Exhausted by the years spent in the conquest of her colonies, her navy destroyed by the British and her merchant fleet under the constant harassment of pirates and privateers, Spain was unable to maintain her possessions in the Caribbean. The plantation system was utterly dependent on a continuing supply of slaves, and the British and Dutch had already taken over the hideous and profitable African trade. Soon the slavers were taking much of the rum and sugar and coffee produced in the islands in exchange for the 50,000 or 75,000 slaves annually imported from Africa. French, Dutch, and English settlers began to spread out from the islands they had occupied and to buy up the plantations that the Spanish—who had never been enthusiastic colonists—were unwilling or unable to operate successfully. Spain's hold on the West Indies was further weakened by the 17th-century wars and territorial disputes of Europe and, in time, England, France, Holland, and Denmark were all able to establish claims to island possessions in the Caribbean.

The sugar-and-rum prosperity of the West Indies reached its height during the 18th century. Supported by the prodigious profits created by a vast slave population, the landowners and the ruling elite lived in lavish splendor unknown elsewhere in the New World. Famous architects were imported to design the Great Houses that were built on the plantations. It is said that in the days when fortunes were made annually on the sugar crop, golden dinnerware was commonplace. Leading dancers and opera singers were paid handsomely to make the trip to the Caribbean for a single night's performance at the home of a planter. The courts of France and Britain buzzed with gossip and excitement when fabulously wealthy Creole planters arrived in Europe for the "season" with their mistresses and their retinue of slaves. A Creole beauty from Martinique, born Marie Joséphine Rose Tascher de la Pagerie, became Josephine, Empress of France.

THE SLAVE REVOLTS

Beneath the thin veneer of French elegance in Haiti there had long been a seething discontent. Sparked perhaps by the revolutions in France and in the American colonies, the resentment of Creoles, freed Negroes, and Negro slaves flared into revolt at the end of the 18th century. Under the leadership of the remarkable Toussaint L'Ouverture and Jacques Dessalines the armies of Napoleon were defeated, and in 1804 Haiti proclaimed its independence, becoming the world's first black republic. In 1821 Santo Domingo overthrew its Spanish government, and shortly thereafter Spain lost all her holdings in South America when no less than five independent countries arose at the call of Simón Bolivar, the Liberator.

By the middle of the 19th century slavery had been forever abolished in the Caribbean, and the old plantation system passed into history. The wealthy planters returned to Europe, abandoning the plantations and letting the sugar mills fall into ruin. The production of beet sugar increased elsewhere in the world; rum ceased to be the popular drink that it once had been. Without the means or the knowledge to revise the dying sugar economy, many of the islands sank slowly into bankruptcy.

The once-great empire of Spain had been reduced to Cuba and Puerto Rico, and in 1898 these too were lost in the Spanish-American War. Cuba was given its independence and Puerto Rico was ceded to the United States. At the beginning of the 20th century, in addition to Cuba, Haiti and Santo Domingo were independent. The French held seven islands, the Dutch six, the Danish three, and Great Britain all the rest.

Though their basic economy improved slowly during the first decades of this century, it was not until after World War II that the Caribbean islands took a decisive, united forward step. That they have been able to surge ahead so rapidly since then is largely the result of two related factors: the phenomenal growth of plane travel, and the far-reaching decision of all the islands to support the Caribbean Tourist Association as a joint venture in the promotion of their greatest natural resources—climate and location. Tourism has already become the largest single industry in some of the islands and its importance is increasing rapidly in the others.

Within the last 20 years the Caribbean area has deservedly become one of the most popular of American playgrounds. In their romantic past and colorful present, in the immense variety of attractions and facilities they offer to the visitor, and, most of all, in their extraordinary sun-and-sea beauty, the islands of the Caribbean have discovered wealth beyond even Columbus' dream of the fabulous treasures of the Indies.

THE CARIBBEAN TODAY

Because it is difficult to generalize about the islands of the Caribbean, they are discussed separately or in small related groups in this guide.

Antigua: Nelson's Dockyard

But you will need some general background information before you make up your mind about the islands you want to visit. Here, then, are some first facts to bear in mind while you are considering the specifics that come later.

PLANNING YOUR TRIP

When to go. The best time is whenever it is most convenient for you. The so-called "season" in the Caribbean runs roughly from the middle of December to the middle of April. Those are the ideal months to escape to the islands in order to miss the chills of a northern winter. The weather in the Caribbean will be dependably warm and, since winter is the dry season in the islands, you can expect the days to be invariably sunny. Everything will be shined and polished, sports and amusements in full swing, the shelves of the shops filled to overflowing, entertainment at its very best.

It is the refugees from northern frost and snow who have decided that the Caribbean is a winter resort. It isn't. The islands are a delight all year round. In August Boston and Chicago are hotter than Jamaica and Barbados. But, until more people discover that they can actually go *south* for a cool summer vacation, you will still be able to enjoy the islands at their uncrowded best between May and October. Those are the months, as we have said, when everything is in bloom. The people have time to be relaxed and friendly. The service in restaurants is attentive and unhurried, you have a wider choice of accommodations, hotel rates are 30–50% lower in luxury resorts and 20–30% lower in other price ranges.

It is possible that solicitous friends will warn you against going to the Caribbean in the late summer or fall—the hurricane season. Well, every few years a severe storm does strike somewhere in the islands, just as storms hit Florida or New England. Once in a while there is considerable damage, and sometimes lives are lost. But the danger in the islands is little if any greater than it is anywhere along the eastern coast of the United States. Today storms are spotted long before they have become dangerous, and all areas that may be affected are alerted. The movement of the storm is plotted, and the people in its path are warned, often days before its appearance. If necessary, ships and planes can be rerouted to avoid danger, and people in the exposed areas evacuated. Storms do occur and nothing can be done to stop them, but they are no longer anything like the danger they once were. If you take the same sensible precautions that you would in a storm at home, you will be in no more danger in the islands than you would in Atlantic City.

Where to go. Only you can decide which of the islands is best for you. There is an endless variety to choose from—luxurious resorts sumptuously equipped to anticipate your whims, escapist islands so remote that you will be the only visiting pebble on the beach. You can bask all day in the sun, or spend all night over a roulette table. You can schedule activities for every waking hour or refuse to move out of your hammock between sunrise and sunset. You can arrange an island-hopping tour that will take you through four languages and halfway around the Caribbean or you can settle in and get to know the back streets of one little town. All of the Caribbean is there for you to choose from. Time, taste, and your budget will be your best guides.

Passports, inoculations, and other red tape. With the exception of Trinidad, Tobago, French West Indies, and San Andres, none of the islands requires that U.S. or Canadian citizens have passports or visas. You should, however, be prepared to show proof of citizenship should you be asked—a birth certificate or documentary identification.

Check with the tourist boards of individual countries to find out what vaccinations, if any, are recommended. If you plan on spending a lot of time barefoot, a tetanus or booster shot doesn't hurt.

Reservations. Nearly eight million tourists from the United States and Canada visit the Caribbean each year. That means that at some times and in some places—particularly during the winter months—planes, ships, and hotels will be crowded. Make reservations, and make them in ample time. They may not always be necessary, but they pay dividends in better accommodations and peace of mind.

Costs. Unless you're traveling on a cruise ship or planning to stay at one of the all-inclusive resorts like Club Med, where all meals and activities are part of the package, it's tricky estimating expenses. Hotels in this guidebook range from under $30 a night to more than $200. A highly-rated restaurant can set you back for more than $50, but you can also eat well for much less than a quarter of that. Other factors to consider: Will you be traveling during the high season or off-season? Do you desire a high-rolling resort town (such as Jamaica's Montego Bay), or a relatively undeveloped spot (like the secluded beaches of San Andreas)? Are you planning to take advantage of the free port shopping values?

Many of the brochures from the tourist boards quote prices for various activities ($75 for an introductory scuba diving course in the Cayman Islands, for example, or $15 for a two-hour horseback ride in Puerto Rico), which will help you estimate expenses. A reliable travel agent can tell you how much to allow for taxis, tips and other expenses.

Climate and clothing. The temperature variation in the Caribbean, north and south, winter and summer, is remarkably slight, usually ranging predictably between 75–90° (F.). Even if you add a few degrees top and bottom as a hedge against the "unusual" weather you normally encounter, you still haven't the problem of packing clothing for changeable weather.

Summer or winter you will need only summer clothing in the Carib-

Casa Blanca, ancestral home of Puerto Rico's first governor, Ponce de Leon

bean. A lightweight jacket, shawl, or sweater is handy for evenings on the water. Jacket and tie are required at some of the more elegant restaurants during high season, but in general dress is extremely casual.

For women, tops, shorts, and skirts that can be worn in various combinations are excellent space and weight savers. Lightweight jersey dresses and separates are versatile. You will need at least two bathing suits, a robe, and whatever else you need for the beach. You'll want a comfortable pair of walking shoes for sightseeing. You will probably want to buy some sweaters and sport clothes in the islands. And finally —as you have been told dozens of times—wherever possible, choose drip-dry fabrics for traveling. They save space, and avoid laundry and cleaning problems. Choose cotton blends for breathability.

Men will fare well enough with a tropical suit or two, and summer slacks and sport coats for informal wear. Sport shirts in reasonable shades and patterns are acceptable. And socks, shirts, underwear, all in the quick-drying synthetics.

Finally, the standard advice: Pack less than you think you need.

How To Get There. With millions of people visiting the Caribbean every year, travel to and among the islands is big business—and getting bigger every day. All of the major islands are now linked to the U.S. mainland with regularly scheduled airline service. Smaller islands are tied into the network through local airlines that provide "island-hopping" service that will land you almost anywhere you are likely to want to go. The whole area has been well served by several ship lines for many years, and both the passenger liners and the passenger-carrying cargo ships have greatly expanded their service. The greatest change has come in the number, style, and comfort of the cruises threading through the islands. Cruises are no longer for the idle rich; many offer moderately priced packages.

Ship and air lines are now competing for your patronage with package tours, cruises, excursions, stopover privileges, and island-hopping arrangements of every possible kind and variety, including combination air-sea cruises that offer you the advantages of both air speed and ocean leisure. Most people find that the best way to work out their own plan is to sit down with a travel agent who has current rates and schedules and a practiced hand at putting together trips to fit various budgets and interests.

The information given here hardly scratches the surface of the possibilities. It will, however, give you some idea of the range of services available. With this as a starting point you can get specific information about rates and schedules either from your travel agent or directly from the carriers themselves.

By plane. The Caribbean area is serviced by more than a dozen major airlines. American, Delta, TWA, and Eastern fly to Puerto Rico while Eastern and Delta fly to Nassau and have regular flights to most of the other islands. BWIA (British West Indian Airways) and LIAT (Leeward Islands Air Transport) cover most of the Caribbean. ALM (Antillean Airlines) flies to the Netherlands West Indies and some of the other islands. Air Canada flies to the Caribbean from Montreal and Toronto. Air Jamaica flies to Jamaica from Canada and many major U.S. cities.

You can fly from New York to Puerto Rico in three and a half hours. Flights to Trinidad, the farthest island in the chain, take about five and a half hours from New York. And the flight from Miami to Nassau, of course, doesn't give you time to read your paper properly.

The islands, spread over an area two-thirds the size of the United States, are connected by a maze of routes flown by big and small lines offering a bewildering variety of trips, tours, and excursions. See individual country listings for more information.

Excursion fares usually require 7–30 days' advance ticket purchase and restriction on length of stay. Below are some peak season samples; all prices are subject to change.

FROM NEW YORK

	Round Trip First Class	Round Trip Tourist	Round Trip Excursion
San Juan	$728	$468	$350
Jamaica (Montego Bay)	$858	$556	$350
Haiti	$688	$476	$329
Guadeloupe	$1090	$694	$505
St. Thomas/St. Croix	$836	$531	$360
Barbados	$1057	$761	$573

FROM MIAMI

San Juan	$522	$418	$199
Nassau	$250	$190	$150
Jamaica (Montego Bay)	$500	$308	$186
Trinidad	$1148	$726	$487

Those are the base rates, but with a little canny planning you will probably be able to shade these prices considerably by taking advantage of one of the many reduced fare offers available now. For example, there are off-season rates in effect with many lines from mid-April to mid-December. The reductions usually amount to about 20 per cent of the tourist fare. A sure way to cut expense on airplane travel is to fly during the middle of the week when fares are lower than on weekends.

Excursions covering various combinations of islands are becoming increasingly popular and plentiful. You can find anything from a three-day quickie out of Miami to a 21-day vacation jaunt from New York.

Charter flights are another way to save from 30–40 per cent off scheduled airfares. Just keep in mind that you often must commit yourself and your money early, and you could lose most or all of your payment if you have to cancel your flight on short notice.

And finally, there are the package tours, the airline equivalent of cruises. These are fixed-time, fixed-itinerary tours which include accomodations in a varied selection of hotel price ranges, meals (or not, again according to how much you want to spend), sightseeing, and airfare. Many include extras such as tax, tips, drinks, and the like. Because they are economical when compared to the rates a tourist would pay if he were to book similar tours on an individual basis, and because they permit him to spend more of his vacation time actually seeing the islands than the ship cruises, these package tours have multiplied tremendously since their introduction. The airlines and major tour operators such as American Express and GoGo Tours offer very economical package tours to most Caribbean destinations. Eastern Airlines has a 3-night package to St. Maarten that ranges from $328–$509 per person, double occupancy. The price varies according to which of six hotels are chosen and U.S. point of departure. Seven-day

Cruise ships anchored at Nassau's Prince George's Wharf

packages range from $468–$1059 and similar packages are available to Antigua, Aruba, the Bahamas, Barbados, Curacao, Guadeloupe, Haiti, Jamaica, Martinique, Puerto Rico, St. Croix, St. Lucia, St. Thomas, and Trinidad. American Airlines 4–8 packages to Antigua, Aruba, Barbados, Curacao, Jamaica, Puerto Rico, St. Maarten, and St. Thomas range from $299–$1389 per person double.

The all-inclusive tour is becoming very popular, and several islands have hotels that specialize in this type of package. There are several hotels in Jamaica which have this package; for instance Couples in Ocho Rios: for $1,770–$1,830 you get 7-nights' lodging, all meals, and snacks, all drinks (including wine with dinner), sightseeing, all water sports, horseback riding, tennis, shows, disco, tips and taxes. You don't even have to pay for cigarettes. This is ideal for the couple who wants to know exactly what their vacation will cost, because after adding on airfare, you literally don't spend anything else except what you may buy in shops, or on local crafts. There are infinite variations, of course, depending on the accommodations you choose. In the so-called off-season, May 1 to December 15, they are offered at substantial reductions.

By ship. The airlines by no means have a corner on the market. There are still hundreds of thousands of people who prefer a leisurely trip and like the feeling of luxuriating in the relaxing comfort of an unhurried ocean voyage. For such a trip the Caribbean is as nearly perfect as any area in the world, and the ship lines have made the most of what nature provided. More than 500 ships call at San Juan, Puerto Rico, alone each year, and you couldn't investigate all the available cruise packages if you made it a full-time job.

During the winter season the luxury cruises to the Caribbean hold the spotlight in the islands. Reading the list of scheduled sailings you would think that half the world's famous ships were threading through the islands. The Queen Elizabeth II, the Cunard Princess, the Nordic Prince, and the Sun Viking are among the grand ocean liners that ply Caribbean waters.

Here again what you pay will depend on the ship, the accommodations, the time of year and the number of days you are aboard. Most cruise lines also have sea-air combination packages which have become very popular. The connections with major airlines throughout the U.S. and Canada are extensive, and the fares are nominal—certainly much less than normal airfare from these cities—and some packages include free air connections. The Cunard Lines' Countess has numerous trips in the Caribbean. A 7-day trip from San Juan to Caracas, Grenada, Barbados, Martinique, and St. Thomas, including roundtrip airfare, ranges from $999–$2,110. Club Sea has an 8-day cruise to Antigua with scuba diving, windsurfing and sailing for only $599, including round-trip airfare from New York. Holland America has 7-day eastern or western Caribbean cruises starting at $1,245 with airfare included. Carnival Cruise Lines has 3-, 4-, and 7-day packages to Nassau from $375–$975. Norwegian Caribbean Lines has several 7-day cruises that stop at Cancun (Mexico), St. Thomas, San Juan, the Bahamas, and other ports for as little as $553. Your local travel agent can give you the total range of cruises and lines, and also has access to up-to-date ratings for individual ships so you can find out exactly what amenities are on board. The more deluxe ships have more to offer, and the prices range accordingly, just as the hotels do.

MONEY

If you cover all of the Caribbean, before you are home you will have had the chance to do business with money of several sorts and sizes— pounds sterling, Haitian gourdes, British West Indian dollars (called *Beewee* dollars), French francs, and Dutch West Indian guilders. You will have had the chance, but if you are like most visitors in the islands, you probably won't have taken it. American and Canadian dollars are accepted everywhere at fair exchange rates, and in most places you will get your change in the same currency. It really doesn't seem worth the bother to get your money exchanged.

How you carry money is a matter of importance, and it is worth repeating once again that it is only ordinary prudence not to carry more cash than you need for immediate use. The safest and most convenient way to keep the bulk of your funds is in travelers checks. Those issued

A calypso band in a Jamaican night club

by American Express and other international banking firms are accepted everywhere.

Some places you may find prices marked only in the local currency. Here are the local currency equivalents at press time but remember that the exchange rate fluctuates, so check on the currency situation before your departure.

Virgin Islands	U.S. Currency	U.S. $1.00 = U.S. $1.00
Puerto Rico	U.S. Currency	U.S. $1.00 = U.S. $1.00
Bahamas	Bahamian Dollar	U.S. $1.00 = BMD $1.00
Jamaica	Dollar	U.S. $1.00 = $5.50
Haiti	Gourde	U.S. $1.00 = Gde. 5.00
British Leewards **British Windwards** **Barbados**	Eastern Caribbean Dollar	U.S. $1.00 = $2.70 ECD
Trinidad and Tobago	Trinidad Dollar	U.S. $1.00 = $3.60 TTR
French West Indies	Franc	U.S. $1.00 = F6.31
Netherlands Antilles	Antilles Guilder	U.S. $1.00 = NA 2.13G
Cayman Islands	Cayman Dollar	U.S. $1.00 = .83 CID

TIPPING

The tipping problem exists in the Caribbean as elsewhere—unfortunately—but it isn't as troublesome as it sometimes can be. Most hotels add a service charge to your bill. When they do, you won't be expected to supplement it with tips when you leave. Otherwise, 10–15 per cent is still sufficient in many restaurants, except in the more elegant and fashionable spots where 15–20 per cent will be expected. It makes sense to try and find out something about the wage levels of the places you visit and tip proportionally, especially for small services. Extravagant tipping works against the tourist trade in the long run.

If you are on a cruise, the tips at the end are a must that you should figure as part of the cost, unless you get a package that advertises "no tipping required." They will probably run somewhere between 10 and 15 per cent of the price of the ticket. The cabin steward will expect about $2 per day per person. The dining steward should have about the same. The barman should get 10 to 15 per cent of your bill, depending on how good a customer you have been, the wine steward $4 or more if you are fussy about vintages. Deck and bath stewards come in for $3 to $4. This scale is none too high, and if you have had the full luxury treatment it should be increased.

HOTELS AND RESTAURANTS

Food and lodging are covered under the individual islands. Both the hotels and restaurants are grouped roughly on the basis of price: De Luxe (****), Expensive (***), Medium Priced (**), and Inexpensive (*) for hotels, with only three categories of restaurants. Because prices often change abruptly and substantially, it seems more helpful to list places according to their relative costs rather to give specific prices. But you can calculate *roughly* that a four-star hotel will cost $180 and up per day for a double room; a three-star hotel will run from $100–$180; a two-star establishment from $60–$100; and a one-star $60 or less. When "AP" appears in a hotel listing, it means the hotel is on the *full American plan* and that three meals a day are included with the price of the room. "MAP" indicates *modified American plan*—breakfast plus lunch *or* dinner included. To some extent price should (and does) reflect quality, but you should remember that modest places are often excellent. Brief descriptive notes are given wherever they seem pertinent and useful.

It will be clear from the listings that in most of the islands there is a wide range of hotels, lodges, cottages, and guest houses. In the more fashionable resort areas, of course, prices are generally higher, and there is a preponderance of luxury hotels. The smaller and more remote islands commonly have few facilities beyond the middle range, sometimes only simple guest-house accommodations.

Most of the hotels and lodges listed in this guide cater primarily to people whose stays in any one place usually do not exceed two weeks. However, if you plan a longer stay or come with your family, you might want to look into renting an apartment or a cottage with kitchen facilities. This type of accommodation is becoming more prevalent in all the islands, and offers the tourist savings on meal costs and flexibility of meal times. One bedroom apartments or studios for two people average from $80 to $120 a day in the winter season; for two bedrooms count about twice that. Of course there are luxury accommodations for much more. A three-bedroom villa on the sea, for example, will rent for up to $2000 a week, can accommodate six people and will include a full staff of cook, maid and gardener. These accommodations are often advertised in *The New York Times, USA Today, San Juan Star,* and other papers. Tour operators and travel agencies often have their own lists.

Restaurant categories and restaurants change with the times. There are restaurants that specialize in local food, continental cuisine, native foods of other countries or a mixture of all. A restaurant specializing in the local cuisine can be very inexpensive, or can be top-priced. A dinner for two at a *** restaurant can run from $40–$75 per person, ** from $30–$40 and * from $15 to $30. A bottle of wine will add $8 to $40 to the bill. This is for a full-course dinner. Many countries have small take-out food stands by the road, but you will have to judge the sanitary conditions.

FOOD

You can eat well anywhere you are likely to go in the Caribbean. You will be visiting islands that have inherited the great traditional foods of France, Spain, and Holland and then, over the generations, have developed their own local variations. The result is often extraordinarily interesting, and you owe it to yourself to sample these island specialties. Unfortunately, you may not often be encouraged to try unfamiliar dishes, for, like their kind everywhere, hotel and restaurant proprietors are inclined to play it safe with a sound but undistinguished international cuisine. But many dining rooms do feature local specialties, and even when they don't they will often be delighted to suggest several once they realize that you are interested.

Fresh seafood abounds throughout the islands. There seems to be no end to the variations you will encounter—lobster in Jamaica and the French islands, a dozen different kinds of fish stews in the Spanish-speaking islands, conch fritters in the Bahamas, flying fish in Barbados, turtle steaks, French fish cakes, chowders, shrimp, crabs—the list goes on and on.

But fish isn't the whole story. There are the famous Spanish favorites —*arroz con pollo,* half a dozen variations of *paella,* roast suckling pig *(léchon asada),* the peas-and-beans combinations, and all the rest. The Creole gumbos are famous, and you will find them in all their guises on almost every menu. The British islands wouldn't be able to operate without their curries—but, unless you're an old hand, beware of the hot ones. When you get around to the Dutch islands, you will encounter Indonesian *rijsttafel,* the "rice table" with its 15 or 20 pungent companion dishes. It goes from soup to dessert, and includes the Holland gin, the Holland beer, and, of course, the Holland cheeses. In Jamaica, the national dish is rice and peas (peas being close to our navy bean) and curried goat, both of which are popular on almost all the islands. Dominating everything is a fabulous assortment of fresh fruits and vegetables, some familiar and many exotic—but nonetheless worth trying. *Ackee,* a vegetable indigenous to many islands, is served with salt fish for breakfast and tastes a bit like scrambled eggs.

Half of the foods of the world seem to have their Caribbean versions, and you can add much to your trip by sampling at least some of them as you go along.

A word about precautions: Water is safe in most of the islands today, and the milk that you will be served has been properly pasteurized. So long as you are in the larger centers, you need have no concern about them. But in the remote and rural areas of Antigua, Montserrat, Haiti, Guadeloupe, Tobago, and Trinidad among others, you cannot be certain. Whenever you are not certain—and it is not enough to have the casual assurance of the person serving you—drink bottled or boiled water. There is only a slim chance that you would get anything to hurt you, but it is only common prudence to avoid even that possibility.

DRINK

In the Caribbean the drink is rum. Period. You can get any of the other potables that you like, of course, but you are bound to feel out of step unless you join the rum bibbers at least part of the time. Many islands have high duty costs added to imported liquors such as scotch. This puts the price of drinks up considerably, so check the price list, for in some cases you will pay more for a scotch and water than you would in New York City.

There is a whole literature of rum, and wherever you go you will encounter authorities and enthusiasts who will endeavor to persuade you that their favorite type is the one and only rum. You can listen while you keep on sampling. There are many different kinds of rum, each with its own distinctive character, and, unless you plan to become an authority and enter the dispute, you can get along quite well without making a study of the subject. There is a light, distilled "brandy" type of rum produced in Haiti that many people find particularly good. Barbados has one that is much like it. And there is a very dark rum made largely in the French islands. Between the two extremes there are a dozen different tints and flavors. The thing to do is to find the one you like and stick with it. Also, overproof rum, called "white light- ning" is available almost everywhere—but beware, because it is 150 proof (75 percent alcohol) or more and most potent.

You will never know how many rum drinks there are until you go to the Caribbean. Some of them will seem like outrageous concoctions to you, but half a dozen or more have become famous throughout the world. The daiquiri is a favorite cocktail everywhere today, as is the ubiquitous piña colada. In addition to staid rum-and-Coke, there is the *El Presidente* (rum with vermouth, lemon, grenadine, and Cura- çao), the *Cuba Libre* (rum, lime, and cola), and, of course, the popular and potent cooler, *Planters' Punch* (dark rum, sugar, lemon, grenadine, and angostura bitters.)

SPORTS

If a sport has anything to do with salt water, you can assume that it is at or near its best in the Caribbean. *Swimming* varies from good to excellent everywhere. The best beaches are probably in Jamaica, Nassau, Barbados, St. Croix, and Antigua, but others are fine by most standards. Conditions are, of course, excellent for snorkeling and scuba diving, and, in St. Thomas, Bonaire, Grand Cayman and Montego Bay, there is a sizeable group of private operators and schools which offer lessons and have all the equipment available. Many hotels have special diving packages which save considerably on quite an expensive sport. *Sailing* and *yachting* couldn't be better. There are charter arrange- ments for parties of two people or more, sailing lessons, hundreds of islands, and trade winds that go on forever. April is the month for races —the Tradewinds Race in St. Maarten, the Caribbean Racing Confer- ence in the U.S. Virgin Islands, and the Sailing Week in Antigua. The island lagoons are perfect for *water-skiing,* para-sailing, windsurfing, and power surfing are also available. *Fishing* is of the best, and there are guides, boats, skippers, and tackle wherever you go. Deep-sea fishing is available almost anywhere, but the Virgin Islands, Puerto Rico, Cayman Islands and Jamaica are the best-known areas. Many world records have been made there for marlin and other fish. There is a Blue Marlin tournament in St. Thomas in August and one in Jamaica in October. The Cayman Islands' Million Dollar Month is a marathon fishing tournament offering some of the biggest cash prizes in the sport. It is held every June.

The land-based sports aren't neglected. There are 18-hole *golf courses* on several of the islands—Jamaica, Trinidad, Nassau, Puerto Rico, the Cayman Islands, and the U.S. Virgins—and nine-hole courses elsewhere. *Tennis courts* are available on almost all of the islands. Almost every hotel has at least one court, and some of the larger establishments have complete complexes with instructors, pros, schools and tennis packages. Some of the best are Dorado Beach Resorts and Palmas del Mar in Puerto Rico, and Buccaneer Beach in St. Croix. Jamaica has more tennis courts in more hotels than any other Caribbean destination. Eden II and Half Moon Montego Bay Raquet Club have varied packages and great facilities. *Riding* is popular, and horses are available on most of the larger islands. If you are a real energy burner, you can find some *rock and mountain climbing* in Jamaica, Haiti, and St. Lucia.

There is fun for the person who takes his exercise as a spectator, too. During the winter season you can see a baseball game—a good one— or a cricket match on many of the islands. Another popular sport is *soccer,* played all year before enormous crowds, and, if horse racing is your fancy, you will find it on many islands.

SHOPPING

No one, presumably, goes to the Caribbean just for the shopping, but it is certainly true that few people are able to resist stocking up on the fine merchandise from all over the world sold in the islands sometimes at prices far below those in the United States—and, indeed, often below those in the countries where the articles are made. A trip through the islands is like a visit to a world-wide merchandise mart—marvelous for the person who can keep a check on his enthusiasms, a sore temptation to those whose bargain-resistance is low.

If you have been out of the United States for 48 hours or more (but remember Puerto Rico doesn't count), you are permitted to bring or send back purchases of up to $400 duty free. You are allowed duty free one liter of liquor. If you are returning from the U.S. Virgin Islands, the amount you may bring in is double. And, if your purchases run high, remember that every member of your party, including the children, has the same allowance except for liquor, which stipulates a 21 year age minimum.

Every island has its own local products in addition to gift items from all over the world. The Dutch islands, Haiti, San Andreas, and the Virgin Islands are free ports—which means that the prices on the things you buy there do not include the usual customs duties. Since U.S. duties run high on some imports, you can save really substantial amounts if you shop wisely and selectively. Price items such as watches and cameras before you leave the U.S., because some discount houses in the U.S. have better prices than those in the duty-free shops. In addition to the free ports, other islands—Jamaica, Barbados, Martinique, and Guadeloupe—have "in bond" shops which give you the same benefits. Your purchases are delivered duty free to your plane or ship.

You will usually get the best selection and the best prices in the islands with ties to the countries where the merchandise is produced. In the *British islands* you will find an array of British woolens and sweaters, Liberty silks, fine cotton, china, glassware, and other products for which Great Britain is famous; the *French islands* will be particularly rich in wine, liqueurs, perfume, designer fashions, and scarves; the *Dutch islands* have unbeatable Delft ware, tiles, china, silver, diamonds, and other precious stones; the *Virgin Islands* have all of the variety of the others, some Danish specialties because of their old ties with the mother country, and the added advantage that the selection of products has been made by Americans who know their countrymen's tastes.

Shopping is covered in detail in the section on each of the islands. You will do well to look through the lists of best buys and shops for each of the islands you intend to visit, and plan your shopping so that you get the full benefit of this buyers' paradise.

. . . AND A FEW QUICK FACTS

Special events and holidays are listed under the individual islands in this guide. All of the islands have New Year's parades and celebrations. St. Croix has a big festival. In most of the islands the explosive Carnival comes on the two days before Ash Wednesday with the goings-on in Haiti, Martinique, and Trinidad the most exciting and colorful. St. Thomas has its Carnival the last week in April. Sailing regattas are held from April through June. In the French islands Bastille Day, July 14th, looks and sounds like our Fourth of July—fireworks, parades, and dancing in the streets. The harvest festivals come mostly in October and November. All-Saints' Day, November 1st, is celebrated with processions and candle-lit cemeteries. At Christmas time there are celebrations everywhere of all kinds—trees, fireworks, carols, parades, and fêtes.

Getting around in the islands is discussed in the section on each island. It is usually no problem. Taxis are generally reasonable, transfer (minibus) service to hotels available on larger islands, and buses crowded but fun. On most islands you can rent a car, with or without a driver, to see the outlying areas. You need only a U.S. or Canadian driver's license.

Newspapers and magazines in English are generally available. *The New York Times, Miami Herald,* and other major U.S. newspapers are flown in daily and found at most of the larger hotels. *USA Today* is sold at newsstands in the major cities throughout the Caribbean.

Medical facilities are more than adequate throughout the islands. Many of the larger centers have excellent modern hospitals, and anywhere you are likely to go you will be able to find English-speaking physicians. In the remoter areas it is always possible to arrange for off-schedule emergency transportation to a hospital on one of the larger islands.

Airmail from the main islands is normally delivered in cities along the eastern seaboard within 48 hours, a day or so later elsewhere in the United States and Canada. Rates vary from island to island, but generally approximate those in the States.

Telephone, cable and telex service between the larger islands and the U.S. is reliable. Most large hotels have their own Telex and cable service at the same rate as in the U.S. A three-minute call from Puerto Rico (direct dial, day rates) to New York is $1.16; from Jamaica, $2.68. Direct dialing is possible virtually everywhere. Some hotels will add service charge for calls made by the operator. The calls northbound are more expensive than southbound, but still reasonable. If you need to be in constant touch with someone, avoid the smaller islands which have few telephone lines.

3

THE BAHAMA ISLANDS

Hundreds of beach-fringed islands in the clear warm blue water of the Atlantic and fanned by a constant breeze, the British Bahama Islands have everything to make them a vacation paradise.

Take some 700 islands and about 2,400 cays and reefs and scatter them over 800 miles of blue sea between Palm Beach, Florida, and the north coast of Haiti. Give them beautiful beaches and snug harbors, stock the waters with game fish, keep a soft breeze blowing and the temperature about 74 degrees in winter and 82 in summer, and the water warm. Add hotels, resorts, and facilities for everything from yachting to shopping, and you have the Bahama Islands.

Of the 240,000 Bahamians living on the 24 major island groups, 85 per cent are black, and 15 per cent are white.

Although as early a visitor as George Washington found the islands lovely, they have not always been so prosperous. Generally flat with little arable land, some timber, and no known mineral resource except salt, they were uncolonized for centuries after their discovery. Yet it was one of the Family Islands (formerly known as the Out Islands) that first brought the Americas into the ken of the Old World. On October 12, 1492, Christopher Columbus hove to off the shore of what most authorities agree was San Salvador, a small island about 200 miles southeast of Nassau. It was the first landfall in the New World.

Within 20 years the Spaniards had rounded up the Indians and shipped them off to die in the mines of Hispaniola and Cuba, and the depopulated islands dropped out of history in the first of many ups and downs.

In 1629 King Charles I of England included the islands in a grant giving Carolina to his attorney-general, Sir Robert Heath, who made no attempt at colonization. Twenty years later, London merchants joined by a group from Bermuda established the first British settlement under the name of the "Eleutherian Adventurers." Their island is known today as Eleuthera, from the Greek "eleutheros," meaning "free." But they had their troubles. The land was poor. They argued. Many of their number gave up and went home. But other adventurous souls began arriving in the islands, and in 1671 the first governor was appointed, with Nassau or, as it was called then, Charles Town, as the seat of the government. The islands also became the base for such pirates as Blackbeard, Vance, and Speed. When word of their activities eventually got back to London, King George I named a former buccaneer, Captain Woodes Rogers, as governor, gave him soldiers, and told him to wipe out the pirates. Rogers hanged some of his old compatriots, pardoned others, and the rest fled.

At the beginning of the American Revolution, an American naval squadron held Nassau briefly during an ammunition raid. Later American Loyalist refugees from the mainland settled on the island of Abaco. The Spanish made their final attempt to keep the islands in 1782, but were driven out one year later.

The sunny islands boomed during the American Civil War as a trading point for outbound southern cotton and inbound guns, but with the war's end they drifted back into poverty, leaving behind as the only evidence of prosperity the ornate Royal Victoria, now closed, but still a visitor's haunt because of its beautiful gardens. American prohibition and rum-running profits brought in enough money to begin a tourist industry; but it wasn't until after the Second World War that a hard-driving group took over and, by dint of hard work and promotion, changed the Bahamas from a millionaires' playground into the fastest growing tourist attraction in the area. About fifteen of the islands have been developed, and building is the Bahamas' third industry.

GENERAL INFORMATION

How To Get There: *By Air:* Delta flies to Nassau daily from N.Y. Eastern has daily flights from several cities. Other airlines offering frequent flights include Air Canada, Pan Am, TWA, United, Aero Coach, Bahamas Express, Caribbean Express, Gull Air, and Air Jamaica. From Miami, Bahamas Air, Eastern, and Chalks Flying Service have frequent service. Walker's Cay Airline serves Walker's Cay from Fort Lauderdale and Rum Cay has its own airstrip for private charters.

Many airlines and travel agencies have packages that include hotels, meals, and hops to one or more islands.

By Sea: Many cruise lines which offer Caribbean cruises out of New York and other ports call at Nassau as their itineraries permit. Your cruiseship directory will list these details.

Regular scheduled service to the Bahamas is available *from Miami* on Costa Lines, Carnivale, Dolphin IV, Emerald Seas, Norwegian Caribbean Line, Norwegian Cruise Line, and Royal Caribbean Cruise Line. *From New York,* Royale Odyssey, Royale, and Sagafjord all have regular sailings.

How To Get Around: Nassau is small enough to tour comfortably on foot. For getting around outside of town, bicycles rent for $10 a day—motor bikes for $24, and car rentals range from $50–$70 a day. Taxis are metered, and are readily available.

Perhaps the most pleasurable way to see the capital city is by horse-drawn carriage. You will find one at the carriage stand in Rawson Square. Rates are $8–$10 per half-hour.

There are a number of boat-rental outlets where powerboats are available at $35 per day for water-skiing, beach-hopping and touring nearby cays. Several agents, such as Playtours (809-32-22931), and Majestic (809-32-22606) offer both day and night tours to Nassau highspots, as well as water cruises around the harbor and nearby islands.

Festivals: The Junkanoo—Bahamas Boxing Day Parade and Mardi Gras —features music, dancing, and parades in native costume on December 26th and New Year's Day. On Grand Bahama Island a festival and costume balls accompany the annual Bahamas 500 ocean power boat race.

Sports: There are championship tournaments year-round in either tennis, golf, or fishing. But the non-champion will also find fine facilities for water and other sports.

Swimming. White beaches abound on all the major islands. From Prince George Wharf, Nassau, you can take the boat to the justly famous Paradise Beach on Paradise Island, beach admission $5.

Skin Diving, Spear Fishing. Clear water and plenty of fish have made the Bahamas a world headquarters for SCUBA diving. You can rent equipment, take lessons on its use and hire guides from Underwater Tours (809-32-23301), and the Underwater Explorers' Club (809-373-1244), in Freeport; or Small Bay Lodge (809-36-82014 or 800-223-6961), on Andros Island.

Water Skiing. Boats and water skis can be rented at Paradise Beach, Bay Shore Marina (809-32-28232/3) and Brown's Boat Basin (809-32-33231). Some of the larger hotels have instructors.

Fishing. Record game fish of all kinds have been taken from Bahama waters. Tournaments are held all year round. The deep-sea inventory includes wahoo, kingfish, dolphin, bonito, blackfin and bluefin tuna, marlin and sailfish. Off the reefs you can get amberjack, grouper, mutton snapper, mackerel, yellowtail and jacks, and on the flats of the outer islands you will find bonefish and grey snapper.

There are plenty of charter boats, and you can make your arrangements through your hotel or at Nassau Yacht Haven. On the Out Islands you will find shore accommodations and charter boats at Bimini and Chub Cay, known for their marlin and bluefin tuna; Freeport and West End on Grand Bahama, known for deepwater trolling, reef fishing, and bonefish; Walker's Cay in the Abacos, where a number of world-record fish have been taken; and Rock Sound Club on Eleuthera. Andros and Eleuthera Islands both have excellent fishing in the deep sea and on the flats.

Sailing and Yachting. The islands provide some of the best sailing and cruising in the world. You can rent small sailboats at the waterfront hotels or motor skiffs at Nassau Yacht Haven, Brown's Boat Basin and Bayshore Marina, Nassau. All kinds of larger yachts can be chartered by the day, week, or month for cruises through the islands. Ministry of Tourism, Nassau, publishes *Yachtsman's Guide to the Bahamas* (Tropic Isle Publishers, Coral Gables, FL 33134) and has a detailed list of charter boats available. You can also make arrangements through your hotel.

Golf. There are 15 championship links in the Bahamas, and many other 9-hole courses. Greens fees average $10–$20 for 18 holes.

Tennis. Most large hotels and many smaller resort hotels have all-weather courts (free to guests, and with a nominal fee to others). Several large hotels have pros in residence. Important tournaments have been staged, and the Bahamas National Open Tennis Championship is held in January.

Night Life: Nassau night life has plenty of bounce, floor shows, dancing, calypso singing, goombay music, bongo drums, strolling troubadours, and lavish shows at the larger hotels. *Blackbeard's Tavern* and the *Drumbeat Club* are among the best of the clubs firmly entrenched in native sympatico. Paradise Island offers *Le Cabaret Theatre,* a lavish floor show. In

World-famous Paradise Beach in Nassau

Freeport opulent sophistication sets the tone in bistros, and performers from London, Las Vegas and New York headline nightclub reviews and all-native shows in any of a dozen plush nightclubs. Nassau's *Bahamian Club* specializes in the elegant savoir faire and quiet atmosphere of Europe's noted casinos, while Freeport's *Princess Casino,* a Moorish palace, gilds traditional games of chance with a more exotic patina. Casino restaurants include the *Crown Room, Garden Cafe,* and *Casino Royale Showroom.*

Medical Facilities: Princess Margaret Hospital, Nassau, and Grand Bahama Clinic, Freeport, modern, with a competent staff of resident doctors.

Other Things To Do: *Movies,* in Nassau, have two shows a day. The *Nassau Music Society* stages performances during the year. At *Nassau Seafloor Aquarium* you can see beautiful marine fauna and at *Ardastra Gardens* flamingos strut in precision drills.

Additional information: Bahamas Tourist Offices are located in the following U.S. cities: 150 East 52nd Street, New York, NY 10022 (212-758-2777); 1950 Century Blvd., N.E., Suite 26, Atlanta, GA 30345 (404-633-1793); 1027 Statler Office Building, Boston, MA 02116 (617-426-3144); 875 North Michigan Avenue, Chicago, IL 60611 (312-787-8203); 2050 Stimmons Freeway, World Trade Center, Dallas, TX 75258-1408 (214-742-1886); 26400 Lahser Road, Suite 112A, Southfield, MI 48034 (313-357-2940); 5177 Richmond Avenue, Houston, TX 77056 (713-626-1566); 3450 Wilshire Boulevard, Suite 208, Los Angeles, CA 90010 (213-385-0033); 255 Alhambra Circle, Suite 425, Coral Gables, FL 33134 (305-442-4860); 437 Chestnut Street, Suite 216, Philadelphia, PA 19106 (215-925-0871); 44 Montgomery Street, Suite 503, San Francisco, CA 94123 (415-398-5502); 1730 Rhode Island Avenue, N.W., Washington, D.C. 20036 (202-659-9135).

Where to Stay

You can find any kind of accommodation in Nassau from guest houses and old-fashioned establishments to ultramodern pleasure resorts. Most of the hotels offer both European and American plan. The hotels on Grand Bahama and the Family Islands are apt to be new and modern.

NASSAU

*Buena Vista Hotel & Restaurant, 6 rooms, centrally located in downtown

Nassau. *Dolphin Hotel, 66 rooms, swimming pool, ocean views, adjacent to public beach. *El Greco Hotel, 26 rooms, pool. *Gleneagles Hotel, 54 rooms, pool, restaurant and bar. ***Graycliff Hotel, 12 rooms, former colonial mansion. Fine restaurant. * Hotel Corona, 21 rooms. **Lighthouse Beach Hotel, 92 rooms. *Marietta's Hotel, 50 rooms, swimming pool. **Nassau Harbour Club, 49 rooms, marina, pool. **New Harbour Moon Hotel, 30 rooms, opposite public beach, short walk to downtown. ** New Olympia Hotel, 50 rooms, opposite public beach near downtown. * Ocean Spray Hotel, 29 rooms, opposite public beach, short walk to downtown. *Parliament Hotel, 12 rooms, air-conditioned, near beach. *Parthenon, 18 rooms, near beach, downtown. No restaurant. **Pilot House Hotel, 120 rooms, swimming pool lounge, entertainment. *Poinciana Inn, 50 rooms, air-conditioned, no credit cards. ***Sheraton British Colonial Hotel, 325 rooms, centrally located, swimming pool, disco. *Sir Charles Hotel, 20 rooms, air-conditioned, no credit cards. **South Ocean Beach Hotel & Golf Club, 120 rooms, pool, 18-hole golf course. * Towne Club, 46 rooms, swimming pool, entertainment.

CABLE BEACH
***Cable Beach Hotel & Casino, 694 rooms, gourmet restaurants, lounges, nightclubs. **Cable Beach Inn, 141 rooms. **Emerald Beach Hotel, 162 rooms, private beach, swimming pool. ***Nassau Beach Hotel, 425 rooms, private beach, swimming pool. *** The Royal Bahamian Beach Club, 170 rooms. On private beach.

PARADISE ISLAND
***Holiday Inn, 535 rooms, beach, pool, 18-hole golf course. ***Loew's Harbour Cove Hotel, 250 rooms, entertainment, disco. ***The Ocean Club, 71 rooms, elegant and sophisticated. **Paradise Island Resort & Casino, 1,200 rooms, gambling, night club. ***Sheraton Grand Hotel, 360 rooms, lounge, disco, casino nearby.

GRAND BAHAMA ISLAND
**Atlantik Beach Hotel & Country Club, 123 rooms, swimming pool, entertainment. **Bahamas Princess Resort & Casino, 565 rooms, 6 dining rooms, swimming pool. *Castaways Resort, 138 rooms, beach privileges. **Coral Beach Hotel, 11 rooms, private beach, swimming pool. **Freeport Inn, 150 rooms, beach privileges, entertainment. **Genting Lucayan Beach Resort & Casino, 200 rooms. ** Holiday Inn Beach Resort, 502 rooms, private beach, swimming pool. ****Jack Tar Village, 416 rooms, largest swimming pool in Western Hemisphere, private beach, American plan. *New Victoria Inn, 40 rooms, swimming pool, lounge. **Princess Tower, 400 rooms, arcade linking hotel to casino. *Silver Sands Hotel, 164 rooms, pool, private beach. **The Windward Palms Hotel, 100 rooms, pool. ** Xanadu Beach & Marina Resort, 184 rooms, on private beach, swimming pool.

FAMILY ISLANDS
Abaco: **Elbow Cay Beach Inn, Hope Town, 30 rooms, private beach. **Hope Town Harbour Lodge, 21 rooms, charming inn with harbor views. *Ambassador Inn, 6 rooms, basic amenities, close to beach. ** Conch Inn, 14 rooms, full-service marina, excellent native food. **Green Turtle Club & Marina, 30 rooms, luxurious suites and cottages with full-service kitchens. **New Plymouth Club & Inn, 90 rooms, Bahamian colonial inn close to ocean beach. *** Walker's Cay Hotel & Marina, 66 rooms, full-service marina with charter yacht and full scuba program.

Andros: **Andros Beach Hotel, 15 rooms, air-conditioned, on the beach, full diving program. ***Small Hope Bay Lodge,* 20 rooms, dive resort, on beach, AP.

Berry Islands: ****Chub Cay,* 35 rooms, on the beach, swimming pool, tennis courts, full-service marina.

Bimini: ***Admiral Hotel,* 18 rooms. ***Bimini Big Game Fishing Club & Hotel,* 49 rooms, luxurious, with pool and marina, beach nearby. ***Bimini Blue Water Marina,* 12 rooms, Hemingway's Bimini hideaway, pool, marina, beach. ***Sea Crest Hotel,* 17 rooms. **Bimini Inn,* 28 rooms, swimming pool. **Brown's Hotel,* 22 rooms, rustic motel on harbor. ***Complete Angler Hotel,* 12 rooms, small historic inn opposite harbor.

Cat Island: ***Bridge Inn,* 12 rooms. ****Greenwood Inn,* 20 rooms. Private beach, disco, entertainment, swimming pool, tennis courts.

Eleuthera: ***Cigatoo Inn,* 26 rooms, hilltop location in Governor's Harbour, beach privileges. ***Coral Sands Hotel,* 33 rooms, overlooks sea and Harbour Island's pink sand beaches. **Rock House,* Harbour Island, 6 rooms, intimate guesthouse, ceiling fans. ***Spanish Wells Beach Resort,*

28 rooms, ocean front, world-famous dive program. ***Spanish Wells Harbour Club,* 14 rooms, simple accommodations overlooking harbor and marina, shares amenities with Spanish Wells Beach Resort. **Hilton's Haven Motel & Restaurant,* Tarpum Bay, 19 rooms, cozy, close to beach. ****Windermere Island Club,* 47 rooms, both casual and elegant, pool, marina, AP.

Exuma: ***Hotel Peace & Plenty,* 32 rooms, freshwater pool, private beach club, overlooks Elizabeth Harbor. ***Hotel Pieces of Eight,* 32 rooms, pool, lovely patio. ****Out Island Inn Village,* 80 rooms, beachfront vacation resort with thatched roof sun shelters and marina. ***Sand Dollar Beach Hotel,* Georgetown, 22 rooms, cozy dining room, overlooks beach.

Long Island: ***Stella Maris Inn,* 45 rooms, private beach, swimming pool, entertainment.

Rum Cay: ****Rum Cay Club,* a paradise for divers, anglers, and sailors, only lodging on island, full American plan packages optional.

San Salvador: ***Riding Rock Inn,* 34 rooms, recently re-opened, only hotel on San Salvador.

Where to Eat

The Bahamas' British background influences the food. However, hotels and restaurants almost everywhere serve American and Continental dishes. Fresh fish is excellent. Native foods include turtle steaks and soups, peas 'n rice, conch chowder, salad and fritters, and lime pie. Chinese and Polynesian restaurants have become very popular.

All the large hotels have dining rooms, many with exchange dining privileges for guests on American plan.

Nassau: *****Cafe Martinique,* Continental menu. *****Bahamian Club,* white-glove service, excellent Continental food, plush decor, dancing. *****Buena Vista,* specializing in the finest Continental and Bahamian

foods. ****Bridge Inn,* specializing in Bahamian cuisine and seafood. ***Cafe Laronde,* mixture of American and European dishes.

Freeport: *****El Morocco,* Princess

Casino, finest service and some of the tastiest Continental and Bahamian specialties on Grand Bahama Island. ****Captain's Charthouse, Polynesian decor, steaks, excellent wine list. ****The Stoned Crab, Taino Beach, seafood and steak house right on the beach. ***International Bazaar Restaurants, varied decors and cuisines at this compound of restaurants range from African to French to Cantonese.

Where to Shop

Nassau and Freeport are the shopping centers of the Bahamas; Bay Street is the shopping center of Nassau. Many leading shops have branches in major hotels. The stores are open from 9 A.M. to 5 P.M., Monday through Saturday. A few shops close either Friday or Saturday afternoon.

There are native handicraft shops all over, with baskets, wood carvings, coral curios, etc. Freeport has developed one of the most intriguing shopping areas in the International Bazaar, a dazzling potpourri of exotic shops and foreign architectures. There are sections devoted to the food and wares of Hong Kong, Paris, India, the Middle East, Scandinavia, Spain, Mexico and the Bahamas.

NASSAU

ANTIQUES, CHINA, AND GLASSWARE

Brass and Leather Shop, imports. Solomon's Mines, Treasure Traders, General Hardware China Shop, Sir Francis Peek, Island Treasure Chest, John Bull.

FABRICS AND FASHIONS

Amanda for cashmere sweaters, women's wear; Scottish Shop has most of above plus children's wear and special knits. Vanité sells children's and women's wear.

PERFUME

The Perfume Shop, Lightbourn's Perfume Center.

TOBACCONISTS

Pipe of Peace, John Bull.

LIQUOR

Arcade Liquor Store, Thompson Bros. Ltd., William Brewer, Beaumont House, Maury-Roberts Co. Ltd., on Bay Street. Captain's Cabin, East Bay Shopping Centre. Rum Keg Liquor Store, Lyfore Cay Shopping Centre. Paradise Island Liquor Store, and Paradise Wines & Spirits, Paradise Island.

NATIVE HANDICRAFTS

The Straw Market, native-crafted baskets, handbags, place-mats, dolls. The price depends on how well you bargain. Nassau Art Gallery, Bahamian art; Johnson Bros., Ltd., beautiful tortoise-shell jewelry. Brass & Leather, Charlotte Street; and Solomon's Mines on Bay Street also carry handicrafts.

TOYS

Carter's Record Shop and The City Pharmacy.

WATCHES AND CAMERAS

John Bull, Carib Shop, Island Camera Shop, Pyfrom's Department Store, Island Tackle and Sports Shop.

FREEPORT, GRAND BAHAMA ISLAND

Bahamian art: *Island Galleria.*

Cameras and film: *The Ginza, L.M.R. Drugs, Oasis.*

Cosmetics: *Casablanca Perfumes, East Sunrise Food Store, L.M.R. Drugs, London Pacesetter Boutique, Oasis.*

Crystal and china: *Island Galleria, Midnight Sun, Oasis.*

Fashions: *London Pacesetter Boutique, Seventeen Shop.*

Health food and groceries: *Coopers Roadway Service Station, East Sunrise Food Store, Fountain of Health Foods, Harbour Lobster & Fish Co.*

Jewelry: *Colombian Emeralds International, The Ginza, Island Galleria, La Sandale, L.M.R., London Pacesetter Boutique, Midnight Sun, Oasis, The Old Curiosity Shop.*

Leather goods: *Oasis.*

Perfumes: *Caribe Bahamas, Casablanca Perfume, L.M.R., Fragrance of the Bahamas, Parfum de Paris.*

Swimwear: *London Pacesetter Boutique, UNEXSO.*

T-shirts: *Beachcomber, L.M.R. Drugs, Rhona's, UNEXSO, The Shipwreck.*

What To See

The over-all impression you get of Nassau—a clean, bright, pink-tinged town of limestone houses and wooden verandas, blue-water sloops, and white beaches—that's the most impressive "sight" in all the Bahamas. Tropical flowers—purple bougainvillaea, white jasmine, yellow allamanda—are everywhere. The air is soft and pleasant. Most of the architecture is early Georgian and present building laws require new structures to conform in many areas.

You can pick up one of the excellent maps of the city from the Ministry of Tourism Bureau right in the center of Parliament Square.

With or without map, the place to start is the center of the city, *Rawson Square.* The square and its government buildings are British and correct, freshly painted, orderly, and well planted. If the *House of Assembly* is in session, you will enjoy attending on Wednesday. You may also be able to watch the proceedings in the *Law Courts* where bewigged justices preside, and handsomely uniformed police keep order. In front of the post office is a lovely garden with a statue of Queen Victoria and behind it is the octagonal building that now houses the *Library and Museum.* It was built in 1799 as a jail.

At the waterfront, island sloops and schooners tie up with produce and livestock from the Out Islands. The native Bahamians are great sailors, and their ships carry most of the freight and produce between New Providence and the scattered island empire. Fishing boats tie up each day to unload big turtles, brilliant tropical fish, and huge lobsters. The liveliest time on the dock is between 6:30 and 9 in the morning Friday, Saturday, and Monday.

From *Prince George Wharf* you can take the boat to *Hog Island* and

Paradise Beach, or you can also hire one of the glass bottom boats for a trip to the *Sea Gardens* about a mile east of the wharf.

At the end of George Street, you will spot *Government House,* the home of the governor, easily identified by the large statue of Christopher Columbus, which, incidentally, was modeled under the direction of Washington Irving.

On the outer edges of the city are Nassau's three old forts. *Fort Charlotte,* to the west, largest of the three, was built around 1790. It bristled with more than 40 guns which never had to fire a shot. Beneath it are fascinating underground passages and dungeons. *Fort Montagu,* at the eastern end of Bay Street and built in 1741, guarded the eastern entrance to the harbor, but not too effectively. The new American Navy captured it in 1776 and again in 1778, and the Spanish took it in 1782. *Fort Fincastle* went up in 1793 near the top of the hill on which Nassau is built, and never had to fire a gun to defend the city. Close to the fort is the famous *Queen's Staircase,* a flight of 65 steps cut by slaves out of solid limestone to provide an escape route for troops of the fort.

Several miles east of the center of town are the crumbling ruins of the watchtower that was supposed to have been used by Edward Teach, the pirate, more commonly known as Blackbeard.

Grant's Town, the main black settlement, and one of the cleanest and neatest in the West Indies, is just over the ridge from central Nassau.

Scheduled tours around Nassau and the island can be arranged through local tour operators.

Some 90 miles from Nassau, Freeport, Grand Bahama offers enormous luxury hotels, challenging golf courses, two casinos, elegant nightclubs, and the usual cornucopia of water sports. The pace is fast and the tone is ultra-modern.

FAMILY ISLANDS

Abaco. Great and Little Abaco Islands and nearby cays form the northernmost group of the Bahama Islands. They were settled by Loyalists who fled from Florida and New York and New England in 1783 and prospered at fishing, farming, lumbering, and boat-building. Several mansions from the prosperous days remain, but the islands now concentrate on tourism, fishing, and boatbuilding.

Andros. Largest of the Bahama Islands, Andros is generally low, thickly wooded, and split into three sections by South, Middle, and North Bights. During the 17th and 18th centuries, it was a home base for pirates, and more recently has become famous for its fishing grounds and Andros Town, among the most luxurious of the island resort communities.

The Berry Islands. Developed as a resort area in the 1960's, the Berry Islands offer long stretches of white-sand beaches sheltered by coconut palms. Both deep-sea fish and bonefish abound.

Bimini. Close to Florida, these tiny islands were once the rum-running capital of the world. And here, we are told, was the Fountain of Youth that Ponce de León spent so much of his time looking for. Today, Bimini boasts unsurpassed Gulf Stream fishing with record catches of marlin, sailfish, kingfish, bluefin tuna, and other fighters of the deep.

Eleuthera. The island was the first of the Bahamas to be settled by the white man. Governor's Harbour in the center of the long, slender island is 300 years old, and descendants of the original settlers, the Eleutherian Adventurers, still live here. The beaches are long and white, the bonefish abound, and there are a number of resorts and hotels. Rock Sound, 25 miles south of Governor's Harbour, used to be famous for the wreckers who lured ships ashore with false lights, and it was called "wreck sound."

Exuma. Both Little and Great Exuma to the south and east of Nassau have excellent harbors and are favorite stopping spots for yachtsmen. The annual Out Island Regatta is held here at George Town during the latter part of April. The accommodations are good in this sailors' and fishermen's paradise and—guess what—there are wonderful beaches too.

Grand Bahama. Some 60 miles from West Palm Beach, Grand Bahama has become a popular resort area, building around the big Grand Bahama Club at West End. Fishing, water sports, golfing, tennis, bicycling along the shoreline, and exploring the interior are all popular.

Great Inagua. Third largest of the Bahamas, Great Inagua is only 67 miles from the northern coast of Haiti. It is a sanctuary for some 70,000 lovely flamingoes, all kinds of colorful wild birds, pelicans and parrots, and—reportedly—wild horses in the interior.

Harbour Island. This tiny spot of an island on the Atlantic side of Eleuthera with its pink beaches as a lure has become more and more popular as a resort. Despite its comparative isolation it now has at least seven hotels and offers all the comforts of the larger islands.

Long Island. Recently emerged as a tourist resort, Long Island, in the Eastern Bahamas, boasts numerous surfing beaches and resorts tailored to attract the upbeat younger set.

Rum Cay. Just to the east of Long Island, Columbus' second landfall is a tiny (under 100 inhabitants) island with miles of secluded beaches and gorgeous reefs for world-class diving experiences.

San Salvador. Landfall of Columbus, San Salvador caters to history buffs and those who crave relaxation amid idyllic, uncluttered surroundings.

Spanish Wells. The town of Spanish Wells is on St. George's Cay near Eleuthera. Descendants of former American Loyalists, the islanders supply fish and greens to Nassau, and now have small resort hotels.

HAITI

One of the most flamboyant islands in the Caribbean, Haiti is rich in African influence and tainted by the excesses of its dictators.

No bigger than Maryland and shaped like the claw of a giant lobster, Haiti shares the island of Hispaniola with the Dominican Republic. It is so mountainous that less than half of its area can be profitably cultivated. Crowded with 6,000,000 people and scarred by poverty, Haiti is not all pretty. But it does have beauty and grandeur. And above all, it does have a vivacity that makes it one of the most exciting islands in all of the Caribbean.

Christopher Columbus established the first recorded European contact with the Western Hemisphere when he landed at what is now Haiti on December 5, 1492. His flagship, the *Santa Maria,* ran aground as he tried to depart on Christmas Eve. When the Spanish colonists failed to develop the island, French buccaneers moved in, and by 1700 they and other adventurous Frenchmen had taken the western end of the island for France. Slaves were imported to work more plantations, and by the middle of the century Cap Français (now Cap Haitien) had become the richest colonial city of the French Empire, shipping vast quantities of sugar, indigo, coffee, cotton, and cocoa from its port. Supported by the labor of thousands of slaves, the Creole planters lived in glittering luxury.

Abruptly the flood of gold ceased. In 1791 black slaves and freed mulattoes revolted. Within a few weeks they had devastated hundreds of plantations and slaughtered some 2,000 whites. More than 10,000 rebellious blacks were killed in reprisals.

The savagely bloody struggles of the next twelve years produced Haiti's four national heroes and the world's first black republic. Toussaint L'Ouverture was the first and most admirable of the leaders. A former slave and coachman, he was put in command of a Negro force after the French—in an effort to prevent encroachment by the British and Spanish—freed the slaves and called on them to help expel the invaders. But when that had been brilliantly accomplished and Toussaint made Governor General, Napoleon dispatched a formidable army under General Leclerc to capture the Haitian leader and destroy his movement. Failing to defeat Toussaint, Leclerc seized him by a ruse and sent him to France where he died in prison. The rebellion, however, continued. Led by Toussaint's most gifted commander, Jean Jacques Dessalines, the Haitians defeated the weakened French, and in 1804 Dessalines proclaimed Haiti independent and himself Emperor.

Two years later, when Dessalines was assassinated, the new nation was declared a republic and Henri Christophe, the most dramatic though not the greatest of the Haitian leaders, became king of the northern part of Haiti.

As strong and fearless as a bull, Christophe had been a waiter before he joined the Toussaint rebellion and rose to be General. He was an inspired and inspiring leader who quickly converted constitutional authority to personal power. His vaulting ambition drove Alexandre Pétion, still another of the Toussaint leaders, to establish a government in opposition in the south. Thoughtful, educated, and politically restrained, Pétion was to become Haiti's first president.

Christophe left a legacy of a different kind to his people. He abandoned the pretense of democracy, had himself crowned Henri I, and filled his court with a ludicrously named pseudo nobility. He promulgated the Code Henri, punished laziness with death, and made virtual serfs out of the slaves he had helped free. Admired, feared, and hated, he outlawed voodoo and forced his countrymen to build bridges, roads, and schools, and make the sugar lands flourish as they had not done for twenty years. He had a mania for building that drove him obsessively to build palaces and châteaux throughout the country. At Milot, some 20 miles south of Cap Haitien, he built the Palace of Sans Souci. For 13 years he drove an army of 200,000 slave laborers to finish the fantastic Citadelle Laferrière. Three years after the Citadelle was completed, Christophe committed suicide.

After Christophe's death, the country was reunited, but for almost a century failed to find effective leadership. In 1915 it was on the verge of national bankruptcy and threatened by German occupation when the United States landed Marines on the island and took over the government. The Americans restored order, bolstered the economy, and trained the Haitian military forces, but after the occupation ended in 1934, political ferment and economic instability reappeared.

In 1957, after five regimes had failed in the preceding seven years, "Papa Doc" Duvalier was elected President. Taking advantage of political unrest, he declared himself President-For-Life in 1964 and, upon his death in 1971, the office passed to his 20-year-old son, Jean Claude. The Duvalier regime also became known for its oppression and excesses that were bankrupting the country. On February 7, 1986, Duvalier was ousted and replaced by a provisional government headed by Lt. Gen. Henri Namphy.

The Citadelle Laferrière of Henri Christophe

Although there has been turmoil since the ouster, no violence has been directed at tourists. Despite occasional protests and general strikes, the country is calm.

More than most, the people of Haiti are the product of their violent past, and what they are is visible through two remarkable windows—art and voodooism. The first you cannot miss. You will hear it in African drum rhythms of the music, feel it in the dancing, see it everywhere in one of the most prolific bursts of creative art that has occurred this century.

Sunday-supplement writers have tried to make voodoo a sensational orgiastic mystery. It's far from that, but it is real and it is practiced by many Haitians. A primitive African ceremonial form of worship, it involves pagan gods, rituals and mysteries known only to the priest (hougan), compulsive and trancelike "possession" of the believers, and sometimes the sacrifice of small animals. The ceremonies are performed at night and include the use of corn flour drawings and symbolic rituals to call up gods or propitiate them. Whatever voodoo is—and it isn't the simple business of incantation and pin-sticking evil charms—it has a firm hold on some Haitians that even generations of Church opposition has not been able to break.

The ceremonies that you will see with a tourist party are likely to be pale in comparison to the real thing. Even so, they are an experience. Some adventurous souls like to strike out on their own and follow the sound of the drums to its source. You might have luck that way. If you ask permission to attend the ceremony, if you are quiet and respectful and don't insult the religion by trying to use a camera, you will probably be welcome to witness a sight you can see nowhere else.

GENERAL INFORMATION

How To Get There: *By Air:* American has daily nonstop flights to Port-au-Prince from New York. Eastern, Pan Am, and Air France fly daily from Miami. ALM Antillean Airlines flies three times a week from Miami. *By Sea:* Port-au-Prince is a popular port of call for cruise ships. The Norwegian Carib Line, Royal Carib Line, Home Lines and Commodore Cruise Lines are among the many companies making frequent stops there.

How To Get Around: Main roads have improved, and it is now possible to drive from Port-au-Prince to Cap Haitien (4 hours) or Jacmel (2 hours). Haiti Air Inter flies daily to Cap Haitien, and several times weekly to Jérémie and Jacmel. The flight to Cap Haitien takes 45 minutes and costs about $60 roundtrip.

Taxis come in three varieties; the most picturesque are the "tap-taps"—multi-colored pick-up trucks decorated on the outside with names such as "God is my Buddy." The inside is generally loaded down with people, while the roof sags under tons of produce—if not more people. More appropriate for tourists are the station wagons with bright red baubles hanging from the inside mirror, which wander through Port-au-Prince taking passengers at twenty cents apiece wherever they want to go in the city. If empty, you may go direct to your destination. If there are other passengers aboard, you will be dropped off in turn. Regular taxis take you there more quickly, at considerably higher cost. The taxis have no meters and the drivers no scruples. Settle the fare before getting in. Drivers also have deals with shops and hotels, so don't depend on their advice.

Or you can rent a car at rates comparable to U.S. prices. A valid U.S. or Canadian license is required. Cars can be rented at Port-au-Prince and Pétionville.

More expensive is renting a car and driver for an hour, half-day, or day. Licensed bilingual guides can be found at the airport or through most hotels.

Among the tour operators are Agence Citadelle, Chatelain Tours, and Southernland Tours.

Language: French, officially. But everyone speaks Creole, a language based on 17th-century French. English is spoken in tourist areas.

Festivals: Haiti's Mardi Gras carnival during the three days before Lent is one of the most exciting, most African in the Caribbean, with parades, historical costumes, and the crowning of a carnival king and queen. Rara, another carnival-like affair, featuring singing and stamping, takes place in Leogane from Good Friday to Easter. Christmas lets loose costumed bands that parade, sing, dance, and carry candles and torches in the streets night or day. Native festivals—including voodoo ceremonies—are held the week preceding the Day of the Virgin, July 16th, at Saut D'Eau (about one hour and forty minutes from the capital). The Carnival of Flowers is an early July spectacle.

Sports: Haiti's two national sports are *cockfighting* and *soccer*. You can see cockfights every Saturday and Sunday in the circular, open-walled stadium called a *gaguère* on the Exposition Grounds in Port-au-Prince, or at smaller but similar structures in the outlying sections of town. Soccer matches are held at the Sylvio Cator Stadium in Port-au-Prince.
Swimming. Most of the hotels have excellent pools. Beaches are not exceptional, but the best are at Cacique Island's Ibo Beach, which has all

watersports, only forty-five minutes from the capital; also good, are Kyona Beach, Club Med and Ouanga Bay, all less than 1½ hours north of the capital, with overnight facilities.

Fishing. Deep-sea fishing is not a highly developed sport in Haiti, but outings can sometimes be arranged through your hotel. Snorkeling and scuba diving are becoming popular. Equipment and instruction are available at *Baskin in the Sun* at Kaliko Beach, *Cap d'Estrees* at Petit-Goâve and *Sand Cay* in Port-au-Prince.

Horseback Riding. Club Med, Ibo Beach and Kaliko Beach, north of the capital, all have riding facilities, as does Cormier in Cap Hatien.

Golf. Bellevue Club has a nine-hole course. It is open to tourists Monday through Saturday.

Tennis. Montana, Villa Créole, Club Med, Kaliko Beach, Jolly Beach, Mont Joli, Courmier, Moulin Sur Mer, Ibo Beach, Royal Haitian and El Rancho all have courts.

Cruising. Day cruises to uninhabited islands of Arcadin are available at Ibo or Kyona beaches. Each morning "yellowbird" catamaran offers cruises from Casino dock in Port-au-Prince to the Sand Cay.

Night Life: African drums keep Haiti's night life throbbing. You'll want to see a voodoo ceremony and a "bamboche," a neighborhood dancing party that raises the thatched roof of the dance hall. Staged and relatively mild, the voodoo you see probably won't include animal sacrifices or "possession," but it will give you an idea of what is going on when you hear voodoo drums pounding in the hills. Although unscheduled, a bamboche is easier to find through your hotel. You'll seldom see any dancing as vigorous.

The leading hotels in Port-au-Prince coordinate their floor shows so that each night a different hotel has something special. Villa Créole, Royal Hatien Hotel, Castel Haiti and Ibo Lélé all have live shows at different times during the week. Check at your hotel for a current schedule. Flamboyant, a club at El Rancho in the mountains above Port-au-Prince, is open every night. El Rancho also has a luxurious casino, as does the Royal Hatien. Both offer blackjack, craps, roulette, and "jackpots," as Haitians optimistically call slot machines. Le Bistro, a restaurant-grill in Port-au-Prince, has a folklore and voodoo show every Friday.

Medical Facilities: There are Ameri-

Coastal sloops and schooners line the harbor of Port-au-Prince

can-trained doctors on call at the larger hotels, several hospitals in Port-au-Prince.

Boil milk everywhere. Use boiled or bottled water outside of Port-au-Prince. Be cautious about fruits and salads. Wash fruits thoroughly if you buy these locally.

Additional Information: The Haiti National Tourist Office, 630 Fifth Avenue, Suite 2109, New York, NY 10020 (212-757-3517); 919 N. Michigan Ave., Chicago, IL 60611 (312-337-1603); 1980 Post Oak South Blvd, Houston, TX 77056 (713-961-9037); 150 SE Second Ave., Miami, FL 33131 (305-337-1603); Office Nationale du Tourisme, Avenue Marie-Jeanne. Port-au-Prince, tel. 2-1720.

Where to Stay

Port-au-Prince: ****Castel Haiti,* 100 rooms, pool, air-conditioned, city and bay views. ****Holiday Inn Le Plaza,* 80 rooms, pool, free transportation to beach. ****Royal Haitian Hotel,* 75 rooms, pool, casino, garden setting.

On the Beach: ****Club Med,* 352 rooms, all-inclusive resort. ****Kaliko Beach Club,* 40 rooms, pool, tennis, water sports. ****Moulin Sur Mer,* restored plantation on 36 acres of land, 6 of which are beach. ***Kyona Beach,* 20 rooms, restaurant, shopping.

Pétionville and the mountains: ****Ibo Lele,* 45 rooms, pool, air-conditioned, Haitian paintings. *****El Rancho,* 110 rooms, luxurious, pool, nightclub, casino. ****Choucoune,* 42 rooms, pool, air-conditioned, roof garden. ****Montana,* 70 rooms, pool, air-conditioned. ****Villa Creole,* 70 rooms, modern, large pool. ***Petit Hotel Caraibe,* 12 rooms, intimate, pool. **Ife Hotel,* 11 rooms, restaurant, air-conditioned.

Cap Haitien: ***Beck Hotel,* 12 rooms, private beach, view. ***Roi Christophe,* 20 rooms, pool, tennis. ***Mont Joli,* 40 rooms, pool, beach, view. ***Cormier Beach Hotel,* 35 rooms, on beach.

Cacique Island: ***Ibo Beach Hotel,* 60 rooms, 30 minutes from Port-au-Prince.

Where to Eat

Haiti's food is French and Creole, and both versions are superb. Creole cooking will delight your palate with guinea hen and orange sauce, *diri et djondjon* (rice and black mushrooms), *langouste flambée* (flaming rock lobster). Sweeter delights are *pain patate* (sweet potato pudding), mango ice cream and pudding, and fresh coconut ice cream.

French wines and champagnes are bargains. Barbancourt rum is among the best in the Caribbean.

RESTAURANTS: **Port-au-Prince:** *** *La Terasse,* at the Holiday Inn, serves French and international cuisine. *** *Les Boucaniers,* at Moulin Sur Mer, has excellent barbecue. ***Villa Créole has a creole buffet. *Le Bistro is a restaurant-grill featuring pizza and crepes. Folklore show every Friday. ***Le Recife,* specialty: seafood. ***Le Rond Point,* Exposition Grounds, excellent Creole cooking.

Pétionville and the mountains: ***La Lanterne.* Paté maison and red snapper are specialties on varied menu. ** *La Belle Epoque,* good ribs. ***Le Gourmet at El Rancho, French haute cuisine. ***Chez Gérard,* French restaurant highly considered by international travelers.

Where to Shop

Port-au-Prince offers beautiful products of native artists and craftsmen —paintings by Haiti's famed artists, mahogany sculpture and wood carvings, voodoo-inspired jewelry, hand-

Just a visit to the Iron Market is a tumultuous adventure

loomed cottons, and excellent hand-woven rugs; Haiti's dressmakers are also becoming well known.

The best buys in liquor are the famous Haitian Rhum Barbancourt and French wines and liqueurs.

Although shops are scattered all over town, many are centered around the Exposition Grounds and along Rue Bonne Foi. Pétionville also has a number of fine shops.

CLOTHING: *Nanotte,* Chemin des Dalles, *Mme. Alexandre Celestine,* Avenue John Brown. *Bagatelle, Bagaille* and *Art et Mode* on Pétionville's main street have both local and European fashions.

HANDICRAFTS: *La Belle Créole,* Rue Bonne Foi near the dock, a department store with good buys in china, sweaters, and watches. *Carlos,* Avenue Pie XII on the Exposition Grounds, gifts, watches, and bargains in French perfumes and liqueurs (also has gift shop branches in several of the hotels). *Mountain Maid Artisans,* embroidered clothing, ceramics and candles. Not to be missed is the *Iron Market* in Port-au-Prince, in which everything from produce to jewelry is sold. Bargaining is expected.

Other shops on Rue Bonne Foi are: *Little Europe,* for perfumes, glassware; *Versailles,* imported fabrics; and *Aux Cent Mille,* for china, glassware, perfumes and gifts.

HANDICRAFT FACTORIES: You can visit the factories, watch the craftsmen work, and buy if you wish. Among the best are, *The Red Carpet,* Pétionville; the *Baptist Mission Church* in Fermate, above Pétionville, features beautiful embroidery. *Haiti Perfume Factory,* 21 Rue Panaméricaine, and the castle-like *Jane Barbancourt* rum factory at Boutiliers are also worth a visit.

PAINTINGS: If you're interested in Haitian paintings, which you can buy for anything from a few dollars to a few hundred, visit *Centre d'Art* on Rue de Sept. 22; *Claire's Gallery,* Rue 3; *Galerie Issa,* 18 Ave. de Chili; *Galerie Monnin,* 382 Blvd J. J. Dessalines; *Musé Gallery,* Angle Rue Geffraud; *Galerie Nader,* 92 Rue de Magasin de l'Etat; *Touche d'Art,* 21 C. Avenue Marie-Jeanne. In Pétionville there is the *Gallerie Marassa* and the *Gallerie Theard Art Co-Op.*

What to See

Port-au-Prince (Port oh PRANCE), metropolis of 500,000 and the capital of the country, reflects the best and worst in the country. Ablaze with sun and flowers, and marked off by broad modern avenues and spacious parks, it lies in a tropical green valley backed by rising tiers of handsome wind-cooled suburbs. The parks are neat landscaped oases, the Presidential Palace is gleaming white in its flowered gardens. But a few steps from the modern thoroughfares the streets narrow to arcaded passages crowded with street merchants, peasant women down from the mountains with baskets of wilted vegetables or scrawny chickens on their heads, insistent beggars who unabashedly demand money. Still further toward the edge of town the streets become unpaved alleys winding through sagging slums where dogs and half-naked children forage together. All this is one small city of exceptional beauty and shocking squalor.

The city faces the bay across a broad, impressive avenue, President Truman Boulevard. Between the boulevard and the waterfront are the *Exposition Grounds.* The buildings, imposing rather than distinguished, were put up for the 1949 Bicentennial and have now been converted to shops, restaurants, and government buildings. The grounds include the lovely park where cruise ships land their passengers, the handsome *American Embassy,* the *Rond Point,* a restaurant and night club, the *Museum of Fine Arts,* and the open air *Théâtre de Verdure* where excellent local musical and dance groups perform. Here, too, is the great center of excitement for the townspeople—the *Gaguère Cockpit,* where cockfights are held every weekend. Also along the waterfront is the *Fontaine Lumineuse,* the tastefully illuminated and much photographed fountain.

Just east of the Exposition Grounds is the fabulous *Iron Market,* two

The formidable Presidential Palace in Port-au-Prince

massive open metal warehouses separated by a minaret-topped entrance. The time to see it as its tumultuous best is on Saturday, but at any time it is an adventure into din and confusion. In hundreds of stalls natives display every conceivable kind of salable merchandise—straw hats and fresh fish, mangoes and mahogany bowls, soap and voodoo drums. And rising above it all like a cloud is the roar of top-of-the-lungs haggling. Take your camera, but be sure to ask permission before you snap any of this bargain bedlam.

A few blocks away is another world—the Champs de Mars. Here is the domed *Palais National,* the handsome white presidential palace with its Hall of Busts where are displayed statues of past presidents and leaders. Around the park are government buildings, memorials, the army headquarters, and barracks. Most interesting is the new *Museum of Haitian Art.* You will also see rarities at the *Museum of the Institute of Ethnology,* and historical exhibits, including the anchor of Columbus' wrecked flagship at the *National Museum.*

Not too far away are the city's two most interesting churches, the *Old Catholic Church,* built in 1720, and the *Episcopal Cathedral of the Holy Trinity* on Rue Pavée. The Catholic Church is one of the few buildings of French colonial days that has survived and been restored. The Episcopal Cathedral is distinguished for the superb murals in the apse which depict scenes from the Bible with great simplicity and in the brilliant colors of Haiti. Painted in 1947, they were forerunners of the art renaissance that has swept across Haiti.

All this is merely the downstairs of Port-au-Prince. The rest—and in some ways the best—is in the rising tiers behind the lower city. Five miles and twenty minutes away over a winding, flower-banked road, **Pétionville** is 2,000 feet higher and 10° cooler than the city. It is the residential section favored by the Paris-oriented elite and the foreign colony. Here, too, many of the more luxurious modern hotels have been built. A few winding miles and 1,000 feet higher is **Boutiliers** with its splendid view of the city. A mile above sea level **Kenscoff** floats in a sea of flowers, the wide native market framed by enormous poinsettias and brilliant bougainvillaea, the mountain slopes awash with fields of flowers grown by the Chatelet des Fleurs and shipped by air to markets in the United States. The road corkscrews still higher to **Furcy** which is perched at an elevation of almost 7,000 feet. Port-au-Prince lies below like a tiny model of a town neatly arranged beside a painted deep blue sea.

Cap Haitien. Less than four hours by road and only forty-five minutes by plane from the capital, Cap Haitien is a tranquil little picture city of 80,000 people that lies at the heart of Haiti's turbulent past. It was the city of Henri Christophe. He defended it, lost it, burned it to the ground, and then rebuilt it. And twenty miles to the south, at the village of *Milot,* he built his own palace and the incredible mountaintop bastion which became his tomb.

Christophe, the slave who became king, enslaved thousands to build *Sans Souci,* conceived as the most magnificent palace in the Western Hemisphere. Even today the faded brick ruins, four stories high and wide as a city block, rise in majestic splendor against the tropic green. The shell of the whole plan is there—the grand double stairway, the ballrooms, the banquet halls, the waiting rooms, and the private apartments for the royal family. It takes little imagination to see these rooms before they were destroyed by an earthquake in 1842, their walls panelled in mahogany, and hung with splendid tapestries, their marble floors cooled by mountain streams that flowed beneath them.

The Black Emperor lived in splendor—and in fear. On the knife-edge crest of a savage peak half a mile high he built *Citadelle Laferrière,* a fortress to stand against the world. For thirteen years an army of men labored to build the battlements, 140 feet high and nearly twenty feet thick at the base, a man-made rock of Gibraltar with storehouses, cisterns, forges and blacksmith shops, treasure rooms, arsenals, quarters for the court, barracks large enough to house a garrison of 15,000 men. On the roof-top parade grounds there were emplacements for hundreds of cannon, and in the magazine you can still see thousands of rusting cannon balls. And all this—every scrap except the stones themselves—was dragged up the rocky paths by chains of sweating slaves.

Not a gun was ever fired from the fortress. Three years after it was completed, Christophe was crippled by a stroke, and terrified that his enemies might capture him, he committed suicide in the Palace of Sans Souci. In secrecy his queen had his body carried by night to the Citadelle and sunk in quicklime. Christophe had built not a fortress but a mausoleum.

The monument can only be reached by hiking the last two steep miles or renting a horse at Milot with an accompanying guide on foot.

There are three centers on the southern peninsula that can be easily visited. **Jacmel** is a coffee town with 17th-century architecture and good beaches nearby. **Les Cayes,** on the southern shore, is best known as the place where Simon Bolívar found refuge when he was forced to flee Venezuela. **Jérémie,** at the northern tip of the peninsula, is tropical and beautiful, handsomely set in a semicircle above its sparkling bay.

Largest city on the northern peninsula is *Port de Paix,* a shipping center. Only a few miles off the coast is *Tortue Island,* once the most famous pirate stronghold on the Spanish Main. Directly south on the gulf is *Gonaïves,* the city where Haitian independence was proclaimed by Dessalines more than a century and a half ago. *Gonave Island,* centered in the gulf, is undeveloped for tourists today. It has a future, however, in its swarming fish, crystal water, exquisite shells, and vast beaches.

PUERTO RICO

As old as the discovery of the New World and as modern as tomorrow, as lush as the tropics and as mild as the spring, Puerto Rico is an exciting "Bootstrap" island where 3,400,000 Americans are remaking their land and their future.

When the Spanish founded the first European settlement on the North American continent at St. Augustine in 1565, Puerto Rico was already an old and rich colony. Ponce de León had long before sailed from San Juan to Florida to search for eternal youth—and to find a fatal Indian arrow. When the Pilgrim Fathers sailed the *Mayflower* into Plymouth Harbor in 1620, San Juan was a century-old bastion of Spanish power that had deprived the English of the riches of Central America, and twenty-five years before had stood off a siege that cost the lives of Britain's toughest sea dogs—Hawkins and Drake.

That is one Puerto Rico—the old Puerto Rico—and much of its stormy four-century history is still there to see. But beside and around the island of the past there has grown another that lives on the verge of the future, a remarkably beautiful country that in less than 40 years has peacefully hoisted itself from below the poverty line to become the island with the highest per capita personal income in the Caribbean and Central America.

A lush and verdant rectangle 100 miles long and 35 miles wide, Puerto Rico is an area about half the size of New Jersey lying 1,000 miles southeast of the tip of Florida at the center of the Caribbean chain. The mountains that cut across the length of the island are brilliant with dozens of varieties of flowering tropical shrubs and trees, and their lower slopes are green with tobacco plants and pineapple fields and coffee bushes growing in the shade of orange trees. Along the fertile coastal plains the cooling trade winds ripple vast plantations of sugar cane. On the northern shore the Atlantic surf pounds in on long sandy beaches sheltered by reefs, and the southern coast is lapped by the quiet waters of the Caribbean.

The northeasterly trade winds cool the island to an ideal 76° average in winter, hold the summer temperature down to 82° or less. They also press the airborne moisture of the Atlantic high against the mountains where it is released in the heavy rainbow showers that produce the tropical rain forest with its giant ferns and exotic orchids on the upper slopes of El Yunque, the 3,500-foot peak at the eastern tip of the island.

Along the Atlantic coast east of San Juan are ribbons of beaches—Luquillo Beach alone is over 2 miles long—and from the great deeps a few miles offshore record-breaking game fish of many kinds have been taken. The southern shore, drier and almost arid in parts, is old and colorful and decidedly Spanish.

Of the 3.4 million people who live on the island, roughly three-quarters are of mixed Spanish, African, and Indian ancestry. The rest represent various races and cultures of the world. Spanish is the official language, but almost everyone speaks English.

Spain misruled Puerto Rico for centuries, and when the United States took over, following the Spanish-American War of 1898, life for the islanders did not improve. Until World War II, one-cropism (sugar), absentee ownership, overpopulation, and poverty made the island virtually a slum.

But in 1947 the government initiated Operation Bootstrap, an economic development program to modernize Puerto Rico. In the four decades since then, the island has attracted $7 billion of investment that has created tens of thousands of new jobs. Life expectancy has risen from 45 to 73 years and illiteracy reduced to less than 2 percent of the population.

Today, tourism is an important part of the island's economy, contributing close to 6 percent to the annual gross national product. More than 2 million people visit Puerto Rico each year for the sunny shores and tropical forests. For Puerto Ricans, however, it is not entirely a paradise. Unemployment is still a problem.

The Puerto Ricans have shown a tremendous talent for forging a

San Geronimo was built in the late 18th century to defend San Juan from pirates.

future for themselves. Now they are turning their energy toward preserving the island's rich Spanish culture and history. This artistic renaissance is being compared to Haiti's art explosion in the 1950's.

General Information

How To Get There: *By Air:* San Juan's Luis Muñoz Marin International Airport, renovated in 1984, is the busiest in the Caribbean.

American, Eastern, Delta, and TWA all have daily nonstop service from many U.S. mainland cities. American flies from Toronto via New York, and Eastern flies from Montreal and Toronto through Atlanta. American Trans Air has daily flights from New York to Aguadilla, on Puerto Rico's northwest coast. Air Puerto Rico, Executive Air, and Virgin Islands Seaplane Shuttle have connecting service from other Caribbean islands. *By Sea:* San Juan is the Caribbean's leading embarkation point. More than 560 ships call each year, including Carnival, Chandris, Costa, Cunard, Exploration, Pacquet, Princess, Royal Viking, Sitmar, and Sun Line.

How To Get Around: In San Juan and its suburbs buses are plentiful, clean, and fast. Stops are marked by a yellow post and sign, "Parada." The fare is $.25 on air conditioned buses. Metered taxis are available everywhere; $.80 for the initial charge, $.10 for each additional quarter-mile.

Goya Foods also operates free trolleys for patrons of San Juan stores. The trolleys travel along La Fortaleza and San Francisco streets to Plaza de Armas.

Outside San Juan you can use airconditioned buses or inexpensive "publicos," five- or seven-passenger cars (with "P" or "PA" on their licenses) connecting all the island cities. "Publico" fare from San Juan to Ponce on the south coast is $2.

Rental agencies offer drive-yourself cars at rates from about $30 a day. A car with driver will cost you about $50 a day.

Complete tours of the city and the island are offered by such agencies as Tour Co-Op of Puerto Rico, Travel Services, Gray Line, Turismo Internacional, Rico Sun Tours, United Tour Guide, V.I.P., Coast Tours, and Will Ray tours. Check at your hotel for details.

Language: Spanish, but English is understood by most people.

Sports: *Baseball* and *horse racing* are the major spectator diversions. Baseball is played at San Juan's Hiram Bithorn Stadium, amateur from February to September, with major league stars competing from October to January.

Surfing is excellent at Rincón, Añasco, Aguadilla, and Guánica beaches. The World Cup Surfing Championship will be held in Rincón in January 1988. There is horse racing Wednesdays, Fridays, and Sundays at El Commandante, on the outskirts of San Juan.

Swimming. The big hotels have pools and the larger resorts are on the beaches. Luquillo, the government-operated beach 30 miles east of San Juan, is the largest.

Water Skiing, Spear Fishing. Luquillo Beach and the Condado Lagoon are centers for water skiing. Scuba lessons are available at the Caribe Hilton (721-0303), the Caribbean School of Aquatics (723-4740), and Coral Island Divers (742-3177), among others.

Fishing. Excellent for blue and white

marlin, sailfish, tuna, wahoo, tarpon, and bonefish. Club Nautico in San Juan is host to the International Billfish Tournament every August.

Boating. Charter yachts, day sail-boats, and motorboats for hire throughout the island. Island sloops with captains can be rented for about $80–$150 per day at Benitz Deep Sea Fishing (723-2292), Castillo Water-sports (724-6161), San Juan Fishing Charters (723-0415), and Torruella Fishing Charter (725-1408).

Golf. Hyatt's Dorado Beach Hotel, and its neighbor, the Hyatt Regency Cerromar Beach Hotel, have 36-hole championship golf courses designed by Robert Trent Jones. Palmas del Mar at Humacao has an 18-hole course designed by Gary Player. Berwind Country Club in Rio Grande and Dorado del Mar Country Club in Dorado have 18-hole courses. Many smaller resorts have 9-hole courses.

Tennis. Most of the larger hotels have courts, and the private clubs generally welcome visitors.

Horseback Riding. Palmas del Mar Equestrian Center, Humacao, (852-4785), and Hacienda Carabali (726-0992) offer trails and instruction.

Night Life: Leading entertainers from the States, Europe, and Latin America, plenty of music and atmosphere are featured at the luxurious night clubs—the Caribe Hilton's Club Caribe and Juliana's, La Concha's Supper Club, the El San Juan's Tropicoro, El Chico Latino Lounge, and Amadeus disco, the newly renovated Ponce de León at El Convento, La Fiesta Lounge at the Condado Plaza, Leonardo's at the Diplomat Hotel, Pegasus at the Carib Inn, and The Sheraton's Salón Carnaval. The Swiss Chalet is a favored late spot. In Old San Juan there are El Convento, La Fonda del Callejón, El Primitive and Ocho Puertas. The big hotels operate government-controlled gambling casinos.

Medical Facilities: Modern hospitals are staffed by U.S. trained doctors and nurses.

Cultural Events: Choose from performances by the Puerto Rico Symphony Orchestra, the San Juan Ballet, the University of Puerto Rico Theater at the Fine Arts Center, or check *Qué Pasa,* the monthly visitors' guide published by the tourist board, for other concerts, stage, and film programs.

Additional Information: Commonwealth of Puerto Rico, Department of Tourism, 1290 Ave. of Americas, New York, NY 10104 (212-541-6630); Suite 903 Peninsula Bldg, 200 S.E. First St., Miami, FL 33131 (305-381-8915); 11 East Adams St., Chicago, IL 60603 (312-922-9701); 3575 W. Cahuenga Blvd., Los Angeles, CA 90068 (213-874-5991); 10 King St.

East, Toronto, Ontario, M5C 1C3 (416-367-0190); 301 San Justo, Old San Juan, P.R. 00905 (809-721-2400).

Where to Stay

SAN JUAN

HOTELS: All hotels listed have pools and air conditioning. De Luxe hotels usually have restaurants, bars, and other services. A few hotels have kitchenettes and efficiencies (as listed).

****Caribe Hilton, ocean front, near ancient Fort San Gerónimo, 676 rooms, night club, tennis. ****El San Juan, ocean front, near airport, 397 rooms, night club, tennis. ****La Concha, ocean front, 234 rooms, night club, tennis. ***Dupont Plaza San Juan, 450 rooms, casino, tennis, beach. ****Carib Inn, 225 rooms, tennis. ***Quality Inn Royale, 152 rooms, rooftop restaurant, ***Condado Beach, 251 rooms, ocean front. ***Dutch Inn, 146 rooms, restaurant, bar. ***El Convento, 95 rooms, night club. ***Candado Plaza, ocean front, 587 rooms. **Ramada San Juan, 96 rooms, ocean front. ***Travel Lodge Hotel, 91 rooms, restaurant, near beach. **Howard Johnson's, 150 rooms, pool, restaurant. ***Best Western Hotel Pierre, free transportation to nearby beach club, 180 rooms. **Excelsior, free transportation to nearby beach, 140 rooms, some with kitchenette. **The Regency, 129 rooms and suites, restaurant. * Tanama, 95 rooms. *Toro, 44 rooms.

CONDOMINIUMS AND GUEST HOUSES: The trend to renting apartments for a vacation is on the upswing. Apartments are advertised in The New York Times, USA Today, and the San Juan Star, and every airline or travel agent has its own list and will gladly quote prices, which are usually reasonable. All apartments have kitchens and maid service; most buildings have pools and are convenient to the beach. Many package deals with local hotels and restaurants are offered. **El San Juan Towers, 319 rooms, beach, tennis. **Jewel's by the Sea, 8 air-conditioned rooms on the beach. **Arcade, 15 air-conditioned rooms and efficiencies, pool. ** Prado Inn, 18 rooms, near beach. * Casa Roig, 16 rooms. **Green Isle, 17 rooms. **El Canario, 20 air-conditioned rooms near the beach. **La Casa Mathiesen, 12 rooms with kitchenettes, pool.

OUTSIDE SAN JUAN

****Hyatt Dorado Beach, Dorado, country and beach resort 15 miles west of San Juan, 308 rooms, cabañas, air-conditioned, nightly entertainment and dancing, two golf courses, pool, 5 tennis courts. ****Hyatt Regency Cerromar Beach, Dorado, on the beach, 520 rooms and suites, two 18-hole golf courses, seven tennis courts, nightclub, air-conditioned. ** Parador Vistamer, Quebradillas, 35 rooms, pool, tennis, golf nearby. *** Parador Montemar, Aguadilla, 40 rooms, mountain top, nightclub. *** Mayagüez Hilton, resort hotel at entrance to Mayagüez, 50 rooms, air-conditioned, pool. **Parador Oasis, San Germán, 150 rooms, near Phosphorescent Bay. ***Hacienda Gripinas, Jayuya, 19 rooms, coffee plantation guest house, near Utuado Indian park, pool, garden. ***Villa Cofresi, Rincón, on the beach, 55 rooms, restaurant, bar, all water sports. **Baños de Coamo, Coamo, 48 rooms, mineral spring pool, tennis. **Boquemar, Cabo Rojo, 41 rooms near beach. ** Copmarina, Guanica, beach-front resort, 72 rooms, air-conditioned, pool. **Meliá, Ponce, commercial hotel, 80 rooms, air-conditioned, golf and swimming privileges. **Holiday Inn,

Ponce, 120 rooms. **Parador El Guajataca,* Quebradillas, 38 rooms, beachfront. **Parador Hacienda Juanita,* Maricao, 21 rooms, former plantation, tennis, walking trails. **La Casa Del Francis,* Vieques Island, 12 rooms. *Sea Gate Guest House,* Vieques Island, 10 rooms, spectacular view. *Parador Martorell,* near famous Luquillo Beach, guest house, 8 rooms. *La Palma,* Mayagüez, commercial hotel, 47 rooms, some air-conditioned. **Parador Villa Esperanza,* 50 rooms, pool, near Phosphorescent Bay. *Posada Por La Mar,* 13 rooms near beach. **Perichi's,* Cabo Rojo, 15 rooms, restaurant, near beach.

Where to Eat

Spanish and Puerto Rican native dishes, particularly sea food, are the specialties. The most popular native dishes include *arroz con pollo* (chicken with rice), *asopao* (a thick soup made with chicken or sea food, rice, and wine sauce), and *paella* (meat or shellfish and rice). Don't miss the *langosta* (lobster) or the *jueyes* (specially fed land crabs).

Rum is the national drink, and you can buy it in almost any shade and inexpensively. Fresh fruit juices are delicious.

RESTAURANTS: **Old San Juan:** *Galanes,* 65 San Francisco St., international cuisine. *La Danza,* Cristo and Fortaleza, Puerto Rican specialties, piano music. *El Patio de Sam,* 102 San Sebastian, steaks and do-it-yourself salads. *La Chaumière,* 367 Tetuán, French cuisine. *Amadeus,* 106 San Sebastian, nouvelle, Puerto Rican. *Tetuán 20,* 20 Tetuán St., Spanish and Puerto Rican. *Casa Nostra,* 211 Cristo, Italian. *La Mallorquina,* 207 San Justo, Puerto Rican and Spanish cooking. San Juan's old-

est restaurant. *La Zaragozana,* 356 San Francisco, Spanish, Cuban and continental cuisine. Spanish atmosphere. *El Convento,* Calle Cristo, continental cuisine, elegant dining in Spanish Renaissance decor, dancing. *Tango's,* 313 Recinto Sur, Argentine. *Farol,* 411 San Francisco, steaks and seafood. *Meson Vasquo,* 47 Cristo, authentic Basque cooking.

San Juan: *Rotisserie,* in the Caribe Hilton, French cuisine. *Dar Tiffany's,* in the El San Juan Hotel, steaks and seafood. *Ali-oli,* in the Excelsior, international cuisine. *Casa Eusebio,* Club Nautico, Puerto Rican and Spanish food. *Che's,* 35 Caoba, Argentine. *Isla Verde,* Los Angeles Marginal, steaks, seafood. *El Cid,* facing Condado lagoon, Spanish dishes are their specialty. *Swiss Chalet,* Pierre, one of the oldest and best restaurants in San Juan. *Le Pavillion,* El San Juan Hotel, French. *Metropole,* Route 37, Spanish and Puerto Rican. *Fornos,* 604 Ponce de León, Puerto Rican. *Fabada,* 603 Miramar, Spanish. *D'Arco,* in the Toro Hotel, American and Puerto Rican specialties.

Out on the Island: Caguas: *Roosevelt Inn,* on main square, delicious pastries. Cidra: *Salón Pomarrosa,* Treasure Island Hotel, typical Puerto Rican cuisine in country atmosphere. Dorado: *Hyatt's Dorado Beach Hotel Dining Room; Ocean Terrace Grill* for dining and dancing; *Su Casa* featuring Spanish specialties. *Hyatt Regency Cerromar Beach Hotel,* supper club and restaurants. Fajardo: *Anchor's Inn,* steaks, seafood. *Hotel Delicias Restaurant,* Puerto Rican and seafood specialties. Humacao: *Candelero,* Puerto Rican *Paradise Seafood,* very fresh fish. *New Hawaii Village,* Chinese food, some American dishes. *Tulio's Seafood,* has Spanish fare as well. Isabela: *Sea View Wonder,* seafood specialties. Loiza Aldea: *Doña Hilda,* international cuisine. *Meson*

Espanol, Spanish. *Mayagüez Hilton Restaurant,* air-conditioned. Parguera: *Villa Parguera Hotel Restaurant,* seafood and other specialties. Ponce: *La Montserrate,* beautiful view, right on the water. *Hotel Meliá Restaurant,* air-conditioned, Puerto Rican and American specialties. *Lydia's,* steaks, seafood, warm atmosphere. Rincón: *Villa Cofresi Hotel,* restaurant and cocktail lounge. Salinas: *Coche,* seafood, grill. San German: *Parador Oasis,* restaurant in a charming country inn, Puerto Rican, international. Santa Isabel: *El Aquarium,* modern, air-conditioned, fresh lobster and seafood specialties. El Yunque: *El Yunque Restaurant,* high in Caribbean National Forest, Spanish and native dishes. Culebra Island: *Seafarer's Inn,* fresh seafood. Vieques Island: *Casa del Francis,* Puerto Rican dishes.

Where to Shop

There are more than 400 stores within seven square blocks in Old San Juan's picturesque shopping district, all restored 16th- and 17th-century buildings. Fifteen minutes away by taxi or "publico" is Plaza las Americas, the largest shopping center in the Caribbean—a modern, air-conditioned mart which houses many local and well-known U.S. retail firms.

Puerto Rico is not a free port, but many products imported from Europe and Central America are cheaper than they are in the United States. Rum is a real bargain, but you must pay a tax on it when taking it back to the States. Cigars from local tobacco are hand-rolled in the old city.

Foremost among Puerto Rico's handcrafts are the small, gaily painted wood religious figures called "santos." Other good buys are ceramics, hand-woven fiber articles, stringed musical instruments, papier-mâché products, hammocks called *cuatos,* and jewelry.

The local art has developed an international reputation and galleries are popular tourist stops.

Tourists interested in viewing basket-weavers, hammock-makers, and other artisans at work should stop by the *Centro de Artes Populares,* Dominican Convent, Old San Juan, for information on craftsmen who welcome visitors.

Arts and Crafts: These centers have been recommended by the Folk Arts Program of the Institute of Puerto Rican Culture: *Centro de Artes Populares,* Dominican Convent; *Plazoleta del Puerto,* Marina, Old San Juan; *Puerto Rican Arts and Crafts,* 204 Fortaleza, Old San Juan; *Mercado de Artesania Puertorriqueña,* Muñoz Rivera Park, Puerta de Tierra; *Mercado Artesania Carabali,* Sixto Escobar Park, Puerto de Tierra; *Artesanos Unidos de Bayamón,* Parque Central, Bayamón; *Los Artesanos,* Barrio Martin González, Carolina; *Artesania Camui,* Route 3, Canóvanas. *Beachcomber,* Route 304, La Parguera.

GIFTS AND SOUVENIRS: *Casa Cavanagh,* 202 Calle Cristo, Old San Juan, and Plaza las Americas, imports from the Far East, Mexican and Puerto Rican objects; *Arca del Tesoro,* Plaza las Americas, articles from around the world. *Crafts Ole,* 105 Fortaleza, Old San Juan, mahogany, straw, pottery.

CLOTHING AND FASHIONS: *Ralph Lauren Factory Outlet,* Calle Cristo and San Francisco, designer fashions; *Barbara Ann,* Tourism Pier 3, Old San Juan, women's and girls' apparel; *Suarez & Hnos.,* 205 Fortaleza, Old San Juan, men's clothing; *Hathaway Factory Outlet,* 203 Calle Cristo, famous label shirts.

DEPARTMENT STORES: *Gonzalez Padin* at Cruz & Fortaleza, Old San Juan; the *New York Department Store,*

San José & Fortaleza, Old San Juan, is the local versions of Macy's. There are also *Penney's,* Plaza las Americas, and *Sears* in Hato Rey.

CIGARS: *Antilles Mfg.,* 325 Recinto Sur, Old San Juan; *Caribe Cigars,* 204 O'Donnell, Old San Juan.

JEWELRY: Calle Fortaleza has several shops with good prices on gold jewelry.

What to See

San Juan will almost certainly be your introduction to Puerto Rico— and a very proper one it is, for this sprawling metropolis of more than one million people contains both the crumbling ruins of the ancient Spanish empire and the glass-and-steel outlines of the island of the future.

The historic city is crowded into seven square blocks of narrow, medieval streets between the fortress walls that guard both shores behind the mammoth pointed bulk of El Morro. From the *Plaza de Colón,* the landside entrance to the old city where the bus routes end,

The Pablo Casals Museum: Casals spent his last 20 years in Puerto Rico.

you will have to walk, for only pedestrians can negotiate the ancient blue cobbled streets. From your starting point it is only a matter of ten or twelve short blocks to the mighty and magnificent fort, *El Morro,* which for more than four centuries has been the city's chief defense, the sharp point of the great stone shield thrust out into the sea. You can go through it on National Park Service tours. It is open from 8 A.M. to 6:15 P.M.

When you walk the ramparts where the sea beats against the massive walls that rise 145 feet straight above the water, you will understand why in four centuries it never fell before a naval attack. Beginning in 1539 it took the Spanish nearly fifty years to build the core of this bastion and another two centuries to complete the outlying fortifications.

You can follow the walls backward along the shore and wind through tunnels to the towers and huge gun emplacements high above the roaring sea. Sections of the wall still remain, but of the four gates that gave access to the city only one, the Gate of San Juan, opening toward the bay, has been preserved. The wall still rises steeply all along the Atlantic shore, and from El Morro you can see it stretching back to the other great fort, *San Cristóbal,* started in 1631 after both the English and Dutch had successfully breached the defenses from the land side. San Cristóbal's back is to the sea and it overlooks the narrow strip of land connecting the city with the main island.

Near the entrance to El Morro are the *Dominican Convent* and *San José Church,* said to be the oldest church in continuous use in the Western Hemisphere. Both were founded in 1532 by the Dominican Friars. Though San José's façade was not added until a century after the founding and the church itself was remodeled in the 18th and 19th centuries, the vaulted Gothic ceiling is an unusual example of the style in the New World. The Convent is a splendid structure done in the Spanish monastic manner.

Only a few blocks or so to the south is *Casa Blanca,* the fine ancestral manor of the family of Ponce de León. The original wooden house, begun in 1521, the year of the governor's death, was destroyed by a storm and two years later Ponce's son-in-law began construction of the present lovely mansion. From 1898 to 1966 it was the residence of the United States Army. It is now a museum of 16th and 17th century Puerto Rican life, and is open Tuesday through Sunday, 9 A.M.–noon, 1 P.M.–4:30 P.M.

A few steps further along the city wall is *San Juan Gate,* completed about 1641, and once the main entrance to the city. It was here that governors and official visitors disembarked and gave thanks for their safe arrival at an overhead oratory before they entered the city.

Just beyond the gate is *La Fortaleza,* for more than four centuries the residence of Puerto Rico's governors and the oldest executive mansion in continuous use in the United States. Begun in 1533, it was destroyed by the Dutch in 1625. It was reconstructed a century later and subsequently enlarged a number of times. Two of the 16th-century towers and a wall still stand. There are daily tours of the magnificent public rooms, terraced gardens, mahogany stairway, and the chapel. Hours are 9 A.M.–4 P.M. Monday through Friday.

In the middle of the old city, at Cristo and Luna Streets, you will find *San Juan Cathedral,* successor on this site to a number of cathedrals. The present circular staircase and Gothic ceiling, both rare examples of medieval ecclesiastical architecture in the Western Hemisphere, date from a building put up in 1540. Damaged repeatedly by hurricane, earthquake, and plundering invaders, the Cathedral was finally reconstructed in its present shape in 1802. The body of explorer Juan Ponce de León lies in a marble tomb near the transept.

The *Casa del Libro,* a few blocks from the Cathedral, is a beautifully restored 18th-century house that now serves as a museum of rare books. Nearby is the beautiful two-century-old chapel *Capilla del Cristo.*

To get an excellent view of the old city and El Morro, drive west around the north shore and take the bridge to *Cabras Island* on the entrance to San Juan Bay. Part of the island has been turned into a pleasant picnic and recreation area, and you can stroll about the ruins of *Fort El Canuelo* which used to help guard the harbor. Most impressive, however, and the reason for your being there, is the view across the bay where you can see the towering, indestructible walls of El Morro, as formidable looking today as they must have been to men-of-war four centuries ago.

In San Juan, modern housing developments ring the city, and high-

La Fortaleza, residence of the island's governors for four centuries

rise condominiums and office buildings dot the metropolitan area. Hato Rey, once simply the outskirts of San Juan, has become the island's financial center. The beach fronts of Condado, Ocean Park, and Isla Verde are lined with luxurious hotels and condominiums, as well as a wide expanse of white sand. The vast and modern Luis Muñoz Marin International Airport is only a quarter of an hour from the city's center in the Isla Verde section of the capital.

OUT ON THE ISLAND . . . 1, 2, 3

San Juan is not all of Puerto Rico. Much of the island's history and much of its Spanish charm you will find only after you have left the capital and gone "out on the island," as the Puerto Ricans say.

By far the most satisfactory way to see the outlying districts is by car. The island is small—hardly more than two-thirds the size of Connecticut—and laced with some 4,000 miles of excellent paved roads. The three main routes—numbers 1, 2, 3, and a few alternates and connecting links—encircle the island completely and provide access to most of the places you will want to see. All of them lead out of San Juan.

East to the beaches, mountains, and rain forest. Route 3 starts out from Río Piedras and runs east through *Carolina, Loiza,* and *Río Grande,* quiet old country villages a little inland from the coast. A little further along is the great curving arc of **Luquillo Beach,** its soft white sand ringed by coconut palms. It is the most beautiful public beach on the island, safe, almost surfless, plentifully equipped with dressing rooms and picnic facilities. A few miles along, in the corner of the island, is **Fajardo,** a good sized fishing port that was hotly disputed for a few days during the Spanish-American War. It and *Las Croabas,* nearby, are now favorites with fishermen and sailing enthusiasts. From Fajardo you can take a ferry for $2 to Puerto Rico's offshore islands, *Vieques* and *Culebra.* Both have lovely beaches.

About midway between Río Grande and Luquillo, a good secondary road (191) turns south to **El Yunque**—the Anvil—the 3,500-foot peak on whose crest and slopes lies the lush rain forest that has been set aside as the *Caribbean National Forest.* An amazing tropical world of giant ferns, enormous cedars, and satinwood draped in tangles of vines, brilliant chattering birds, and climbing wild orchids, it is dotted with splashing falls and cool, shaded pools. It is crisscrossed with hiking paths and horseback trails, and at the top there is an observation tower looking out over the contrasting sweep of the coastal plains and beaches. There is an attractive terraced restaurant, called *El Yunque.*

On the way back to San Juan take the coastal road (187). It's a delightful little excursion into an area that has been little changed by time—you still cross the Loíza River in a hand-poled ferry—and the unpaved drive along the shore is one of the most scenic on the island.

West to luxury, rum, and history. As Route 2 swings out of San Juan around the bay, it passes *Cataño*. Just outside Cataño is the Bacardi plant where tour guides will show you and explain the interesting process of distilling rum. In nearby Dorado, on three miles of shining beaches are the Hyatt Dorado Beach and Hyatt Regency Cerromar Beach Hotels, sister hotels of luxury built by Laurance Rockefeller. A few miles along is *Vega Baja,* a popular beach resort in the heart of the citrus groves.

Continue west and you'll hit the new *Rio Camuy Cave Park,* 300 acres of canyons, caverns, and sinkholes, as well as one of the world's largest underground rivers. There are guided tours and a trolley to transport you from the visitors' center to the cave entrance. Close by is the *Arecibo Observatory,* with the largest radar/radio telescope in the world, and the *Caguana Indian Ceremonial Park,* built as a place of worship by the Taino Indians more than 800 years ago.

The drive along the coast further west is where the mountains narrow. The coastal plain is more rugged and dramatically scenic. Past *Isabela* two ancient and colorful towns, **Aguadilla** and **Aguada,** a little way down from the tip of the island, contend for your attention. Both claim to be the spot where Columbus landed with his imposing retinue on his princely second voyage in 1493.

Southwest for phosphorescence and Old World charm. **Mayagüez,** a city of 100,000 on a fine harbor halfway down the western coast, is the third largest city of the island and the commercial and shipping center of the west coast. Some of the finest seafood to be had in the area is available there. Adjacent to the Mayagüez branch of the University of Puerto Rico is the Tropical Agricultural Research Station, established by the U.S. Department of Agriculture at the turn of the century. Visitors can wander through the lush gardens and admire the orchid collection and other flora.

San Germán, southeast and inland, is an extraordinary little museum piece of a city preserved from the earliest days of the Spanish colonization. Founded on the south coast in 1512, it was removed some half a century later to its present site, and for many years rivaled San Juan in importance. It long ago gave up the race—its population is today less than 38,000—and settled back gracefully into the serene Spanish atmosphere of centuries ago. It has retained an air and an appearance that make it one of the most captivating cities on the island. The streets are lined with gracious old buildings, the patios bright with flowers. In the cool of evening the whole population turns out to stroll in the traditional Spanish manner in the plaza.

Most famous of San Germán's ancient buildings is the *Porta Coeli,* a magnificently preserved little church on a shallow hill above the plaza which is thought to have been founded by Columbus' son, Diego. Though it has not been used for worship for many years, the altar and the beautifully carved wooden pillars are still intact and the pulpit sounding boards and the heavy studded door still in place. The church has one unique and distant tie to mainland United States. Every December a flock of swallows arrives from San Juan Capistrano in California. Porta Coeli has been lovingly and authentically restored in a way that befits what is possibly the oldest church in the New World. Also in San Germán is the coeducational Inter-American University, founded in 1912. It has a beautiful campus. **Cabo Rojo,** on the arid southwestern tip of the island, was for years the hideout of a pirate of considerable local infamy, Roberto Cofresi. Washed by coastal waters are vast, glittering white flats where thousands of tons of salt lie drying in the unremitting sunlight. Here too the University of Puerto Rico has established a Marine Research Center, where creatures of the deep are studied in their natural habitat.

On the coast south of San Germán is **Parguera,** a little fishing resort much favored by Puerto Ricans and visitors alike. Its chief attraction is **Phosphorescent Bay** which at night shimmers and gleams with the eerie light of millions upon millions of microscopic creatures called dinoflagellates. The slightest disturbance in the water activates their luminescence, a fragile phenomenon especially beautiful on moonless nights.

Ponce, Pearl of the South. *Ponce* is an attractive anachronism in Puerto Rico. Second of the island's cities with a population of nearly 220,000, Ponce dominates the whole southern coast, is a major business center and manufacturing area as well as the busiest port in the Caribbean; yet it has about it the distinct air of a provincial Mediterranean town. In appearance and attitude, it is the most Spanish of the larger cities, although at 200 years old, it is only a youngster among its elders. Against the background of luxuriously balconied resort hotels, it presents the handsome *rejas*—framed balconies of its beautiful colonial mansions.

Ponceños are justifiably proud of their beautiful Museum of Art, collected and donated by industrialist Luis Ferre, the former governor. The city is distinguished by having not one but two spacious central plazas separated by the impressive *Cathedral of Our Lady of Guadalupe.* A second distinguishing feature immensely popular with all visiting color photographers is the *Parque de Bombas;* the old firehouse, painted in bold red and black stripes, Ponce's colors, and otherwise ornamented with bright green and yellow accents. More relaxing are the aging horse carriages which will trot you for hire around the plaza and through the lovely shaded streets. And for recreation there is the gracious and sample-dispensing *Don Q Rum Distillery.*

THE VIRGIN ISLANDS

The American Virgin Islands offer a near-perfect climate, free-port shopping, and a variety of pleasures—from the wild tropical paradise of St. John to St. Thomas' big resorts and sophisticated night life.

All the color of the Caribbean and all the comforts of home—the beautiful Virgin Islands combine the best of two worlds. These sun-drenched American outposts, each with its special brand of charm, are examples of island life at its best.

About 40 miles east of Puerto Rico, the American Virgins—more than 50 islands, islets, and cays—rise steeply from a sea of undiluted blue. There are no rivers to muddy the clear waters, no crowds to despoil the sands, no long rainy days to ruin vacations.

North and east are the British Virgins, peaks of the same extinct volcano chain, rising from the same sea. Once they were the lairs of pirates and privateers waiting to spring on homeward bound Spanish galleons. Now the British Virgins are one of the world's best yachting areas.

Lying right in the path of the tradewinds that come down from the northeast, the Virgin Islands enjoy a climate that—the islanders claim —is just the thing for hay fever and arthritis. Almost every day is warm and sunny, and the year-round temperature averages 80 with a low of 70 and a high of 90. The 45 inches of annual rainfall come in brief showers invariably followed by bright sunshine. Most of the 110,000 inhabitants are wholly or partly descended from the slaves who worked the rich sugar plantations.

For many years the fighting Caribs kept settlers away, and the first semipermanent European residents were chiefly privateers and pirates. By 1671 the Danes, through the instrument of the Danish West Indian Company, began colonizing first St. Thomas, then St. John. They got plantations working, welcomed all comers, from pirates to religious refugees, and in 1733 bought St. Croix from the French. Except for angry raids by the British to wipe out the pirates peddling their wares in St. Thomas and to control the islands during the Napoleonic wars, Denmark held the islands until 1917.

The sugar plantations of St. Croix worked by slaves produced a fabulous crop and the islands grew rich. The planters built Great Houses. The Virgins were at one of the corners of the slave-and-molasses route, and through the ports traveled ancestors of blacks living today all over the Americas. Twice the slaves revolted, and once they held St. John for six months until the French sent a force from Martinique. By the time the slaves were freed in 1848 blacks outnumbered whites on the island by almost 15 to one.

During the Civil War, the United States had found it difficult to blockade the South without a Caribbean port. Negotiations began for purchase of the islands. Bargaining went on until World War I, when the Government paid 25 million dollars and the American flag flew over the Virgins.

Prohibition went into effect in 1920 and dealt a terrible blow to the islands' one industry—rum—and Congress had to vote funds for the islanders' relief. For the next 25 years progress in the islands was slow. Then, after World War II, came the flood of tourists. The establishment of major industries and refineries followed. Partly because of their unique position as a free port, today the Virgin Islands are a shipping center and a mecca for bargain-hunting tourists.

ST. CROIX (Sant Kroi)

Though a late-starter in tourism compared to St. Thomas, St. Croix, the largest of the Virgins, is a paradox of charming houses and farms, and a huge oil refinery; of bustling ports, and crystal clear reefs and beaches. Yet, with all the activity, St. Croix remains the most reserved, even serene, of the islands.

Until the Danes took over, the island passed through many hands. The Caribs drove Columbus off before he had time to do much more than name the island Santa Cruz. Fifty years later the Dutch started a little settlement on Christiansted Harbor, were driven out by the English, came back, were thrown out again by the English. Spaniards from Puerto Rico massacred the English. Chevalier de Bois, who had colonized Caribbean islands for France, drove out the Spanish and took possession. He persuaded the King of France to sell the island to him and his fellow Knights of Malta, but unhappily the Knights were hardly pioneers. The empire lasted 14 years. France took the island back.

Meanwhile, the Danes had turned St. Thomas into a bustling port colony, and in 1733 they purchased St. Croix, asked only that squatters on the island swear allegiance to the Danish crown. Under Danish rule the sugar lands of St. Croix became some of the most productive in the world.

The first blow to this fabulous prosperity came in 1826 when the U.S. adopted a tariff on sugar to protect southern growers. Then, in 1848, the slaves were freed. In 1878 the contract laborers that worked the big estates rioted and burned some of the Great Houses and the factories. There wasn't any money to rebuild.

The planters tried cotton, then began raising cattle, continuing whatever sugar and rum production they could. They rejoiced when the U.S. took over, for the terms of the treaty permitted the islands to continue as a free port. But with U.S. prohibition, the rum business stopped and the plantations went back to the bush.

But things are different now. One problem facing St. Croix's 57,000 people is just how far to go in exchanging the quiet rural air for the bustle of business—tourist or otherwise. Other problems—of a political nature—caused considerable uneasiness in the early '70's, but they have been resolved, and the island is back to normal.

General Information

How To Get There: *By Air:* American and Pan Am offer nonstop service from New York to St. Thomas, continuing to St. Croix. Eastern provides similar service from Miami. There are frequent 35-minute flights to St. Croix from San Juan, Puerto Rico, on Aero Virgin Islands, American Eagle, Crown Air, Eastern Metro Express, and Virgin Air. The V.I. Seaplane Shuttle offers frequent direct service from downtown St. Croix to downtown St. Thomas and St. John; also San Juan to St. Thomas and St. Croix. *By Sea:* Cruise ship lines leaving various eastern U.S. ports and making frequent calls include Holland America, Sitmar Lines, Home Lines, Carnival Lines, and Epirotiki.

How To Get Around: The taxis are reasonable and most rates are fixed. If you ask, the driver will tell you what the fare will be before you get in. You can hire a taxi with driver for about $20 for two hours of sightseeing with or without friends.
Renting a car. Several agencies rent cars in both Christiansted and Frederiksted on St. Croix, for about $25–$30 a day. But prices vary widely and advertisements are often misleading—be sure to read the fine print. You can drive (on the left-hand side of the road) by showing your U.S. license. Good maps of the island are available at the Department of Tourism, Scale House, Christiansted St. Croix, USVI 00820, 809-773-0495. The roads are

serviceable, and you can't get lost for long because all the roads lead to the main Center Line Road.

Sports: You will find this a haven for all water sports.
Snorkeling and Scuba Diving: Buck Island Reef, just off Christiansted, contains one of the world's most beautiful marine gardens. Administered by the National Park Service, the underwater trail has a number of signposts describing the local flora and fauna. Daily trips are made from the Christiansted waterfront, or boats and equipment can be hired through your hotel or any of the many water sports centers.
Swimming. The big resorts and hotels have pools. The best beaches are Pelican Cove, Davis Bay, St. Croix By The Sea, in Christiansted; at Cramer's Park 10 miles beyond; and Magic Isle, Royal Harbour Beach, and Stony Ground Coral Resort in Frederiksted.
Spear Fishing. You can rent equipment, explore coral reefs and wrecks around the many coral reefs.
Fishing. Deep-sea and small boats for hire. During the winter, bluewater men take sailfish, blue marlin, white marlin, wahoo, kingfish, yellowfin tuna, dolphin. Bonito and blue marlin run in the summer. Shallower waters abound in snapper, amberjack, tarpon, and the fierce fighting bonefish, particularly on the flats off the south shore of St. Croix and even at the western end of Christiansted harbor.

Boating. Sailboats of all kinds can be rented or chartered for short or long sails on the steady trade winds.

Golf. The Buccaneer has an 18-hole course on its grounds. Rockefeller's Fountain Valley Golf Course is an 18-hole championship course designed by R. T. Jones.

Tennis. The Tennis Club near Christiansted and some hotels have courts.

Horseback Riding. Sprat Hall in Frederiksted (809-772-0305) specializes in horseback riding. You can make arrangements through your hotel.

Festivals: On St. Croix, New Year's Eve is known as "Old Year's Day" and in Frederiksted a traditional fair is held complete with Maypoles and jig dancing. In fact, from the week before Christmas until Three Kings Day is one long festival of calypso music and strolling troubadours of Puerto Rican ancestry singing "aguinaldos," or Spanish Christmas carols. July 4, Independence Day, is celebrated on all three islands.

Night Life: The larger resorts provide regular dances and entertainment during most of the year. Popular late spots with a fair share of fun and rhythm include Club Comanche, Old Quarter, King Christian, Pentheny Pub, and Anchor Inn of St. Croix at Christiansted; the Beach Hotel of St. Croix, the Buccaneer Hotel, Cane Bay, Grapetree Bay, and St. Croix By The Sea, nearby.

Medical Facilities: U.S.-trained doctors and nurses staff modern hospitals.

Additional Information: Virgin Islands Tourist Information Office, 1270 Avenue of the Americas, New York, NY 10020, 212-582-4520; 343 Dearborn St., Suite 1003, Chicago, IL 60604, 312-461-0180; 7270 NW 12th St., Suite 620, Miami, FL 305-591-2070; 1667 K St., Suite 270, Washington, DC 20006, 202-293-3707; P.O. Box 4538, Christiansted, U.S. Virgin Islands 00820, 809-773-0495.

Where to Stay

HOTELS: ****Buccaneer,* Christiansted, 140 rooms, on 240-acre estate, beach, tennis courts, golf, overlooks the water. ****St. Croix By The Sea,* Christiansted, 67 rooms, newly renovated pool built into the Caribbean. **Cane Bay Plantation,* 30 rooms, at base of Mt. Eagle. ***Hotel on the Cay,* 55 rooms, on small island across from Christiansted, beach, tennis, water sports. **The Inn of St. Croix,* 28 rooms. **King Christian Hotel,* 38 rooms, downtown. ** Queen's Quarter Hotel,* 72 rooms, on hill, 4 miles to beach. **King Frederik on the Beach,* 24 rooms, pool, on beach. ***Caravelle,* nestled in Christiansted Harbor, 44 rooms with sea view, pool. ***Gentle Winds,* on beach, some kitchens available. 135 rooms. ***King's Alley,* set in private garden overlooking harbor, 22 rooms, all with private balconies, freshwater pool. ***Anchor Inn,* 25 rooms, all overlooking harbor, pool. ***Sprat Hall,* oldest plantation greathouse on St. Croix, Frederiksted, 12 rooms, private beach, all water sports, riding. ** Club Comanche,* Christiansted, 43 rooms, overlooks harbor, pool, dock. **Charte House,* 32 rooms overlooking charming courtyard, pool, Christiansted. **Lodge Hotel,* 19 rooms. ** The Frederiksted,* 41 rooms. **Tamarind Reef,* 20 rooms, on beach, comfortable. ****Carambola Beach Resort & Golf Club,* 156 rooms, 18-hole championship golf course, all-weather tennis courts, beachfront, swimming pool, AP. ****Grapetree Bay,* 48 rooms, freshwater pool, beach, watersports, tennis, MAP. ***Queen's Quarter,* 50 rooms, free beach shuttle, MAP. **Cane Bay Reef Club,* 9 suites with kitchens, balconies, on sea. ** Cathy's Fancy,* 21 rooms with kitchenettes, beachfront, freshwater pool. ***Coakley Bay,* 20 rooms, sea view from balconies, restaurant. ***Pink Fancy,* 13 rooms, in National Historic Register.

COTTAGES AND EFFICIENCY APARTMENTS: **Caribbean View, 20 rooms, Christiansted. ***Granada Del Mar Condominiums, 35 units, 2 and 3 bedroom apts. overlooking water, pool, tennis. **Northside Valley Villas, 11 apts., near Frederiksted. ****Mill Harbor, 86 apartments, newly-renovated pool, beach, watersports. ***The Waves, Cane Bay, 10 units, ocean view, near golf courses. ***The Reef, Teague Bay. 101 oceanview villas with full housekeeping facilities. Pool, beach, golf, tennis. ***Coakley Bay, 100 units, pool, fine view. ** Holger Danske, Christiansted, 44 rooms, on the waterfront. **Cottages By The Sea, Frederiksted, 14 cottages, on private beach, all housekeeping facilities. **Turquoise Bay, Christiansted, 7 cottages on the water. ** Sugar Beach, Christiansted. 23 beachfront condos, fully equipped. *Bay Gardens, 10 fully-equipped condos overlooking Christiansted. ***Colony Cove, 60 units, luxury beachfront resort. ***Estate Carlton Condos, 42 units on Old Sugar Cane Plantation. ***Questa Verde Condo, 11 suites in townhouse overlooking harbor. **** Arawak Cottages, 8 efficiency units on white sand beach, MAP. **Chenay Bay, 20 efficiency cottages on beach, entertainment.

Where to Eat

The local seafood, particularly lobster, is delicious, and the native chefs turn up some tasty Creole and Danish dishes. Most popular American foods are served with the emphasis on such items as charcoal-broiled steaks.

RESTAURANTS: ***Top Hat, Christiansted; specializes in Danish food. ***La Grange, Frederiksted, excellent Danish food, reservations only. ***Cafe de Paris, Christiansted, continental dishes, famous for lobster blinis. ***Kings Alley, Christiansted. ***Anchor Inn, Christiansted. *** Caravelle Hotel, Christiansted. *** The Cellar, Christiansted. ***Persian Virgin, garden restaurant in Frederiksted, specialties are Mezza and Shish Kebab. ***Mother Tongue, Frederiksted. ***New England Lobster House, Christiansted, popular with locals. ***Smithfield Mill, Frederiksted, elegant dining at a restored sugar mill. **Clover Crest, Frederiksted, excellent island cooking. **McConnell's, Frederiksted, Creole and American food in an old West Indian building. **Tivoli Gardens, Christiansted, cozy, restaurant in garden setting.

Where to Shop

The Virgin Islands are free ports; this means that there are real price bargains and that purchases up to $800 in retail value may be brought back duty free by each visitor. And that can include one gallon of liquor and all the cigarettes and cigars you want. Also there's no limit on gifts under $100 mailed out from there.

Wares range from local Caribbean products to European fashions, jewelry and designer clothes. Gucci, Givenchy and Courrèges have boutiques here. Perfume and liquor prices are among the lowest in the world. Store hours are 9 A.M.–5 P.M. Monday through Saturday, but most stores open on Sundays and holidays when cruise ships are in.

GIFTS: Cavanagh's, Christiansted, Dynasty fashions, imported jewelry, gift items; Compass Rose, Christiansted, Japanese jewelry and art objects; Continental, Inc., Christiansted, imported fabrics, china, and perfumes; Danish House, Christiansted, fine Danish and other imported china, porcelain, and silver; For Him, Christiansted, English sportswear; Little Guard House, Christiansted, woodcarvings and European antiques; Pan Am Pavillion, Christiansted, wide

variety of shops; *Violette's Boutique,*
Caravelle Hotel, Christiansted, gifts.
LIQUOR: *Carib Cellars, Trade Winds,
Comanche, King's Cellar, Crown*

*House, Dam's Liquor Store, The Gal-
lery Wine and Spirits Shop,* all in
Christiansted; *Moorehead's* in Frederiksted.

What to See

Christiansted, capital of St. Croix, solidly Danish and colorfully tropical, is one of the most lovely towns in the West Indies. Its roofs are red.
The buildings glow softly in pastels of every hue, and scattered about
are the blooms of all kinds of tropical flowers.

The *Waterfront Area* and the *Old Town Square* were named a National Historic Site in 1952, and have retained all the character of
centuries ago. Walking about the old town, you will find the wise Danes
designed the stone buildings with overhanging second-floor balconies
which shade and protect the streets and transform them into cool
arcades.

The Dutch *Fort Christiansvaern,* dating from before 1645; the *Steeple Building,* which began as a church around 1690; the picture-post-
card *Danish Post Office;* the *Public Library,* which now houses the *St.
Croix Museum;* and the original *Customs House,* now used by the
Chamber of Commerce, are all on Christiansted's waterfront. At the
corners of the roads you will see old cannons inverted and imbedded
as markers.

Up the street is the lovely restored *Government House,* whose gardens are just as they were in the days when Christiansted was the
capital of the Danish West Indies. Be sure to visit the charming ball-
room with its replicas of original Danish furnishings given by the
Danish Government.

Fifteen miles away is the little town of **Frederiksted,** far different
architecturally from the capital. In 1878, fire swept through the town,
destroying most of the old houses. The Danes and other residents
rebuilt in Victorian style, with lacelike trim of iron and wood, cupolas,
gingerbread, and curlicues.

The town is built along open water, and oceangoing freighters and
cruise ships anchor in the roadstead. Small boats move the goods and
passengers onto the docks. The most historic building and principal
sight in town is the *Old Danish Fort,* built in 1760 and strangely plain
and stark in comparison to the later, decorated buildings. There are
good white-sand beaches close to the town.

Between Christiansted and Frederiksted, and all over the island, are
the old plantations and the ruins of the Great Houses where the planters lived. They almost all have strange names: Upper Love, Jealousy,
Whim Great House, Lower Love. The circular stone towers all over the
island were once the bases for grinding windmills that overlooked great
fields of tasseled sugar cane.

Through the good offices of the St. Croix Landmarks League and its

"Open-House Tours," you will want to see some of the loveliest restored mansions, particularly *Whim Great House,* an early French château that was spared during the slave and other uprisings and has been completely restored.

ST. THOMAS

While St. Croix grew rich on the land, St. Thomas drew its wealth from trade brought by the steady winds to the great harbor of Charlotte Amalie, strategically located between the Old World and the New. The trade now is tourists, and St. Thomas provides more facilities and collects more money per square mile than any other resort area in the Caribbean. It is a free port, and most visitors come from San Juan or from the cruiseships for a day of shopping—or for the yachting.

St. Thomas is the home of the largest charter fleet in the world where every imaginable type of yacht can be rented "bare" or complete with captain, cook, and crew, from 10 to 110 feet, to go anywhere at any time. The fishing is unsurpassed, and boats out of St. Thomas hold a large number of world records.

The island is 13 miles long and less than 3 miles wide. Inlets, bays, little islands, and cays lie on every shore, and on the south a narrow peninsula juts out into the Caribbean to protect the harbor of Charlotte Amalie. Behind the bay, the town climbs the steep hillsides with houses and resorts and hotels that have given Charlotte Amalie the sobriquet of "night club of the Virgin Islands."

The mingled backgrounds and racial heritages of the 51,000 inhabitants of St. Thomas give the island a cosmopolitan air and virtually every language under the sun is spoken here including the lyrical down island "patois." Though no longer the largest in population, St. Thomas remains the political hub of the islands.

While England, France, and Spain were squabbling over St. Croix and richer islands to the west, 100 Danish settlers moved onto St. Thomas in 1672. They developed the harbor and parceled the island into estates. The plantations did well, but the slave traders and the local merchants operating in a wide-open free port did better.

Slavers sailed straight from Africa on the trades, and for 30 years made St. Thomas the biggest slave market in the world. New England sailing captains traded barrel staves for rum, and ships flying just about every flag on the globe stopped in the harbor on their way to and from the Western Hemisphere. Charlotte Amalie was one of the world's richest ports.

The end of slavery and the coming of steam wiped out the prosperous trade. Later, cruise ships brought tourists, and since World War II St. Thomas has developed its harbor, its beaches, its hotels and resorts into a tourist and shopping paradise.

General Information

How To Get There: *By Air:* American and Pan Am offer nonstop service from New York to St. Thomas. Eastern provides similar service from Miami. There are frequent 35-minute flights to St. Croix from San Juan, Puerto Rico, on Aero Virgin Islands, American Eagle, Crown Air, Eastern Metro Express, and Virgin Air. The V.I. Seaplane Shuttle offers frequent direct service from downtown St. Croix to downtown St. Thomas and St. John; also San Juan to St. Thomas and St. Croix.

By Sea: Charlotte Amalie is a popular port-of-call for most of the cruise ships out of New York and Miami.

How To Get Around: Taxi service is excellent and cheap. Rates are fixed. Drive-yourself cars are available at very reasonable rates—a Volkswagen will cost you $25–$30 a day, gas and insurance included. You do have to get a Virgin Island license—$2 at the police station, on presentation of your U.S. license. And, as you'll soon find out, you drive on the lefthand side of the road.

Festivals: The biggest holiday of the year occurs in mid-April, when the islanders used to celebrate the sugar harvest. It is one of the most colorful carnivals in the West Indies. A Calypso song contest is held for the coveted title of Calypso King and Queen the week before, followed by coronations, dancing in the streets, two parades—one for adults and one for children—and various races and competitions.

Sports: Be on the lookout for the big name yachts which grace the harbor every winter. Fishing and boating are fantastic here. You can also watch baseball every Sunday, horse racing on holidays at Sugar Estate Racetrack, and you can take part in the monthly lottery, which is under government control.

Swimming. Many of the resort hotels have pools. Among the best beaches are those at Magen's Bay, Morningstar, Lindbergh, Sapphire Beach Club, Pineapple Beach Club, Pelican Beach Club, and Bluebeard's Castle.

Snorkeling and Scuba Diving. Many reefs and colorful tropical fish close to shore. Instructors and guides are readily available.

Fishing. You can rent boats for every kind of fishing, which is excellent.

Boating. Sailboats, motor boats, rowboats, and cruising yachts all can be chartered for short trips or long. There are many good yacht agencies, but Antilles Yachts and Bob Thompson, Inc. are among the most all-around and efficient. The St. Thomas Sheraton and Red Hook have some of the best known (and some say the best) captains in the business. For information call the Virgin Island Charter Yacht League, 809-774-3944. Or, make arrangements through your hotel.

Golf. College of the Virgin Islands and The Herman Moore Municipal Golf courses have 9 holes. Mahogany Run has a championship 18-hole course.

Tennis. You can play at the larger hotels and at the municipal courts.

Night Life: There is plenty on St. Thomas. Frenchman's Reef and Jimmy's are most popular, providing big-name bands for dancing every night, plus entertainment. Ditto for Bluebeard's Castle. The Caribbean Beach Club features calypso, while among the popular bistros are Sebastian's, Big Bamboo and Cheetah.

Medical Facilities: U.S.-trained doctors and nurses staff the modern Knud Hansen Memorial Hospital.

Other Things To Do: A number of boats at the Sheraton Marina and Red Hook offer day sails to nearby St. John, where you can swim, snorkel, and picnic. For the adventurous, sail a Sunfish around Sapphire Beach or Bluebeard's Beach.

Captain Cook's glass-bottom boat makes hour-long trips from the Charlotte Amalie waterfront through the harbor where you can view colorful underwater life. There are also informative 2 hour trips by Safari Tours around St. Thomas, St. John.

Additional Information: Virgin Islands Tourist Information Office, 1270 Avenue of the Americas, New York, NY 10020, 212-582-4520; 343 Dearborn St., Suite 1003, Chicago, IL 60604, 312-461-0180; 7270 NW 12th St., Suite 620, Miami, FL 305-591-2070; 1667 K St., Suite 270, Washington, DC 20006, 202-293-3707; P.O. Box 6400, Charlotte Amalie, U.S. Virgin Islands 00801, 809-774-8784.

Where to Stay

HOTELS: ****Frenchman's Reef, 500 rooms, pool, beach, tennis, ****Bluebeard's Castle, 120 rooms, overlooking Charlotte Amalie, pool, free transportation to the beach. ***Carib Beach, 90 rooms, overlooking Lindberg Beach, calypso entertainment. ***Island Beachcomber, 47 rooms, convenient to airport on beautiful beach. ***Morningstar Beach Resort, 24 rooms, popular with the "in" crowd. ***Bolongo Bay Beach & Tennis Club, 77 beachfront units, all water sports. ***The Windward, 150 rooms, pool, centrally located in Charlotte Amalie. **"1829," 19 rooms, colorful old manor house in town. **Magen's Point Hotel, 42 rooms. Near lovely Magen's Beach. **Mafolie, 23 rooms, overlooking the harbor, popular local restaurant. ***Villa Blanca Hotel, 12 rooms situated on site of the old St. Thomas Club. ****Point Pleasant Hotel, 149 rooms, recently renovated, on Smith Bay, MAP. ****Limetree Beach Hotel, 84 rooms, on secluded cove minutes from Charlotte Amalie, MAP. ****Virgin Isle Hotel, 240 rooms, recently renovated and expanded, MAP. ****Sea Cliff Beach Hotel, 100 rooms plus villas, ocean views, MAP. ***Ramada Inn, 150 rooms, at Yacht Haven, recently renovated, lounge, pool bar. ****Secret Harbour Beach, 60 suites, elegantly furnished, full kitchens, beachfront location. ****Stouffer Grand Hotel, 329 rooms, deluxe beachfront resort, MAP. ***Blackbeard's Castle, 11 rooms, historic site, town and harbor views. **Galleon House, 14 rooms, charming and friendly. **Harbor View, 8 rooms, renowned inn and fine restaurant overlooking town and harbor. ***Inn at Mandahl, 8 rooms, gourmet restaurant. ***Limestone Reef, 10 rooms, secluded location, panoramic views. ***Sapphire Beach, 30 rooms, unsurpassed beach, all watersports, gourmet restaurant. **Villa Olga, 8 rooms, home of noted Chart House restaurant.

EFFICIENCIES, COTTAGES, CONDOMINIUMS: ****Cowpet Bay Villas, 75 apts. overlooking the yacht club on the east end. ***Pavilions and Pools, 24 units, private pool with each room. ***Sea Horse Cottages, 25 units, with pool. ***Watergate Villas, 100 units, condos with pools. ****Anchorage Beach, 30 deluxe, fully-equipped condos, on beach. ****Crystal Cove, 80 full-equipped superior units. **** Harbour House Villas, 25 condos, pool, tennis, restaurant. ****Pineapple House Villas, 20 units, short walk to beach. **Red Hook Mountain Apartments, 10 units, quiet, comfortable, short walk to downtown. **** Casablanca Villas, 10 charming and secluded villas, very luxurious. *** Sign of the Griffin, 7 cottages with private patios.

GUEST HOUSES: **Maison Greaux, 9 rooms, overlooking harbor. **Island View, 11 rooms, spectacular view. ** Miller Manor, 32 rooms, overlooks the harbor. **Beverly Hill,* 12 rooms, beautiful views, close to town, MAP. **Bunkers Hill View,* 18 rooms, close to Main Street, tv. **Danish Chalet,* 14 rooms, close to town, overlooks harbor. *Domini Hus,* 7 rooms, in-town location. *Ramsey's,* 16 rooms, home-style, use of kitchen.

RESTAURANTS: ****Au Bon Vivant,* at Constant Great House, French and elegant. ****L'Escargot,* excellent French cuisine, overlooking the water. ****Frigate* at Mafolie, Continental, breathtaking view. ***Hotel 1829* for German food. ***Chart House* at Villa Olga, continental fare in the former Russian Consulate and historic island home. ***Harbor View,* for elegance and haute cuisine. **Kum Wah* for Chinese dishes. ** *The Dove* at Scott Beach, seafood or barbequed ribs on the beach, specializing in backgammon. *The Greenhouse,* downtown. *Sparky's Waterfront Saloon,* weird and worldly, open until they feel like closing, impromptu entertainment, fun. **Bird of Paradise,* dining by the sea, 15 minutes from C.A. ***The Old Stone Farmhouse,* recently renovated, in the hills a 20-minute drive from C.A., magnificent food. ***Agave Terrace,* at Point Pleasant, in a garden overlooking down-island views, reservations necessary. **Alexander's Cafe,* Austrian restaurant in Frenchtown. *The Bridge,* at Yacht Haven marina, casual dining. *Dockside Inn at Compass Point,* where boaters eat fish & chips, chicken fried steak, and draft beer. *Drake's Inn,* popular gathering spot for drinks and hors d'oeuvres. ** *Entre Nous,* delightful country French cuisine. **Eunice's Terrace,* local West Indian food featuring conch and whelk. **Fiddle Leaf,* nouvelle cuisine in open-air candlelit setting. **For the Birds,* Tex-Mex food and Margaritas at Compass Point. ***Green Parrot,* Continental cuisine served on outdoor terrace on far side of island. *Horse Feathers,* pizza and subs at harbor's edge in Red Hook. ** *The Inn at Mandahl,* glass-enclosed restaurant/bar with unforgettable views, famous Planter's Punch. **Island Beachcomber,* attractive tropical excellent wine cellar. ***Raffles,* elegant tropical atmosphere at Compass Point featuring seafood and international cuisine. *Sinbad,* in restored Bakery Square building, Middle Eastern cuisine including felafel and kafta, extensive vegetarian selections. ** *Sparky's Cloud Room,* island atmosphere and West Indian food on eastern end of island.

Where to Shop

St. Thomas is a free port, and its shops carry just about anything you might want in the way of imports at the lowest possible prices.

All liquor, including local rum, and U.S. cigarettes are very cheap.

Some of the best buys in imports include Scandinavian, British, Italian, Mexican silverware; French perfumes, lace, petit point, and leather goods; Italian leather goods and jewelry; Swiss and German watches and clocks; German and Japanese cameras and optical goods; European glassware and china; Scottish and Austrian sweaters.

PERFUMES AND FRENCH IMPORTS: *French Shoppe, A. H. Riise Gift Shop, C. & M. Caron,* and many of the other shops.

GIFTS: *Scandinavian Silver Center* and *Maison Danoise* specialize in Scandinavian porcelain, china, and silverware. The *Continental, Inc.,* carries all kinds of imports including Lalique crystal, silverware, English china, British woolens on bolts. *Riise Gift Shop* and *The Bolero Shops* both carry Austrian china, French and Belgian crystal, Madras, all kinds of silver, jewelry, perfumes. *Little Switzerland Gift Shop* specializes in watches, music boxes, and clocks. *Stoner's of St. Thomas* has fine imported jewelry, leather goods, china, and glassware. *Majesty of the East* specializes in fine imports from Japan and India.

SPORTSWEAR: *Cavanagh's* has excellent resort fashions. *Cosmopolitan, Inc.* for French and Italian clothes for adults and children. *The Shoe Salon* for Charles Jourdan and Salvatore Ferragamo shoes.

LIQUOR: *A. H. Riise, Bolero, Al Cohen's, Sparky's,* and many others.

BOOKS, PRINTS, PHOTOGRAPHIC SUPPLIES: *Paper Book Gallery* offers a great variety of best-sellers, hundreds of art prints, maps, frames, greeting cards, and art supplies. *Ad Lib Book Center* carries a wide selection of books, records, and greeting cards. *Steele's* carries photographic equipment.

What to See

Although bustling these days, **Charlotte Amalie** is still a venerable town. The present police station is encased in old Fort Christian, built by the first Danish settlers nearly 300 years ago.

Emancipation Park near the waterfront, where the slaves were declared free in 1848, is a good place to start. Near the park is old *Fort Christian,* named after King Christian V by the early Danes. It has served as a church, courthouse, jail, and governor's residence since it was built in the mid-17th century. The fort is the oldest building on the island and is currently used as a short-term jail.

The *Waterfront* itself is lovely. Each day at dawn and again at dusk the interisland boats come in with fresh produce, meat and fish, and native products. On Saturday, the area is turned into a native market ablaze with colors and filled with odors.

A short and delightful walk will take you through *Beretta Center,* the cluster of colonial terra cotta warehouses with old doors and locks and hinges. Now many of the warehouses are transformed into tourist shops, selling a fantastic assortment of merchandise from all over the world. Its narrow alleys and winding lanes, the tropical flowers on every hand make it a sightseeing experience as well as a shopping expedition.

Just past the *Street of 99 Steps* is the handsome *Government House,* residence of the governor. Murals inside depict the history of the island. Opposite Government House is *Quarters B,* once the German consulate and famous for its lovely staircase said to have been taken from an old ship. On Denmark Hill you will find the *Danish Consulate,* built as a private home by the former Danish governor, and the *Lutheran Parsonage,* both excellent examples of Danish architecture of the 1880's. Another fascinating relic of those years is the *Grand Hotel,* opened in 1841 when the island was still fabulously rich. It now houses a hospitality center, restaurants, and shops.

Don't miss the lovely old churches. The *Nisky Moravian Mission* includes a seminary and school based on and built into the remains of the 1777 church. The *Dutch Reformed Church* was one of the first of that faith in the New World. Also see the 18th-Century *Frederick Evangelical Lutheran,* and the *Jewish Synagogue,* one of the oldest in the Western Hemisphere.

Bluebeard's Castle Tower is an excellent example of a fortification of the old days. On another hill is *Blackbeard's Tower,* which actually was supposed to have been the home of the famous buccaneer and pirate Edward Teach.

Driving around the mountainous island you will get some wonderful views of the shore, the blue sea and cays, and the islands in the distance.

From *Drake's Seat,* where the great buccaneer Sir Francis Drake is said to have reviewed his fleet, you can see both the Caribbean and the Atlantic Oceans. Near *Red Hook,* you will find an excellent view of nearby St. John and the many islands of the British Virgins.

On the north side of the island, the vegetation is more lush and the beaches are even better. Don't miss *Magen's Bay, Coki Point* and *Sapphire Beach* for soft white sand, turquoise sea, and magnificent views.

ST. JOHN

Just 3 miles across the water from St. Thomas lies the unspoiled tropical island of St. John, the most lovely chunk of mountains, greenery, coves, and bays still unadorned by civilization in the Caribbean.

Beautiful, rimmed with white-sand beaches and one huge harbor, the island has approximately 2,760 people. Its hills and mountains are covered with tropical vegetation, including a bay-tree forest that supplies St. Thomas with the leaves to make the famous men's toilet water.

On the eastern side is the huge harbor of Coral Bay, where the first colonizers settled, and on the west, facing St. Thomas, is Cruz Bay, the only town and island capital. Between, the mountains rise to a peak of more than 1,200 feet.

Although the "roads" on St. John are being improved, you still travel by jeep. But then there are no traffic lights, blaring horns, or neon signs. Since 1956, about two-thirds of the island's 20 square miles have been the Virgin Islands National Park, a gift of Laurance S. Rockefeller, made to insure the unspoiled tropical wilderness for generations. If you want rest, swimming, and water sports on a paradise island, there are a few resort hotels to accommodate you. But, no matter what your preferences, if you stay on St. Thomas or St. Croix you should spend at least a day exploring the unspoiled islands and beaches, among the best in the world—or a night or two camping at beautiful Cinnamon Bay and Mayo Bay.

When Rockefeller first came to the island, the population was down to around 700, and the land was a wilderness. He bought much of the acreage and gave it to the government for the National Park. He also purchased Caneel Bay Plantation, where he built a resort which he turned over to the Jackson Hole Preserve, a nonprofit organization.

General Information

How To Get There: Daily ferry service is provided from Red Hook, about six miles east of Charlotte Amalie on St. Thomas to Cruz Bay and Caneel Bay, St. John. Caneel Bay has private ferry service. Antilles Air Boats flies from St. Thomas to Cruz Bay Harbor; V.I. Seaplane also provides service.

Sports: *Swimming.* Superb. St. John is rimmed with beautiful beaches.
Fishing. You can fish with line in some of the finest fishing grounds in the world along the many coral reefs. You can also go deep-sea fishing off the shore.
Boating. You can rent sail or other boats through Trade Wind Charter Boats in Cruz Bay.
Tennis. There are courts at Caneel Bay.

Medical Facilities: The island has a hospital dispensary with an attending doctor and nurse.

Additional Information: Virgin Islands Tourist Information Office, 1270 Avenue of the Americas, New York, NY 10020, 212-582-4520; 343 Dearborn St., Suite 1003, Chicago, IL 60604, 312-461-0180; 7270 NW 12th St., Suite 620, Miami, FL 305-591-2070; 1667 K St., Suite 270, Washington, DC 20006, 202-293-3707; P.O. Box 200, Cruz Bay, U.S. Virgin Islands 00830, 809-776-6450.

Where to Stay

****Caneel Bay Plantation,* 171 rooms, superb setting on the beachfront of three bays, luxurious, all water sports. ***Estate Zootenvaal,* 4 cottages, deluxe. **Huldah Sewer's Guest House,* 20 rooms, centrally located. **Maho Bay Camp Resort,* 96 units, in National Park. **Serendip,* 10 condos, informal and relaxing. ***Lavender Hill Estates,* 12 rooms, terraces and spectacular views. ****

Virgin Grand Beach Hotel, 285 rooms, largest pool in the Caribbean, beachfront activities. ****Gallows Point,* 32 units, new pool and deck. * *Bethany Condos,* 6 units with decks. **The Cruz Inn,* 17 rooms, charming West Indian-style inn, short walk from town. ***Cruz Views,* 10 condos in hillside village setting. ****Gifft Hill,* 23 luxury units with pool. *** *Havens With Ambiance,* 12 units, water views, beach and tennis nearby. ***Intimate Inn,* 6 rooms at secluded hilltop retreat. **Raintree Inn,* 11 rooms, private baths, in-town location. **St. John House Rentals,* 6 modern-style villas with decks. ***St. John Villas,* 7 private hillside cottages, each with jacuzzi. *Selene's,* 5 fully-equipped efficiency apartments. **The Lost Chord,* magnificent home in secluded setting, indoor/outdoor dining, views minutes from Cruz Bay and beaches. **St. John Passion,* luxuriously furnished home on south side of island. Holiday Homes of St. John, Vacation Homes, Moran Real Estate, Private Homes, Star Villa, and Vacation Retreats lease private houses on the island at a variety of prices. *Campsites and cottages* are available at Cinnamon and Mayo Bays in the National Park. Cottages go for about $35 a day, and tents and tentsites are also available.

Where to Eat

The specialties are island turtle steaks and lobsters.

Fish frys are special events that occur fairly frequently. It's said that if you go once, you'll want to come back for more. They're generally held on Friday or Saturday nights from 6:30 P.M. to midnight at Pond Mouth. In addition to fish and johnnycake and other West Indian dishes, there's entertainment by local bands (professional and "scratch") and dancing to reggae, rock, and calypso music.

Although many guests dine at their hotels, or hire cooks for rental units, there are many fine restaurants on the island.

The ***Sugar Mill* at the Caneel Bay Resort is one of the loveliest dining rooms in the world. They serve a special steak and lobster buffet four days a week. The ***Ship Lantern* in Cruz Bay is one of St. John's finest restaurants, featuring gourmet fare. The ***Upper Deck* is virtually a must-go tradition on St. John, featuring candlelight dining with a fabulous view.

The **Bamboo Inn* in Cruz Bay specializes in West Indian cuisine; reservations are required. ***Meada's* has only six tables, but some of the best island cooking in the Caribbean; reservations absolutely necessary.

The *Bird's Nest* features good food and good service in a casual setting, displays local paintings. *Captain & Cook Fisherman's Fleet* is the crossroads of Cruz Bay, and famous for its conch fritters. The *Dockside Pub* has deli sandwiches and cold drinks. *Joe's Diner* has casual fare, and assorted ice cream flavors. *The Moveable Feast* is a casual deli restaurant at Mongoose Junction. The **Lime Inn* at the Lemon Tree Center serves breakfast, lunch, and dinner, and has entertainment most nights. The **Lobster Hut* for fresh lobster rolls and conch fritters, fish and chips.

For ethnic foods, try **The Rain Tree Inn* which features Mexican cuisine and the **Cafe Roma* for Italian specialties.

For island specialties and West Indian fare try **Fred's* (live music in the evening), and **Ric's* restaurants. The **Back Yard* is a cozy spot with vintage movies and live entertainment. *Red Beard's Saloon* in Coral Bay serves up lunch, dinner, and old movies on Wednesday and Sunday evenings.

Where to Shop

The natives make attractive baskets out of black vine which are sold as souvenirs at Cruz Bay and at the hotels.

St. John has a branch of *Sparky's* where you can buy perfume, liquor or jewelry. *The Dock Shop* has men's and ladies' fashion, *Sailor's Delight* features men's clothes and nautical gifts. *The Batik Shop* carries a large selection of original hand-dyed fabrics. *Stitches I* and *Stitches II* feature t-shirts and beachware. *The Posh Bosun Box* has great gifts for the mariner.

The Blue Moon Boutique in Lemon Tree Center is a quaint island boutique that is a one-stop for island memorabilia. Beside the center, *The Sky's the Limit* features unique island art. *The Art Project* features the finest Caribbean arts and crafts. *Local Color Memories* offers the largest collection of hand-painted tropical clothing in the Caribbean.

Mongoose Junction provides an appealing cluster of shops including *Gold and Silversmithing, The Canvas Factory,* the *Donald Schnell Studio,* and the *Fabric Mill.*

What to See

The best sights are those of nature. You can make arrangements through your hotel or one of the travel agencies in St. Thomas to take guided trips through the *National Park,* one-day visits to the island, or a boat trip around St. John, stopping at your own particular beach for a swim and a picnic.

You can walk the *Trail* from Cruz Bay to Coral Bay at the other end of the island. It was once used by the Arawak and Carib Indians, and you will see still undeciphered Indian inscriptions on the rocks above Reef Bay. Coral Bay harbor is larger than any other on the islands, and on a high cliff are the ruins of the old fort that once controlled the entrance.

Spotted about the island you will find the ruins of the old plantations, and some of the windmills, and at *Mary's Point* you may see the cliff where the rebelling slaves are supposed to have jumped to their deaths. A must for snorkeling enthusiasts is a trip to Trunk Bay where the National Park Service maintains an underwater trail with markers pointing out the flora and fauna of the reef in crystal clear waters.

THE BRITISH VIRGIN ISLANDS

Scattered north and east of the American islands and only fifteen minutes by air from St. Thomas are the British Virgin Islands. These 40 islands (a total 59 square miles) of green hills and beautiful harbors, unmarred by the accoutrements of modernity are the yachtsman's dream. Every Captain Mitty can imagine himself a privateer churning through the Sir Francis Drake Channel, so named by the commander himself in 1595; or hunting for booty in the caves of **Norman Island,** which is supposed to have been the prototype for Robert Louis Stevenson's "Treasure Island"; or diving off **Dead Man's Chest,** a rocky cay where Blackbeard marooned 15 pirates and gave rise to the ditty.

More than 500 wrecks lie on the infamous Horseshoe Reef off **Anegada,** the most northerly and isolated of the group. The packet steamer "Rhone" sank during a hurricane over a century ago on **Salt** island, so named for a large and still worked salt pond in its center. Bert Kilbride is an internationally recognized expert on the history of these wrecks and is only too happy to arrange diving parties and show you through his well documented collection in his fascinating museum. Kilbride's Underwater Tours is located on Saba Island, a small gem on the eastern end of North Sound, Virgin Gorda (P.O. Box 40, Virgin Gorda, B.V.I.; 809-49-42746).

The "fat virgin," **Virgin Gorda,** boasts the plush, 500 acre resort, Little Dix Bay, and the eerily beautiful Baths, a cathedral-like arrangement of huge boulders over crystal pools. The Virgin Gorda Yacht Harbor Marina offers every modern convenience for vacationing yachtsmen, and "Drake's Anchorage" on **Mosquito Island** will handle the landlubber too.

The once private domain of **Peter Island** has been transformed into a luxurious tourist attraction, but with tasteful understatement. There are rustic guest cottages on **Jost Van Dyke** where a Quaker colony flourished in the 1700's; a trip over to **Little Jost Van Dyke** for dinner and unique entertainment at the "Last Resort" is a must.

The principal island is Tortola, approximately 29 square miles in size. In the harbor of Road, Tortola's capital city, two man-made cays, Wickham Cay I & II, comprise a concentration of hotels, marinas, and other tourist services. The area has developed rapidly and many new projects are being planned. Many fine hotels and guest cottages are located here, but expect to pay with travelers' checks, as most places will not accept credit cards. No visit is complete without a hike up to Mount Sage forest, or Joe's Hill Distillery, a glorious relic that still produces a few barrels of fiery rum. Airports are situated on Anegada Island, Virgin Gorda and Tortola.

General Information

How To Get There: *By Air:* There is no direct jet service to the B.V.I.'s but connecting flights are available from San Juan, Puerto Rico; Antigua; St. Thomas; and St. Croix.
By Sea: There are three daily round-trip ferries between St. Thomas and Tortola; and roundtrip service to Virgin Gorda on Tuesday and Thursday.

How To Get Around: Taxis with government-regulated rates are available on Tortola and Virgin Gorda. Rental cars, mopeds, and bicycles are also available.

Sports: Fine sailing, fishing, snorkeling, and scuba diving. B.V.I. is considered the capital of "bare boat" charters; boats can be chartered through most hotels and guesthouses, or directly from The Moorings, Ltd., 1305 U.S. 19 South, Suite 402/403/408,

Clearwater, FL (813-530-5651; 800-535-7289); Caribbean Sailing Yachts, Ltd., Box 157, Road Town, B.V.I. (809-49-42741); West Indies Yacht Charters, 2190 SE 17th Street, Fort Lauderdale, FL 33316; Tortola Yacht Charters, 5825 Sunset Drive, South Miami, FL 33143; Stevens Yachts, Inc., 252 East Ave., East Norwalk, CT (800-638-7044).

Medical Facilities: Tortola has a fine and inexpensive government-supported hospital.

Where to Stay

Tortola: ****Prospect Reef Resort,* 131 rooms, 6 lighted tennis courts. *** *Long Bay Hotel,* 44 rooms, on beach. ****Treasure Isle Hotel,* 40 rooms, marina facilities and freshwater swimming pool. ****Moorings—Mariner Inn,* 40 rooms, tennis, swimming

Ruins of an old estate. Tower in the background was a sugar mill.

pool, yacht charters. ***Sugar Mill Hotel,* 20 rooms, beach and swimming pool. ***Fort Burt Hotel,* 7 rooms, water sports available. ***The Castle,* 32 rooms, air conditioned, freshwater swimming pool. ***Sebastian's on the Beach,* 29 rooms, watersports available. **Sea View* Hotel, 20 rooms, swimming pool. ***Village Cay Resort Marina,* 13 rooms, marina facilities. ***CSY Yacht Club,* 8 rooms, charter yachts. ***Smuggler's Cove Hotel,* swimming beach and snorkeling reef. **B.V.I. Aquatic Hotel,* 14 rooms, short walk from West End pier. **Cane Garden Bay Beach Hotel,* 27 rooms, beach bar and restaurant. **Tamarind Country Club Hotel,* 4 rooms, freshwater pool and secluded beach. ***Maria's by the Sea,* 11 rooms, freshwater swimming pool. ***Frenchman's Cay Hotel,* 12 rooms, freshwater pool and tennis court. ****Little Dix Bay Hotel,* 84 rooms, beach tennis, snorkeling, AP. ****Biras Creek Hotel,* 32 suites, beach swimming pool, marina facilities, AP. ****Tradewinds Resort,* 38 rooms, beach bar, tennis, MAP. ****Bitter End Yacht Club,* 40 rooms, elegantly furnished, marina facilities, AP. ***Fischers Cove Beach Hotel,* 20 rooms. ***Ocean View Hotel,* 12 rooms, near beach.
Anegada: ****The Reefs Hotel Anegada,* 12 rooms, beach watersports, AP. **Peter Island:** *****Peter Island Hotel,* on private island, 52 rooms, pool, tennis, and marina facilities, MAP. **Mosquito Island:** ****Drake's Anchorage Resort Inn,* 10 rooms, 4 beaches, fine food, AP. **Guana Island:** ****Guana Island Club,* 15 rooms, private island hideaway, AP. **Jost Van Dyke:** ****White Bay Sandcastle,* 4 cottages, beach and snorkeling.

Where to Eat

Fresh fish and local lobster are is-land specialties. At the ***Bitter End* and ****Drake's Anchorage,* you can select your own lobster from saltwater traps. ****Peter Island Yacht Club* and ****Little Dix Bay Hotel* have outstanding menus and unsurpassed buffets. ***Foxy's* on Jost Van Dyke and ***The Last Resort* on Little Jost Van Dyke are fun and popular places. ***Carib Casseroles* and ***The Pub* offer good lunches in Road Town. The ***Fort Burt Hotel & Restaurant* in Road Town serves elegant dinners in a 300 year-old fort overlooking Sir Francis Drake Channel; reservations required. ***The Conch Shell Point* on Beef Island specializes in seafood and native dishes.

Where to Shop

The *Sunrise Bakery* sells delicious local baked bread. *Gertrude O'Neal* has local handicrafts. The *Cockle Shop* carries locally-made jewelry, keyrings, books, postcards, fabrics, and other appealing gifts. The *Pusser's Company* store is a combination gift shop air-conditioned bar, and collection of nautical items. The *Shipwreck Shop* is a West Indian store where locals and tourists enjoy browsing. In the *Wickham's Cay,* the *Pace Setter* features formal and casual clothing; *Bolo's Record Shop* carries a good selection of West Indian music. On Virgin Gorda, the *Pelican's Pouch Boutique* features casual wear made of cool natural fibers. The *Wine Cellar* carries a wide assortment of liquors and wines. The *Virgin Gorda Craft Shop* and *Kaunda's Tropical Handicrafts* features work of native artisans.

Additional Information

British Virgin Islands Tourist Board, 370 Lexington Avenue, Suite 412, New York, NY 10017 (212-696-0400); *British Virgin Islands Tourist Board,* P.O. Box 134, Road Town, Tortola, B.V.I. (809-494-3134).

ST. KITTS, NEVIS, ANGUILLA

St. Kitts, Nevis and Anguilla are an unspoiled world of beaches, views, and great historical spots, with no neon night-club lights.

ST. KITTS

St. Christopher, usually called St. Kitts, is peaked with rocky mountains and green fertile fields of sugar-cane and cotton.

About 33 miles long and 5 miles wide, the volcanic island lies about 185 miles southeast of Puerto Rico. Anguilla is just 70 miles to the north, Nevis just 2 miles southeast. The 43,000 people, who are almost all black, raise sugar and sea-island cotton, do some handicrafts, distill their own rum. They are good seamen.

Columbus found the island on his second voyage in 1493, and named it, but it was never colonized until Sir Thomas Warner, the English pioneer of the West Indies, took settlers ashore in 1623. At about the same time the French arrived. They divided the island, and lived in peace for a while, joining to resist both the fierce Carib Indians and the Spanish. From St. Kitts both French and English settlers carried their flags to claim islands north and south and west, which is why it's called the "mother colony of the West Indies." The island was also something of a battleground, passing back and forth between the British and French until the Treaty of Versailles in 1783 gave it to the British for the last time. Britain held it as a colony until the formation of the West Indies Federation in 1958, which was dissolved in 1961. In 1983 St. Kitts and Nevis became independent democracies following the British system of government.

General Information

How To Get There: *By Air:* BWIA and Pan Am fly weekly from New York and Miami; American flies to Antigua or St. Martin and connects to L.I.A.T. or Winnair.

How To Get Around: The capital of Basseterre and the harbor are best explored on foot. There is a good road circling the island, and you can take a taxi around it for a fixed fee, or rent a drive-yourself car.

Language: English

Festivals: New Year's Day is celebrated with parades and steel bands, as is Boxing Day, December 26.

Sports: *Swimming.* Conaree Beach and Frigate Bay, both with good surf. *Fishing.* You can hire boats through your hotel.
Tennis. Your hotel will make arrangements for you to play on the tennis-club courts.
Mountain Climbing, Hiking. Enjoyable, with the best climb up to the cloud-touched peak of Mount Misery.
Bird Watching. Migratory birds in great variety are seen between October and December.

Night Life: Most of the hotels have steel bands in for dancing.

Medical Facilities: Doctors trained in the United Kingdom and Canada staff Joseph N. France General Hospital in Basseterre and Pogson Hospital in Sandy Point.

Additional Information: *St. Kitts and Nevis Tourist Board,* 414 E. 75th St., New York, NY 10021 (212-535-1234); *St. Kitts and Nevis Tourist Board,* Box 132, Basseterre, St. Kitts, W.I. (809-465-2620).

Where to Stay
***Fairview Inn,* Basseterre, 18th century great house with cottages and pool, MAP. ****The Golden Lemon,* Dieppe Bay, 20 rooms, 18th century great house setting for 20th century comfort, AP. ***Fort Thomas Hotel,* Fort Thomas, 64 rooms with all facilities, MAP. ****Banana Bay Beach Hotel,* Banana Bay, 10 rooms, AP. ***Ocean Terrace Inn,* Basseterre, 45 rooms, MAP. ****Jack Tar Village,* 250 rooms, pool, tennis, golf, casino, MAP. ****Rawlins Plantation,* 10 rooms, pretty country inn, MAP. * Conaree Cottage,* two cottages on Conaree Beach. ***Frigate Bay Beach Hotel,* 45 rooms, pool, golf, overlooking bay. **Sun & Sand,* Frigate Bay, 15 free-standing beach cottages, pool, golf. ***Leeward Cove,* 10 one- and two-bedroom condos on beach at Frigate Bay. **Island Paradise,* 40 one- and two-bedroom condos on Frigate Bay. There are also a number of boarding houses and beach cottages.

Where to Eat
You can dine either at your hotel, or at *The Palm, The Ballyhoo, The Georgian House,* or *Fisherman's Wharf,* in Basseterre; and *The Anchorage* at Frigate Bay. The local rum is good, potent, and cheap. Specialties of the native cooks are fish and lobster.

Where to Shop
English imports and native-made straw goods, embroidery, and tortoise-shell jewelry are the best buys. The shops are all centered around the Circus and along Fort Street and side streets.

What to See
Basseterre is a lovely old West Indian town built around a "Circus" —traffic circle—with an ornate tower clock in its center. The harbor bustles with schooners carrying produce to and from neighboring islands. If you're on St. Kitts when one of the large ships is anchored outside, don't miss the sight of the sailing tenders ferrying goods back and forth. The native sailors really know how to handle their boats.

The great sight on the island is the fantastic fort on Brimstone Hill, with its walls rising 700 feet, parade-ground cannon pointing out across the sea, and its view of Sint Eustatius in the distance. It took thousands of slaves over 100 years to complete the huge fortress. *Brimstone Hill Fort* may have been the inspiration for Henri Christophe, who was

The "Circus" in Basseterre, capital of St. Kitts.

supposed to have been born on St. Christopher, to build his Citadelle in Haiti.

There are a number of relics of the old French and English days. At the pretty village of *Half-Way Tree* you will find the big tamarind tree that marked the boundary between the English- and French-owned halves. Near the village of *Old Road* is the place where Sir Thomas Warner landed with his first band of settlers. They established the first permanent settlement at *Sandy Point* to the northwest. Near here, too, you will find Sir Thomas' grave on the grounds of *St. Thomas Church.*

If you like mountain climbing, there are two delightful hikes to be made on the island. You can climb up to *Mount Misery* to see the virgin forest and the crater, or up *Verchilds Mountain* to Dodan Pond, a lovely lake in the old volcano's crater.

NEVIS (NEE-vis)

Mountainous, beach-rimmed, quiet Nevis, unquestionably one of the most handsomely endowed islands of the Caribbean, has been left with its natural beauties untouched.

Dominating the 36-square-mile island is Nevis Peak, 3,232 feet high, and two lesser volcanic mountains, Hurricane Hill in the north and Saddle Hill in the south. The shore is rimmed by coral reefs and mile after mile of palm-tree-shaded beaches.

The 10,000 people are almost all black descendants of slaves, grow cane, cotton, and copra, and fish the bright blue waters.

Although the island is quiet now, it wasn't always so. 150 years ago Nevis' big thermal baths had made it the first fashionable Caribbean playground. The wide streets of Charlestown and Newcastle were thronged with planters and their ladies come to take the waters.

The island has been British since the early days, and the now almost-deserted village of Newcastle was once a center of British commerce. Alexander Hamilton was born on Nevis, and Captain Horatio Nelson of the H.M.S. *Boreas* came here to get fresh water for his ships from a palm-shaded lagoon, and here he met and married the pretty young widow Frances Nisbett.

Life moves slowly on Nevis and tranquility is still the prevailing mood despite its recent discovery by tourists.

General Information

How To Get There: *By Air:* LIAT operates regular flights from St. Kitts to Nevis. There are also direct flights from Antigua and St. Martin a few times a day. Winnair also provides service.

By Sea: Each morning (except Thursday and Sunday), a boat leaves Basseterre, St. Kitts, for Charlestown, Nevis, and returns in the afternoon. The 11-mile voyage takes 45 minutes.

How To Get Around: The island has good roads, and you can tour the tiny capital of Charlestown on foot and drive to other spots. Taxis are available for hire.

Language: English.

Sports: You can swim in the pool at the Golden Rock Estate or at the deserted white-sand spots like Pinney's Beach. Fishing is good if you have your own equipment. You can rent sail or power boats, or go spearfishing and snorkeling. You can hike up the mountains, particularly Nevis Peak, and ride horseback, watch cricket, or go shooting in season (see St. Kitts).

Night Life: Minimal.

Additional Information: St. Kitts and Nevis Tourist Board, 414 E. 75th St., New York, NY 10021 (212-535-1234). St. Kitts and Nevis Tourist Board, Basseterre, St. Kitts, W.I. (809-465-2620).

Where to Stay

HOTELS: ****Golden Rock,* Gingerland, 12 rooms on an old sugar estate, pool, beaches, overlooks the sea, MAP. ****Pinney's Beach,* 60 rooms, beach tennis, snorkeling, MAP. **** *Nisbet Plantation Inn,* 30 rooms, beach, tennis, MAP. *****Montpelier,* 28 rooms, built on site of historic sugar works where Nelson married Fanny Nisbett in 1787, MAP. *** *Croney's Old Manor,* 12 rooms, 17th century estate, MAP. ****Rest Haven,* Charlestown, 37 rooms, MAP. *** *Zetland Plantation,* on slope of Mt. Nevis, 22 rooms, elegant, MAP. **** *Cliff Dwellers,* 14 rooms, overlooks beach, MAP. ***Hermitage Plantation,* 12 rooms in old home, MAP.

Where to Eat

Fish and lobster are best. The hotels are on the American Plan.

What to See

Charlestown is a quiet little town of red-roofed white stone houses and wide, quiet streets. On the edge of town you will find the foundations of an old house and staircase, the gate before which is labeled "Hamilton House." This is where Alexander Hamilton was born in 1757, the illegitimate son of a Scotsman, James Hamilton, and Rachel Fawcett, who lived on Nevis. He left here as a young boy to work in the Virgin Islands before going on to America and immortality.

About half a mile south of Charlestown are the old thermal baths at *Bath House,* the grand hotel built right over the warm springs. In the other direction on the round-island road is reef-protected *Pinney's Beach* with a gradual slope and clear water, the best on Nevis—and one of the best in the Caribbean. If you take the road further along toward the north, you will follow the shore through the village of *Cotton Ground* and then the remains of the once-busy town of *Newcastle,* which flourished in the days of the island's first popularity. Near Newcastle are the old *Nisbett Estate* and the lagoon where Nelson got fresh water to supply his ships. In the rectory of the old *Fig Tree Church* you can see the marriage register signed by Nelson.

On the eastern side of the island the beaches boom with the Atlantic surf. At little *Zion Hill Village* the road turns west again through breathtaking rugged mountain scenery, then back to Charlestown.

ANGUILLA (An-GWILL-uh)

About 70 miles northwest of St. Kitts and Nevis and 11 miles from St. Martin lies Anguilla, 16 miles long, about 4 miles wide, and edged all around with 30 white sand beaches.

Both the beaches and the fishing are excellent, and you can rent boats.

The island is covered by low foliage and scrub vegetation. The 7,050 natives grow peas, potatoes, corn, and sea-island cotton on small farms and work the government-owned salt ponds that spread over 50 acres.

General Information

How To Get There: *By Air:* Winnair flies from St. Martin several times daily.
By Sea: Boats make continuous daily runs from St. Martin; passage takes about 20 minutes.

Sports: *Swimming.* Some of the finest beaches in the Caribbean.
Duck Shooting during the winter season. Bring your own equipment for *snorkeling, spear-fishing, skin-diving* and *water-skiing.*
Boating. Anguilla's biggest events are the racing boat competition on Easter Monday, Anguilla Day (May 30th) and during the August Carnival Week. Everyone turns out on the beach to watch, and the boats are colorful and unique.

Night Life: Minimal.

Additional Information: *Anguilla Tourist Bureau,* 40 E. 49th St., New York, NY 10017 (212-752-8660).

Caribbean Tourist Association, 20 E. 46th St., New York, NY 10017 (212-682-0435).

Where to Stay

****Cinnamon Reef,* on Little Harbor, 14 villas, pool, tennis. ****Coral Bay Resort,* in Corito, 16 rooms, pool. ****Cul de Sac,* in Blowing Point, 6 rooms, pool. *****La Sante,* on Barnes Bay, 40 villas, pool, tennis. *****Malliouhana Hotel,* on Meads Bay, 41 rooms, pool, tennis. ****Mariners Hotel,* in Sandy Ground, 27 rooms. ****Rendezvous Hotel,* on Rendezvous Bay, 20 rooms, tennis. ****Shoal Bay Villas,* on Shoal Bay, 9 rooms. *****Carimar Beach Club,* on Meads Bay, 19 units. *****Cove Castle,* on Shoal Bay West, 4 units, tennis. ****Easy Corner Villas,* in South Hill, 11 units. Inexpensive guesthouses, apartments, villas, and cottages are also available.

THE FRENCH WEST INDIES

Warm, verdant, lavishly endowed with French charm and tropical beauty, Guadeloupe and Martinique, the undiscovered islands of yesterday, are today's newest destinations.

The western border of France is a long way from Europe. It is in Guadeloupe and Martinique, 1,200 miles southeast of Florida in the great curve of the Lesser Antilles. With a handful of tiny off-island dependencies, these two islands are the westernmost *départements* of France, and the 700,000 people who live there are full-fledged citizens of the French Republic—cinnamon-colored *citoyens* with a Gallic verve and a Caribbean grace that is remarkable even in an area where beauty is commonplace.

Three hundred miles south of Puerto Rico, Guadeloupe is a butterfly-shaped island that is actually two—flat and fertile *Grande-Terre* as the northeast wing and the lush and mountainous *Basse-Terre* to the southwest. They are joined by a bridge over a narrow passage called *Rivière Salée*. A few miles off the southern shore lie the eight little clustered *Iles des Saintes,* and the larger sugar cane island, *Marie Galante.* The former leper island of *Désirade* is just to the east. Far to the northwest some 150 miles, past Antigua and St. Kitts and Saba, is the half-island *St. Martin,* Sint Maarten to the Dutch, who own the other half. And an hour's boatride or a ten-minute flight from St. Martin lies *St. Barthélemy.*

A hundred miles to the south of Guadeloupe is Martinique, a lovely varied island which once produced Napoleon's Josephine and Louis XIV's Madame de Maintenon, and now produces the *Martiniquaises,* saffron-hued beauties who are among the most attractive women in all of France.

GUADELOUPE (Gwa-de-LOOP)

Guadeloupe is everything in the Caribbean—great expanses of sugar cane and banana trees on the low, fertile island of Grande-Terre, and on the rugged twin island of Basse-Terre stark, volcanic peaks with their slopes a tangled rain forest. The capital of the twin-island *département* is little *Basse-Terre* with a population of 26,000, on the southwestern tip of the island of the same name. But the metropolis and commercial center is *Pointe-à-Pitre* (62,000) on Grande-Terre just south of the point where the butterfly wings are joined.

The history of the island is standard—with variations. Columbus, cruising north, went ashore on Marie Galante in 1493 and named the island for his flagship. And the main island he saw to the north he named in honor of the Monastery of Guadeloupe in Spain. But the Carib Indians who occupied the island drove off both Columbus and the later Spanish explorers, and it wasn't until 1635 that the French were able to plant a permanent colony there.

Sugar cane and cacao made the island wealthy centuries ago, and one-crop sugar economy made it poor later. But since World War II, it has begun to share in the travel bonanza. It has French and creole cuisine, splendid beaches, full-service resorts and cozy hotels. Jacques Cousteau rated its west coast as one of the world's ten best diving areas.

General Information

How To Get There: *By Air:* American flies regularly from New York. Eastern flies from New York and other U.S. cities via Miami. Air France flies from Miami and San Juan. Air Canada flies from Montreal and Toronto. Air Guadeloupe serves all of the Guadeloupe archipelago daily. LIAT has flights from most neighboring islands. *By Sea:* Cunard, American Canadian Cruise Lines, Chandris, P.&O., and Pacquet are some of the dozen or so cruise lines that call at the island.

Entry Requirements: France recently announced that visas are required to enter its possessions, where previously a passport wasn't even necessary. Visas can usually be obtained upon arrival. For further information, contact the French West Indies Tourist Board, 610 Fifth Ave., New York, NY 10020 (212-757-1125).

How To Get Around: The buses are colorful, inexpensive, and harrowing. Taxis are plentiful, but the driver may not speak English. Night fares are 40 percent higher than day rates. There are a dozen car rental agencies, and driving yourself may be the best way to see the island. Guadeloupe's 1,225-mile road network is one of the best in the Caribbean.

Language: French.

Festivals: The carnival starts just after New Year's, includes parades and dancing in the streets, and builds to a climax on Mardi Gras and Ash Wednesday. Most interesting is the mid-August *Fête des Cuisinières,* a colorful and unique paean to the joy of cooking. High Mass at the cathedral in Pointe-à-Pitre is followed by a five-hour feast.

Sports: *Cockfighting* is in season from November through April. *Horse racing* can be found at Bellecourt, Baie-Mahault, and the St. Jacques Hippodrome at Anse Bertrand. There is an 18-hole Robert Trent Jones *golf course* at St. François, adjacent to the Hamak and Meridien hotels.

Swimming. Good at any of the main beaches or at the little ones you'll find when you circle the island. Among

the best are Le Gosier near Pointe-à-Pitre, St. François, Le Moule, Ste. Anne.

Fishing. The season for barracuda and kingfish is January to May; for tuna, dolphin, and bonito, it's December to March. For boat rentals contact *Thalassa* in Bas du Fort (tel. 82.74.94), or *Guadeloupe Chartaire* in Pointe-à-Pitre (tel. 82.34.47).

Sailing. Sailboats and motorboats at most hotels and the Yacht Clubs in Pointe-à-Pitre and Basse-Terre.

Hiking, Mountain Climbing. Excellent, but you'll need guides. You can make arrangements through the *Organization des Guides de Montagne* in Basse-Terre's lush Parc Naturel (tel. 81.45.53), or climb the volcano Mt. Soufrière and see steaming sulphur and water vapor.

Night Life: All the major hotels have discos and nightclubs. There is one casino at St. Francois and another in Gosier.

Medical Facilities: Good French-trained doctors and hospitals.

Additional Information: French West Indies Tourist Board, 610 Fifth Avenue, New York, New York 10022; (212-757-1125); Office Departmental du Tourisme, 97181 Pointe-a-Pitre, Guadeloupe, F.W.I. (tel. 82.09.30).

Where to Stay

****Meridien St. Francois* in St. François. Pool, beach, 272 rooms. ****Hamak,* 56 rooms. 18-hole golf course. ***Club Mediterranée,* good food and complete sports facilities at reasonable prices. One is at Fort Royal, Basse-Terre, the other, the largest, at Caravelle on Grande-Terre. ***Auberge de la Vieille Tour,* Gosier, 82 rooms, pool, on beach. ***La Creole Beach,* 156 rooms, scuba, in Gosier. **Bougainvillée,* conveniently located in Pointe-à-Pitre. 32 rooms. ****PLM Marissol,* 200 rooms, Bas du Fort, overlooking Grand Bay, ten-

nis, pool, water sports, night life. *** *PLM Sun Village,* 92 rooms, tennis, pool, water sports, disco. **Auberge de la Distillerie,* 12 rooms, Vernou. ** *Ecotel Guadeloupe,* 44 rooms. *** *Novotel Fleur D'Epee,* 180 rooms, Bas du Fort. ***Arawak,* Gosier. 160 rooms, on beach, tennis, pool, water sports.

Where to Eat

Food is French and good in almost all restaurants. The island specializes in sea foods and spicy Creole dishes—turtle, stuffed crab, curries. **La Vieille Tour,* Gosier, for excellent French cuisine and good wine cellar. **La Créole Chez Violetta* in Gosier, has excellent seafood and local specialties. **Chez Rosette,* Gosier, for creole food. ***La Plantation* in Bas du Fort, French and creole cuisine. ** *Chez Paul,* Matouba, specializes in Creole and Indian food. *Madame Jerco,* St. François, small, typical local bistro. *Le Barbazar,* in Pointe-à-Pitre, is a local favorite.

Where to Shop

French imports are found in many of the shops—perfumes (20% off when paid for with Travelers Cheques), glassware, Parisian ready-to-wear, Hermès scarves, and, of course, the best French brandies, wines, and champagnes. The island specializes in dark, rich rums.

In native handicrafts good buys are the doudou dolls in the dresses of the ladies of Guadeloupe, fishermen's hats from Les Isles des Saintes, carvings made of aromatic vetivert wood, shell work, beads, and Creole hats made from madras to match your summer dress.

Rue Frébault is the shopping street in Pointe-à-Pitre. Stores observe the French lunch hour and are open from 8 A.M. to 12 noon, and 2:30 P.M. to 6 P.M.

Among the best shops on Rue Frébault are *La Maison du Rhum,* which lets you sample before buying; *Le Bambou,* a good selection of madras fashions; and *Au Caraibe,* which offers the best of the local handicrafts. *Rosebleu* has a good stock of French cosmetics, accessories and crystal, as does *Vendôme.*

What to See

The butterfly shape of Guadeloupe, the "Emerald Isle," is completely outlined by the coastal roads. From them you will see the best of the island—the beaches and pounding surf on Grande-Terre, the jungles and mountains on Basse-Terre.

From Pointe-à-Pitre you can drive along the southeast coast to *Gosier,* the main resort town and site of most of the island's hotels, restaurants and night clubs.

A little further along is the sugar town of **Ste. Anne** with its excellent beach and little *St. François,* where the Place de la Victoire commemorates the defeat of the invading British in 1794. Just beyond the town is *Pointe des Châteaux,* the easternmost point of Guadeloupe. The sea pounds against the high, ragged cliffs, slashes into the blowholes, and throws spray high into the air. Five or six miles offshore lies the former leper island of *Désirade.*

About midway up the eastern coast is the delightful beach *Le Moule,* shaped like a giant horseshoe. Centuries ago the Caribs battled the colonists here for possession of the island, and in a cemetery close by the sea they buried the dead. Over the years wind and surf have worn down the shore and uncovered skeletons and skulls embedded in the beach rocks.

Looking at the map you would think it no more than twenty miles from Pointe-à-Pitre to the city of Basse-Terre, but the way the road winds around the cliffs along the shore makes it more than twice that distance. It is a fabulously beautiful drive, not to be missed on any

Policemen enjoy traffic lull in noon-day sun in Pointe-à-Pitre

account. Get a car *with* driver, and spend your time looking. This is the rugged part of the island where the people get their living from the sea and not from the land. All along the shore you will pass tiny fishing villages where big fish nets hang drying in the trade winds.

Near *Trois Rivières* is the *Archaeological Park,* a grotto of pre-Columbian rock carvings beside a rushing stream. It is one of the few places you can see Carib art in a setting chosen by the men who swept across the Caribbean long before Columbus was born.

The road swings inland to **Basse-Terre,** the political capital and the banana capital of Guadeloupe. It is a handsome little city between the sea and looming *Mt. Soufrière,* neat with green, shaded parks and a pretty seventeenth-century cathedral.

From Basse-Terre past *Fort Richepance* which guards the harbor, there is a road to the interior that winds through the foothills of Soufrière to **St. Claude,** a cool summer colony, a place so high that sometimes clouds hang about the houses, hiding the town in a misty blanket. Other notable stops include the *Hindu Temple* at Changy and the new *Maison du Café* at Vieux Habitants, a museum devoted to local coffee production. Refreshments are available.

You can drive part of the way up 4,813-foot Mt. Soufrière, but the climb from the end of the road takes up to three hours depending which approach you take. It doesn't have to be a difficult climb, but it is tricky, and you shouldn't attempt it without a guide. Part of it is through the luxuriant rain forest, part over slopes of gray volcanic ash, potted with steaming bogs. At the top there is a small stone shelter—a cramped little building, but a welcome refuge from the wind-whipped clouds that often hang around the old cone.

ILES DES SAINTES (Eel day SANT)

A handful of lush, green islands called Iles des Saintes lie six miles south of *Trois Rivières.* **Terre de Haute,** with a population of about 1,500, is the largest of the group. Almost all of the men are seamen, and they are said to be the best in the Caribbean. It used to be said that there were active smugglers in the area, carrying on a lively and lucrative business in high-duty goods imported unofficially from the neighboring islands.

Whatever else they are, the seamen are camera-shy but irresistibly photogenic, for they wear a strange kind of headgear called *sallakos*—shallow, white, cloth-covered sun shades built on radiating ribs of thick bamboo, which resemble nothing so much as small parasols made with a framework to fit over the head.

Brought here years ago by Indonesian laborers, the hats are most attractive and, of course, much admired by visiting ladies for beach wear. Good accommodations are available at the *Bois Joli Hotel* with 21 rooms.

MARIE GALANTE (Ma-REE Ga-LAHNT)

Round little Marie Galante, about two hours and twenty-five miles south of Guadeloupe, is the sugar island best known to visitors as the place where the women wear the colorful and informative *madras et foulard* costumes. The madras headdress is tied with the number of "points" indicating the girl's marital status: one point, fancy free; two points, engaged; three points, married; four points, looking again.

ST. BARTHELEMY (San Bar-te-le-MEE)

About 125 miles northwest of Guadeloupe, at the beginning of the Lesser Antilles, is St. Barthélemy (called St. Barts by its friends), a slip of an island known for its tranquillity as well as its scenery. St. Barts, with a population of 3,500, is the only island in the Caribbean that can lay claim to Swedish ancestry. It has a magnificent harbor at *Gustavia,* beaches that are good for swimming, a climate that is year-round ideal. There are no high-rises, casinos, or movie theaters, and very few night-clubs on the island. St. Barts has about 430 hotel rooms in all. Recommended are **St. Barth Beach Hotel,* 36 rooms; **Taiwana Club,* 9 rooms; ***Hotel Manapany,* 20 cottages, which all have tennis courts; and ***Hotel Hibiscus,* 11 rooms, which overlooks the harbor and is a favorite with yachtsmen.

Loulou's Marine (tel 27.62.74) in Gustavia is another sailors' haven. The stock is limitless, the staff speaks English, and the bulletin board is a treasure-trove of yachting information.

The way to get to St. Barts is by regular daily flights from St. Thomas, St. Martin, San Juan, or Guadeloupe or by hydrofoil from St. Martin.

SAINT MARTIN (San Mar-TAN)

The half island called St. Martin, just north of St. Barthélemy, also belongs to France. The other half, called Sint Maarten, is owned by the Dutch (See *The Netherlands Antilles*). The Dutch have the biggest city, *Philipsburg,* and the airport, but the French, of course, have the food. Marigot, the capital, has outgrown its sleepy fishing village image and is now a thriving resort town, with new boutiques, marinas, and restaurants to satisfy its growing numbers of tourists. The highest point on the island is *Mt. Paradis,* which rises to 1,728 feet, but most of St. Martin is rolling hills. There are more than 30 beaches, and most hotels rent equipment for snorkeling, scuba diving, water skiing, parasailing, and windsurfing.

****La Belle Créole,* 156 rooms, across Marigot Bay, and *** L'Habitation,* 253 rooms, at Anse Marcel, are the newest hotels. There is also ****Samanna,* 85 rooms; ***PLM St. Tropez Beach,* 118 rooms;

and ****Le Pirate,** 105 rooms. ****Palm Plaza,** 21 rooms, is a good moder-
ately-priced hotel in Marigot. In Grand Case try the secluded *****
Grand Case Beach Club,** 76 rooms, and the *****Club Orient Nudist
Resort,** 84 rooms, if it suits your fancy.

Restaurants here are very French and very expensive. *La Vie En
Rose,* in Marigot, is the island's best, but dinner can run $80 per person.
Maison Sur le Port, with a good poached lobster in pink pepper sauce,
and *Davids,* with its conch fritters and relaxed atmosphere, are a bit
more moderately-priced. Both are in Marigot.

American serves the island from New York, Dallas and San Juan;
Pan Am from New York and Miami; and Eastern from Miami. There
are also daily flights from Guadeloupe and St. Barts on Air Guadeloupe
and Air St. Bathlemy. Juliana Airport is on the Dutch side.

MARTINIQUE (Mar-teh-NEEK)

Largest of the Windwards, lush and lovely Martinique is known for
its French charm, excellent cuisine, chic women, and its carnival season
between New Year's and Lent. About 350,000 people live on the island,
about 100 miles south of its sister *département,* Guadeloupe.

Discovered by Columbus and taken by the French in 1635, the
"Island of Flowers" became rich on the slave-worked sugar plantations, so rich and brilliant that St. Pierre, then the capital, was called
the "Little Paris of the Caribbean." But like its neighbors, Martinique
sank into poverty with the end of slavery. It still has the flowers—
bougainvillaea, hibiscus, and orchids in every wall cranny the year
round; broad and all but deserted beaches; and fine French and creole
food. The hotels range from 300-room establishments to small family-
run places.

Best time of year in Martinique is between November and April
when the temperature is down and the air is dry. And that is when you
are likely to be there, for that is the fabulous carnival time. Shortly after
New Year's the masqueraders begin to appear in the streets of Fort de
France, singing and dancing dressed as pirates, Napoleons, Josephines,
cowboys, Charlie Chaplins, and dozens of other outrageous and uni-
dentifiable characters.

The buffoonery, parties, and parades keep growing, reaching fever
pitch five days before Lent, when all non-carnival activities cease.
Unlike elsewhere in the world, the festival here continues through Ash
Wednesday, the first day of Lent. The mythical Bois Bois, king of the
carnival, dies that night.

On that final day, as many as 30,000 revelers, masked and costumed
in black and white, crowd the streets at dawn to form the carnival
king's funeral procession. By noon, rum and excitement have conquered inhibitions. Long lines of dancers, mock mourners, and trum-
peters lead the funeral corteges on their winding routes through the
town. All day long the tempo increases, the music becomes more

hypnotic, the dancing less restrained. At dusk the crowds begin to converge on the *savane* where a great funeral pyre is waiting for Bois Bois. The fire is lit as the dancers whirl and shout, and the king is hurled to his finish. Dancing continues until about midnight, when all festivities halt and processioners gather to march slowly behind the coffin of Bois Bois, signaling the beginning of Lent.

General Information

How To Get There: *By Air:* American flies from New York; Eastern flies from New York and other U.S. cities via Miami. Air France has flights from Miami and San Juan; Air Canada from Toronto and Montreal. Air Martinique and LIAT link Martinique with many of the Caribbean islands.

By Sea: Fort de France is a popular port-of-call for cruise ships. Home, Norwegian America, Costa, and Holland-America Lines are among the many that stop at Martinique.

How To Get Around: The island has more than 200 miles of paved roads, most of them curved. The buses are cheap, but clean, and faster than necessary. Taxis are government regulated. There are more than a dozen car rental agencies on Martinique.

Language: French. English is understood in tourist areas.

Festivals: All the Catholic holidays are celebrated. Carnival and Mardi Gras just before and on Ash Wednesday are the big celebrations.

Sports: *Golf.* An 18-hole Robert Trent Jones course is at *Trois Islets,* 18 miles from Fort de France.

Swimming. The beaches south of Fort de France are white while the northern beaches are mostly gray sand. The best are in the south, notably Plage des Salines, near Ste. Anne, and Diamant, with its landmark Diamond Rock offshore.

Boating. Your hotel can make arrangements for you to go sailing. Most seaside hotels have a variety of small boats to rent.

Fishing. Sea and fresh water fishing in the rivers. Your hotel, again, for arrangements.

Horseback riding. Trails and riding lessons offered at Ranche de Galochat at Anse d'arlet, Black Horse in Trois Islets and La Cavale near Diamant-Novotel.

Mountain Climbing, Hiking. Guides will take you up Mont Pelée.

Night Life: The beguine in its original and uninhibited form is the Saturday night diversion. The most lively spots are the hotel night clubs at the *Méridien* and *La Batelière.*

Medical Facilities: Good French doctors and modern hospitals.

Additional Information: French West Indies Tourist Board, 610 Fifth Avenue, New York, NY 10020 (212-757-1125); Office Départemental du Tourisme, Fort de France, Martinique, F.W.I. (tel. 63.79.60).

Where to Stay

***Bakoua Beach,* 99 rooms, air-conditioned, pool. ***PLM Carayou,* Pointe du Bout. Pool, beach. 210 rooms. ****Meridien Martinique,* Pointe du Bout. Pool, beach, 303 rooms. ***La Batelière,* Fort de France. Pool, beach. 215 rooms. *** *Buccaneer's Creek Club Med,* 300 rooms, all-inclusive, Ste. Anne. *** *Leyritz Plantation Hotel,* 50 rooms, in Basse-Pointe, restored plantation, very elegant. ***Manoir de Beauregard,* in Sainte Anne, 27 rooms, restored plantation, wonderful beaches on island nearby. **Auberge du Varé*, 12 rooms in Case Pilote. **Malmaison*, 19 rooms, air-conditioned. *Latitude*, 90 rooms. In Carbet with pool and beach. ***Novotel Diamant*, 173 rooms, in Diamant. **Victoria Hotel*, 20 rooms in residential area, Fort de France. **Bambou Hotel*, 40 rooms, in Anse Mitan. *Impératrice*, 24 rooms, air-conditioned. *Lafayette*, 24 rooms, Fort de France. **Diamant Les Bains*, 15 rooms, Diamant.

Where to Eat

Good French cuisine spiced with traditional foods of Martinique. Best native foods include *colombo*, an Indian dish of beef (or pork) and rice, stuffed crabs, excellent crayfish, baked yams, palm hearts, roast mutton.

RESTAURANTS: ***La Grand' Voile*, Fort de France, the best French food on Martinique. ***Le d'Esnambuc*, Fort de France, wonderful seafood. **Escalier*, Fort de France, authentic creole cookery. **Leyritz Plantation*, near Basse Pointe, seafood and creole cooking.

French imports of all kinds are good buys—perfumes, fine wines and brandies. Also excellent Danish silver, china, and glassware.

Best local products are the delightful doudou dolls dressed like local belles, Creole hats made from madras, ceramics, handmade gold jewelry that is sold by the weight, and, of course, rum. An interesting souvenir is one of the brightly colored patchwork tapestries which depict life on the island.

Among the best shops, all in Fort de France, are:

Roger Albert, Rue Victor Hugo, with a wide assortment of goods, particularly French perfumes and other imports; *L'Imperatrice Hotel Shop,* local handicrafts and souvenirs; *Au Printemps,* outstanding novelties, doudou dolls and French crystal and china.

Roger Albert, Cadet Daniel, and *Derogatis* all carry fine selections of imported and local jewelry. Among the best wine and spirit merchants are *La Marine,* Rue Victor Hugo; *H. Sequin,* Rue Victor Hugo; *Héritiers Clément,* Rue Ernest Deproge; *La Régence,* Rue Blenac; *La Rode,* and *Le Petit Marseillais* nearby.

What to See

Martinique's bustling capital, **Fort de France,** fronts on the big bay, and is built around a handsome savannah, a green central square with tall palms and mango trees. Here statues pay the proper honors to the two main figures of the island's history, the Empress Josephine and Victor Schoelcher, who worked to free the slaves more than a century ago. During the week the savannah is hustling with the business and trading carried on in the shops and cafés that line its sides, and on Sunday the crowds stream through it to Mass at the Cathedral whose strange iron steeple was, alas, felled by a storm.

Josephine was born just across the bay at *Les Trois Islets,* and was a Creole beauty of 16 when she left for France. She came back to Martinique during the French Revolution, but later returned to Paris where at 33 she married Napoleon and later was crowned *Impératrice des Français.* In Les Trois Islets there are the ruins of the house where she was born, the church where she worshiped, and a little museum with mementos of her days of glory.

St. Pierre, successor to the city destroyed in 1902 by Mt. Pelée

On a peninsula at the southern end of the island is *Diamant-Novotel,* with its splendid white sand beach, and *Rocher du Diamant,* the off-shore rock known as His Majesty's Ship Diamond Rock. In 1804 a company of 120 English sailors took, fortified, and held the rock against the French fleet for a year and a half until they ran out of powder. To this day, whenever a British ship of war passes HMS Diamond Rock, it dips its flag in salute.

Ste. Anne's Beach on the southwestern tip of the island is a day's excursion for which you should hire a guide. After you have had a swim and lunch—the guide will catch a lobster and cook it while you bask on the white sand—you can drive on a little further to the *Savane de Pétrification,* a strange desert-like valley of petrified trees.

Some 15 miles north of Fort de France are the strange and moving ruins of the old capital, *St. Pierre,* the historic city that was destroyed in a mighty blast of fire and lava from *Mont Pelée* in 1902. In less than one minute nearly 30,000 people were killed—every person in the city except one condemned prisoner in his dungeon. The jungle has over-grown many of the buildings, covering the ruined walls, stone stair-ways, and courtyards. A little town has grown up at the edge of the buried city, and a museum has been set up to house the few bits of the city that were salvaged.

You can climb Mont Pelée, going about halfway up by car, and then hiking to the summit from there in about two hours. There's no danger. Mont Pelée is expected to remain quiet now for many centuries. A guide, however, is recommended.

Finally, you should not miss seeing the *Grande Ballet de la Martinique,* a troupe of 25 singers and dancers, and one of the best folk dancing groups in the Caribbean. They perform weekly at the major hotels.

ANTIGUA

As British as its most famous resident, Admiral Nelson, Antigua offers a ring of sunbright beaches and the finest sailing waters of the Caribbean.

At the shoulder of the Antilles chain 300 miles southeast of Puerto Rico, little Antigua (fifteen miles across, with a population of some 85,000 in its 108 square miles) is an ideal retreat—a dry, mild climate, dazzling coral beaches, day-after-day sun, and the never-failing gentle trade winds that make it a yachtsman's paradise.

English planters from St. Kitts settled the rolling, hilly island in 1632, squabbled with the Indians and the French for possession for a generation, and since then have been developing the place in proper British colonial fashion. The Duke of Clarence, who later became King William IV, served a tour here. So did Horatio Nelson who in 1786–88 built the dockyard which bears his name in landlocked English Harbour.

Since becoming fully independent in 1981, Antigua's industries are growing and the island looks forward to a new and happy prosperity.

GENERAL INFORMATION

How To Get There: *By Air:* BWIA and Eastern fly non-stop from Miami. Eastern also flies in from San Juan. Air Canada, BA and LIAT fly from several cities.
By Sea: Freighters of the Booth Line, Atlantic Lines, and Spanish Royal Line stop regularly as do others.

How To Get Around: Taxis are plentiful, rates are fixed for longer trips. Roads are not of the best, but they are usable. Drive-it-yourself cars are available for $30–$40 dollars a day.

Festivals: Exciting time is a week-long carnival starting the end of July. Carnival festivities include steel bands, parades, dancing, and "jump ups."

Sports: Cricket, of course, and all the water sports, as well as soccer and netball.
Swimming. Most hotels are on the beaches. Best sands are at Fort James, and Dickenson Bay.
Fishing. Equipment is available for deep sea and spear-fishing, both excellent.
Boating and Sailing. The best in the Caribbean. There is a special sailing week at the end of April. All kinds of boats can be hired by day, week, or longer. Commander V. E. B. Nicholson of V. E. B. Nicholson & Sons.
Hunting. Shooting on nearby Barbuda—deer, duck, pigeon, and guinea fowl.

Golf. Cedar Valley Golf Club has 18 holes, and Half Moon Bay Hotel has a nine-hole course.

Horseback Riding. Most hotels can arrange for horses.

Tennis. Courts at a number of hotels and clubs.

Night Life: The island has some of the best steel bands in the Antilles. All the hotels have dancing most nights of the week. Gambling casinos are now situated at the Flamingo Club and Casino, Halcyon Cove Beach Resort and Casino, and the St. James Club. A number of small night clubs have become popular, among them Tropics, Chips, and Belaire. Antigua's Hells Gate and Harmonites steel bands play all over the island, and are famous throughout the West Indies.

Medical Facilities: British- and Canadian-trained doctors and nurses staff Holborton Hospital at St. John's.

Additional Information: Antigua Department of Tourism and Trade, 610 Fifth Ave., N.Y., NY 10020, (212-541-4117); Antigua Department of Tourism, P.O. Box 363, St. John's, Antigua, 20029 (809-462-0480).

Where to Stay

****Anchorage,* 99 rooms, African rondavels, beach cottages, air-conditioning, all water sports. ****Pineapple Beach,* 33 rooms, on beach, special activities for teenagers. ****Curtain Bluff,* 60 rooms, on the beach. ***Galley Bay Surf Club,* 30 rooms, beach. ****Half Moon Bay,* 100 rooms, beach, golf, tennis. ***The Inn,* 25 rooms, overlooks Dockyard, beach rooms. ****Jolly Beach,* 475 rooms, beach. ***Halcyon Cove Beach Resort and Casino,* 104 rooms, on beach, water sports. ***St. James Club* at Mamora Bay, 100 rooms, on beach. ***Runaway Beach Club,* 50 rooms and beachfront villas. ***Barrymore,* 20 rooms, friendly, beautiful flowers. ***Blue Waters Beach,* 35 rooms, dancing, swimming. ***Atlantic Beach Hotel,* 24 rooms beachfront. ****The Admiral's Inn,* 14 rooms in English Harbour. ***Callaloo Beach Hotel,* 16 rooms, in Morris Bay, lovely gardens. *****Long Bay,* 20 rooms, on beach, excellent food, water sports, dancing. ***Cortsland Hotel,* 30 rooms. ***Antigua Mill Hotel,* 33 rooms, near airport, free transfer to beach. ***Flamingo Club & Casino,* 50 rooms. ***Catamaran Hotel,* 11 rooms, charming setting on beach. *****Hawksbill Beach Hotel,* 70 rooms on beach. *****Siboney,* on Dickenson Bay, 12 suites. ***Sandpiper Reef Resort,* on Hodges Bay, 40 rooms. *****Jumby Bay Resort,* on private island, 38 suites.

Where to Eat

The grilled lobster can't be beaten, and the British cooking is sometimes spiced with Creole dishes. Rum's the drink.

The Spanish Main is a local favorite, serving West Indian food. ***Le Bistro* serves French cuisine; ***Brother B's,* local fare; ***Dubarry's* and *Lobster Pot,* American Food, and *****Colombo's,* Italian specialties.

Where to Shop

Most shopping is concentrated on a few streets in the heart of St. John's. Warri, a game of African origin, is Antigua's most popular game. A warri board and instructions makes

an unusual gift and is available at local handicraft stores such as the *Local Handicraft Centre and Arawak Crafts.*

English woolens and linens are excellent buys, and native products are worth the money. Shop for original ceramics, hand-woven straw bags, slippers, hats, and native-made tortoise-shell jewelry. Scotch is the cheapest in the Caribbean.

Y. de Lima features the latest in beach wear and resort fashions. *Shipwreck Shops* specialize in Caribbean handicrafts. *Kalil Shoul* specializes in sea island cottons, cashmere sweaters, Liberty of London silks and cottons, Irish and English linens, English suitings, and English bone china. *Coco Shop* for resort clothes and imports. *Handicraft Workshop* shows arts and crafts. For liquor: *Quin Ferrara.*

Other attractive stores are: *Antigua Pottery, Madeira Shop, John & Francis Anjo, Calabash Shop, Kensington Court Shops, Pink Mongoose,* and *Treasure Cove.* A new shopping mall, *Redcliffe Quay,* has both shops and restaurants.

What to See

Capital of Antigua is low **St. John's,** a bustling miniature business center wrapped around a handsome harbor. It's no gem for the sightseer—see the *Cathedral,* the three-centuries-old barracks, and the ruins of old *Fort James* on the rim of the harbor, and you have had it.

The best of the island is fifteen miles away on the other side of the island, **English Harbour.** Here is where Nelson's Leeward Island Squadron was based, and thanks to the fine restorations that have been made through the efforts of the Society of the Friends of English Harbour, the installations today look much as they did in Nelson's era. There is the *Dockyard* itself with all of the old workshops. Best of the restorations is the *Admiral's House,* furnished in the style of the period and with some of Nelson's own possessions. On **Shirley Heights** stand *Clarence House,* the stone home where the future William IV lived, and the old fortifications and the *Block House* that guarded the Dockyard below.

Fig Tree Drive (don't be misled, when an Antiguan says, "fig," he

Looking down on the concealed fortifications at Nelson's Harbour.

means banana) is one of the island's loveliest tours—through the "rain forest" and along a beautiful stretch of coast.

Devil's Bridge, especially on a windy day, is a must for those who like to be reminded of the power as well as the beauty of the sea.

There is more to the island—the villages, the old plantations with their ruined sugar mills, the harbors and always the marvellous beaches.

BARBUDA (Bar-BOO-da)

Some 30 miles north of Antigua is Barbuda—more than half the size of Antigua with a population of hardly more than 1,200. Remote and almost unvisited, it has its attractions—crystal-clear water, superb fishing, excellent hunting, treasure hunting on shores where scores of plunder-laden ships are known to have foundered. The whole island was once a great slave farm owned by a rich planter. If you are looking for an island away from everything, if you want excellent bird shooting and beaches where you can be alone with a few sandpipers—Barbuda is for you. *Coco Point Lodge,* with its 32 rooms, offers first class hotel accommodations. LIAT flies to Barbuda from Antigua.

MONTSERRAT (MONT-se-RAT)

Antigua will give you sequestered seclusion—at a price. But 30 miles south on the ruggedly beautiful little island of Montserrat you can rent real solitude for a song. If you really do want to escape from the people you have known all your life, and if you actually are happier without the plush appurtenances of a planned vacation world, Montserrat may be the spot for you.

Montserrat is unique, likeable, and little—a sea-dot of some 30 square miles occupied by 12,000 hard-working people, most of them descendants of African slaves. They are friendly and agreeable, but as yet they have not turned their attention solely to providing creature comforts for you. They are busy with their own concerns—raising cotton, vegetables, and peanuts for export, and raising cane which they keep at home to make into rum.

There is, as usual, a story about the settlement of the island, and this time there is reason to believe it—evidence that is audible if not visible. It is said that in the 1630's a group of Irish settlers wearied of their English cousins on St. Kitts and moved en masse to Montserrat. That may or may not be true, but there can be no question that the Irish were there in numbers, for you can still hear the Irish lilt in the language that the natives speak today.

The island runs up to a 3,000-foot volcanic peak—called Chance's Peak—but the slopes are gentle enough to be arable. There is ample rain in season to keep the mountain well forested and to make the farms and plantations fertile.

The only town of any consequence is the capital, **Plymouth,** with a population of a little more than 2,000. It has a *Government House*— a really splendid old residence—and most of the island's hotels.

But it isn't the town that you are here for. It is the island itself—its mountains, its green hillside farms, its beaches of black or white sand, its remoteness, and most of all, the friendly dark Caribbean islanders with the sound of old Ireland in their mouths.

General Information

How To Get There: LIAT has daily flights from Antigua (which take only 14 minutes).

How To Get Around: A jeep for those in a hurry. Horses or mules for escapists. Taxi fares are standardized and self-drive cars may be rented at reasonable rates.

Sports: Cricket is the local sport.
Swimming. Excellent on a number of good beaches.
Tennis. Popular, and there are a number of courts.
Hunting. Sounds unlikely, but one of the favorite sports is frog hunting—with a noose. The victim, called crapond, is the biggest you've ever seen—and delicious.
Golf. Beautiful *Belham River Valley Golf Club* has nine holes.
Riding. Virtually limitless trails. Arrangements can be made through your hotel.

Medical Facilities: Two doctors and a small hospital.

Additional Information: Montserrat Tourist Bureau, 40 E. 49th St., New York, NY 10017 (212-752-8660).

Where to Stay: ***Vue Pointe,* 28 cottages, 12 rooms, pool, on the beach. ** *Coconut Hill,* 10 rooms. * *Wade Inn,* 10 rooms. ***Montserrat Springs Hotel,* Richmond Hill, 29 rooms, deluxe. ***Shamrock Villas,* 50 units, deluxe oceanview apartments.

About 250 estate-sized houses and villas—most with magnificent views and pools—are also available for rent. Contact: Montserrat Enterprises, P.O. Box 270, Plymouth, Montserrat, W.I. (809-491-5270).

BRITISH WINDWARDS

British by tradition, Gallic in manner and Caribbean in outlook, the Windwards are islands where the past lives on in the present and the future is always pleasantly remote.

DOMINICA (Doh-mi-NEE-ka)

Dominica is a mood piece—background for a tale by Graham Greene or a more malevolent Maugham. Though it lies squarely between Guadeloupe and Martinique, it is one of the least visited of the larger islands (290 square miles) of the Antilles chain. Fiercely beautiful, tropically lush, and forbiddingly rugged, it remains untamed, likely to please the exploring botanist more than the relaxing vacationer. Along the shore on the leeward side, it gets a modest 70- or 80-inch annual rainfall, but the mile high volcanic peaks that split the island from north to south milk the moisture-laden clouds so continuously that almost unbelievable recordings of up to 300 inches a year have been made in the interior. The high slopes are a tangle of almost impenetrable tropical vegetation, so steep and so scarred by mountain torrents that only within the past few years has it been possible to build a usable road entirely across the island, and there are still central areas that have never been explored.

Not that Dominica is an uninhabited jungle. Some 80,000 people, mostly black, live on the island, 8,500 of them in the capital city of Roseau on the southwestern coast. To supplement tourist dollars they cultivate bananas, cocoa, copra, and spice—and by raising the luscious fruit that goes into Rose's Lime Juice.

General Information

How To Get There: Leeward Islands Air Transport (LIAT) has daily connecting flights with international carriers out of Antigua, Guadeloupe, Martinique, or Barbados. Air Caribe, Air Guadeloupe, Air Martinique, and Winlink fly there from various islands.

How To Get Around: By bus, taxi, or rented car.

Language: English and a French patois.

Sports: *Swimming* is fine at splendid deserted beaches on the northeast coast and in the river pools. There are

fish in the waters, but proper boats and tackle are scarce. *Sail-* and *power-boats* are both available at Roseau. *Hiking* and *climbing* are limited only by your time and stamina. But you will need a guide. There is some small bird *hunting.* The Castaways, Reigate Hall, and Anchorage Hotels in Roseau have *tennis* courts.

Night Life: Local "jump-ups" and occasional community dances.

Medical Facilities: There are good doctors and dentists and an up-to-date hospital in Roseau, a smaller hospital with a resident doctor in Portsmouth.

Additional Information: Dominica Tourist Board, P.O. Box 73, Roseau, Dominica, W.I. (809-445-2351/2186); Caribbean Tourist Association, 20 E. 46th St., New York, NY 10017 (212-682-0435).

Where to Stay

Accommodations are limited, hotels are small, pleasantly informal, and reasonably priced. Many feature open-air dining.
In Roseau: **Anchorage Hotel,* 36 rooms, on water, MAP. **Sisserou Hotel,* 20 rooms, on water, MAP. **Reigate Hall,* 17 rooms, overlooks town. **In Castle Comfort:** **Evergreen Hotel,* 10 rooms, newly-renovated, on water, MAP. **Excelsior Hotel,* 12 rooms, newly-renovated, MAP. **In mountains:** **Springfield Plantation,* 6 rooms, MAP. **Emerald Pool Resort,* 10 rooms, MAP. **North of Roseau:** **Castaways Beach Hotel,* 27 rooms, on the beach.
Guesthouses and cottages are also available. Plantation houses can be rented by the week, month, or season, with or without housekeeping service.

Where to Shop

Carib baskets and grass rugs are prime souvenirs that can be purchased in Roseau at *Dominica Handcrafts* on Hanover Street, *Caribana Handcraft* on Cork Street, the *Island Craft Cooperative,* and *Bernard's Handcrafts* on King George V Street, *Tropicrafts* on Turkey Lane, and *Bon Marché* on Old Street. Other good buys include soaps made from fresh coconut oil, leathercrafts, Hillsborough cigars and cigarettes, and recordings of traditional "jing-ping" folk music.

What to See

Roseau is a pleasant town with a French-English look, a Saturday-morning native market, and Little Fort, an 18th-century relic. **Portsmouth,** the harbor town, is at the northwest corner 16 or 18 miles away —by launch. But it is more than twice that distance by the only road, a spectacular cliff-hanger that first crosses the island from the southwest corner to the northeastern tip and *then* swings a little southwest to get to Portsmouth in the northwest. It's confusing when you drive it, too—and rough and wonderfully exciting. It takes you past the best beaches, and then cuts back around the flank of the majestic 5,300-foot *Morne Diablotin.*

The excursion to the Carib Reservation is Dominica's big trip and can be made by jeep or car. The Caribs are a shy people but are becoming integrated. They make distinctive baskets and canoes, and their handicraft can be purchased at the Reservation.

ST. LUCIA (St. LOO-she-a)

A temperate climate varying between 70 and 90 degrees, 238 square miles of mountains and valleys lush with the greens and pinks and reds of tropical forests, a volcano still bubbling, sulphur springs, a fine harbor, splendid beaches, and a population of over 120,000 make St. Lucia an appealing destination.

For 150 years the French and British battled for possession of the strategic island—twenty-one miles north of St. Vincent and twenty-five miles south of Martinique—which Columbus purportedly discovered on St. Lucia's Day (June 15) in 1502. The resident Caribs took kindly to no colonizer; they murdered British and French indiscriminately. Nevertheless, the island remained a prize. Fourteen times the rival powers captured and recaptured St. Lucia until, in 1803, the island settled down with British rule and a French cultural heritage.

St. Lucia's half-French, half-English manner is relaxed. The harbor is deep and lovely, convenient for both cruise ships and yachts. The airport servicing inter-island flights is handily next to one of the island's best beaches, and just outside the capital city. And the volcano is—a volcano, a polite one but not extinct and none the less exciting for being well-mannered.

General Information

How To Get There: *By Air:* BWIA has direct flights from New York and Miami, while Eastern flies in from San Juan and Miami. LIAT also offers connecting flights from Antigua and Barbados. Air Martinique and BA also have service. American flies from eight U.S. cities via San Juan.
By Sea: The harbor at Costries is a port of call for many cruise ships including Cunard, Costa, Princess, Sun Line, Paquet, Chandris, Windstar, the Sea Goddess, and the Explorer Starship.

How To Get Around: Buses, taxis, chauffeur-driven cars, and hire-cars are available. There are fixed taxi rates for the usual sightseeing trips. Roads are mountainous and narrow.

Language: English, officially; French patois among the natives.

Sports: British all round: soccer, rugby, and cricket.
Tennis: Most hotels have tennis courts, but if not, there are several courts in and around Castries where you can play.

Petit Peton rises a dramatic 2461 feet straight out of the Caribbean

Boating and Fishing. Boats, from canoes to yachts, can be rented or chartered. Marlin, tuna, kingfish, mackerel, tarpon, and dolphin run off the island and make for excellent sport-fishing.

Swimming. Excellent almost everywhere on the island. Three fine beaches are north of Castries: Vigie, just outside the city; Choc Beach; and Reduit Beach, at the north end near Gros Islet. (Good swimming, too, on Pigeon Point.)

Golf. 9 holes at North Point and La Toc.

Night Life: Most hotels have nightly dance music and shows several times a week. Local night spots are *Salt and Pepper* and *Green Parrott.*

Medical Facilities: Hospitals in Castries, Soufrière, Vieux Fort, and Dennery are staffed by doctors trained in Britain or Canada.

Additional Information: St. Lucia Tourist Office, 41 East 42 Street, New York, NY 10017 (212-867-2950); St. Lucia Tourist Board, P.O. Box 221, Castries, St. Lucia, W.I. (809-452-4094).

Where to Stay

****Cunard La Toc Hotel & Suites,* 256 rooms with view of ocean. Golf, tennis, swimming pool. ****Hotel Cariblue,* 102 rooms spectacularly located on northern tip of the island. Beach, pool, tennis, golf, horseback riding, water sports. ***Halcyon Beach Club* at Choc Beach, 88 cabana-style rooms with patios. Beach, water sports, tennis. Outdoor dining and dancing. ***Club Med St. Lucia,* Vieux Fort, 256 rooms; beach, tennis, water sports. ***The St. Lucian,* 183 rooms, on beach, tennis, water sports. **Bois d'Orange Holiday Village,* 14 apartments. **East Winds Inn,* 10 cottages, La Brelotte Bay. ***Estate Cas-en-Bas,* 10 rooms, in Gros Islet. **Vigie Beach,* 56 rooms, outside Castries. **Hurricane Hole Hotel,* 10 rooms, on bay. ***Dasheene Resort,* 23 villas and suites, Soufrière. **The Islander Apartment Hotel,* 20 units. **Morne Fortune Apts.,* 12 units, fine views. *Villa Hotel,* 30 rooms, fine location above Castries and the harbor. **Anse Chastenet Beach Hotel,* Soufrière, 37 rooms on lovely hillside overlooking bay and own beach. ****Couples,* 100 rooms, idyllic hideaway (couples only). *Kimatrai Hotel,* 20 rooms. **Green Parrot Inn,* Castries, superb restaurant, pool, spectacular views. **Smuggler's Village,* efficiency apartments, close to golf and horseback riding. **Harmony Apartel,* 21 efficiency apartments with fully-equipped kitchens. **Marigot Bay Hotel,* 47 rooms, balconies and air-conditioning.

Where to Eat

Hotels offer a variety of plans regarding meals, but on nights out you'll find the best meals at *Green Parrott, Coal Pot, East Wind's Inn, San Antoine, Capone's,* and *Rain.*

Where to Shop

British items head the list: woolens, china, silver, and sweaters. For the liquor allotment, there is Scotch and British gin as well as rum. Native handicrafts are worth investigating. Shopping in Castries, along Jeremie Street, Bridge Street, and William Peter Boulevard. Shops close at 4 P.M. and on Wednesday afternoons.

What to See

At the eastern end of St. Lucia's landlocked harbor, one of the finest yacht anchorages in the Caribbean and well able to host large cruise ships, is **Castries,** the island's capital. A few miles down the west coast is **Soufrière,** the second largest settlement. Both cities have the modern Caribbean look, for fires (the last in Soufrière in 1955) destroyed many of the old buildings. Some French stone houses and others of traditional British brick do remain as mementos of colonial days. But, for the most part, the cities are new, open, and bright.

At Castries the docks jutting into the harbor are busy with yachts and commercial vessels carrying sugar, cocoa, bananas, and copra. Five minutes north of the city is the three-and-a-half-mile stretch of *Vigie Beach.*

The road north from Castries ends in Cap Estate, a major summer home community. Near it, just offshore, is Pigeon Island, recently connected to the mainland by a causeway and now called Pigeon Point. It is a national park with beautiful white sand beaches and ruins of an 18th century fort and barracks. A perfect spot for a picnic.

South of Castries, though there's no Pigeon Point, there is Soufrière. A new road has replaced the tortuous old spine-tingler which used to connect St. Lucia's main settlements, but you may still prefer a pleasant boat ride to Soufrière. As you come across the deep bay, you'll have an excellent view of the island's two striking peaks, *Gros Piton* and *Petit Piton,* rising sharply from the water. Once in Soufrière, a charming harbor town, drive or be driven (guides and cars are always at hand) to the volcano. The road goes right up to the crater, a steaming, hissing place which needs no guide or publicist to say that it's dramatic. The steam, by the way, is the island's safety valve, releasing subterranean pressure which might otherwise cause it to blow its top in disastrous fashion.

Vieux Fort, at the southern tip of St. Lucia, is worth a visit, and there are little fishing villages which make pleasant destinations for boat trips. The drive up to *Morne Fortuné* and through the inland rain forest should also be on your list. For the hardy, the view from the top of Gros Piton (2,619 feet) or Petit Piton (2,461 feet) is superb. Those without rock-climbing experience should settle for the top of the lighthouse on *La Vegie,* where the view is merely splendid.

ST. VINCENT

Hilly, green-forested little St. Vincent, like its neighbors, is part British, part French, with a dash of West Indian lightheartedness to make things comfortable. Neat and pleasant, it depends on bananas and on a near-monopoly in arrowroot (the readily digested starchy base for baby food and canned soups) to make it a bit richer and a bit more businesslike than its neighbors.

Though the island's economy languished for a time with the passing of slavery, it is relatively flourishing now. The soft French patois mingles with the lilting accent with which the West Indies tempers clipped British speech. And these gentle ways of speaking are indicative of St.

Vincent's busy but unhurried way of life. Not so dependent on a tourist trade as many of its neighbors, the island is a fine place for visitors who prefer their tropics unspoiled, and their pleasures as uncomplicated as lazing on fine, sunny beaches, or climbing the forest-shaded mountain for the fine view from the top.

General Information

How To Get There: *By Air:* LIAT flies from Antigua and St. Lucia.
By Sea: Many cruise lines make St. Vincent a port of call.

How To Get Around: You can hire cars with or without drivers at low daily rates from a number of garages in Kingstown. Or use the local buses.

Language: English.

Festivals: The ten-day Carnival with its dances, parades, and steel band competitions, takes place the last Sunday in June to the first Tuesday in July. The Nine Mornings celebration takes place December 16–24.

Sports: *Cricket* at Arnos Vale, Kingstown.
Swimming. Fine water for snorkelers and skin divers. Tyrell Bay is the best beach.
Boating. Excellent. The nearby Grenadines are superb yachting waters.
Fishing. Good, particularly out of the delightful fishing villages of Layou and Barrouallie. One of the great thrills in St. Vincent is to go out with the men who go whaling for black fish, an expedition right out of Moby Dick. Make arrangements through the St. Vincent Tourist Board, Kingstown, St. Vincent.
Tennis. Kingstown Tennis Club. Aqueduct Golf Club also has courts as well as 9-hole golf course.
Mountain Climbing, Hiking. Mount Soufrière is a good, not-too-strenuous climb. Hikers enjoy Dorsetshire Hill and Mount St. Andrew.

Night Life: Quiet. The Sugar Mill Inn and other hotels have dancing Satur-

day nights, and there are occasional parties at private clubs.

Medical Facilities: Kingstown has a modern hospital.

Additional Information: St. Vincent & Grenadines Tourist Office, 801 Second Ave., New York, NY 10017 (212-687-4490). St. Vincent Tourist Board, Kingstown, St. Vincent, W.I. (809-457-1502). Caribbean Tourism Association, 20 East 46th St., New York, NY 10017 (212-682-0435).

Accommodations are adequate but not luxurious, the prices are low.

HOTELS: ****Treasure Island Beach Resort,** 10 apts. on beach. ****Villa Lodge,** 10 rooms, 100 yards from beach. ****Sunset Shores,** on beach with pool. 20 rooms. ***Tropic Breeze Apartment Hotel,** 12 rooms. Charming. ***Haddon,** 15 rooms, Kingstown. ***Heron,** Kingstown, 15 rooms. *** Kingstown Park Guest House,** 20 rooms, walking distance to town. **** Cobblestone Inn,** Kingston, 20 rooms overlooking harbor. ****CSY Marina & Hotel,** Blue Lagoon, 19 rooms. **** Grand View Beach Hotel,** Villa Point, 12 rooms. ***Mariners Inn,** Villa Beach, 21 rooms, watersports. **** Rawacou Resort,** Mt. Pleasant, 10 rooms. ******Young Island Resort,** on private island, 29 rooms, beach, pool, tennis.

Where to Shop

Among the best buys are English woolens and other fabrics, and Scotch whiskies—all very inexpensive. Best local buys include sea island cotton goods, native handicrafts of straw and shell, and, of course, rum. You can watch local artisans make baskets, pottery and rugs at the *Craftsmen Center.*

What to See

The island is small—eighteen miles long and eleven miles wide at the middle—and though it ranges from foam-whitened beaches to high, green-forested volcanic peaks, it is not difficult to see.

Start in the capital, **Kingstown,** lushly tropical and solidly British from ground up: the bustling waterfront which bustles most on Saturday morning when the boats (and buses) come in loaded with produce for the native market; the three lovely old churches, ornate *St. Mary's, St. George's Cathedral* with its murals, and the *Methodist Church* and quiet English houses which might have been transplanted from London, or—more likely—from Plymouth and Penzance. Kingstown's *Botanical Garden* is the oldest in the West Indies. Its prize exhibit is a breadfruit tree directly descended from the one planted on St. Vincent by Captain Bligh himself. (He took two trips to get the ancestral tree there; the first was interrupted by the world's most famous mutiny.) There are reminders of the island's earlier history in the collection of Carib relics in the library and at *Fort Charlotte,* worth the trip for the fine view from the high cliffs which protect the city.

Going inland you cross the rich *Mesopotamia Valley* below the island's backbone of volcanic mountains. Tallest of the mountains is *Soufrière.* (And if the name seems familiar, that's not surprising; the favorite name for all Caribbean volcanoes seems to be "Sulphurous.") St. Vincent's Soufrière proved itself more than merely sulphurous in 1902 when, along with Martinique's Mont Pelée, it erupted unexpectedly and destructively. It has since been silent, and in its crater now holds not lava but a crystalline lake.

The ascent of Soufrière is not dangerous but it does take some stamina. You can approach the mountain from *Chateaubelair* on the west coast (via Wallibu by boat, then up the volcano on foot) or from *Georgetown* on the east coast (making the first lap by jeep or on horseback, then on foot). Either way, plan to take your time (and a guide), for the mountain is steep; and take lunch and a lightweight raincoat, too. The view at the top, whether into the blue, blue lake or out across the island to the Caribbean is a more than fair reward for the climb. It's the most dramatic aspect of St. Vincent.

THE GRENADINES (GREN-a-deens)

Scattered over the sixty miles of sea between St. Vincent and Grenada are the Grenadines, a host of tiny islands that collectively add up to no more than thirty square miles peopled by some 7,000 descendants of African slaves. Nobody seems to know just how many of these little tropical gems there are—the best guess seems to be in the neighborhood of 600—but only a scattering of them are big enough to bear names, still fewer are populated, and only a very few have any facilities for travelers, and those are of the most modest sort.

A few of the larger Grenadines are more than names. *Bequia* (population: 4,000), only an hour or so by boat from St. Vincent, is a big six square miles, has several excellent beaches, and a vast amount of quiet. Largest of all is *Carriacou,* a cotton-growing island of thirteen square miles and a population of 8,000—more than half of the total for the whole group. Carriacou's annual regatta in the first week of August attracts international patronage.

If you want to explore the Grenadines, you will need lots of time, the best map you can get—but not much money.

Where to Stay

****Petit St. Vincent,* on Petit St. Vincent. On the beach, tennis. 22 rooms. ****Palm Island Hotel* on the beach on Prune Island. 22 rooms. **Crystal Sands Beach Club,* 8 rooms, Canouan Island. **The Cotton House,* 19 rooms, on Mustique Island. **Frangipani Hotel,* 11 rooms. On Bequia Island. **Bequia Beach Club,* Friendship, 10 rooms, MAP. ****Friendship Bay Hotel,* Bequia I., 27 rooms, MAP. **Sunny Caribbee Hotel,* Bequia I., 25 rooms. **Lower Bay Guest House,* Bequia I., 5 rooms. ***Julie's Guest House,* Port Elizabeth, Bequia I., 20 rooms, MAP. **Charlie's Guest House,* Mustique I., 6 rooms. *****Salt Whistle Bay Club,* Union I., 22 rooms, MAP. ****Anchorage Yacht Club,* Union I., 10 rooms. ***Clifton Beach Hotel,* Union I., 10 rooms, MAP. ** Clifton Beach Guest House,* Union I., 4 rooms, MAP. **Sunny Grenadines Hotel,* Union I., 10 rooms.

GRENADA (Gre-NAY-da)

To many visitors Grenada is the Sleeping Beauty of the Caribbean. The island has a charm that is as pervasive as the smell of spice that hangs over it. Its spotless capital with its colorful buildings crowding the deepwater dock and the red-roofed houses climbing the semi-circle of hills behind it is one of the most beautiful harbor cities in all of the Caribbean. Its climate is tropical, but benignly so, with cool interior heights and moderating trade winds. Its 90,000 people, mostly descendants of the slaves, reflect a nice blend of the English and French heritage of the island. They are graciously hospitable, perhaps a bit livelier than their neighbors on some of the other islands. The island has at least two of the finest natural beaches in the West Indies. Watered by heavy rainfall in the interior, the valleys are lushly green and splashed with brilliant tropical flowers, the hills aromatic with orchards of lime, shaded nutmeg, and cocoa.

Grenada's tranquil beauty belies its bloody past. Though Columbus sighted the island, the Caribs held off would-be colonizers for more than a century thereafter. In 1729 the French cannily bartered two bottles of brandy and some baubles for it, but they bought hostility instead of land. When the Caribs attacked with their stone-age weapons, they were driven to the tip of the island where—at a place still called Le Morne des Sauteurs (Jumpers' Cliff)—many of them leaped to death on the surf-washed rocks below. Every Indian survivor who could be found was exterminated. Nor was that the end of bloodshed on Grenada. There followed more than a century of intermittent war between the powers during which the island was won and lost time and again by the French or British. Even after England established her ownership in 1783, there were recurrent slave revolts, massacres, and reprisals, and not until the final abolition of slavery was there anything like peace on the island.

The end of slavery was the island's salvation. Most of the great sugar plantations were abandoned and sugar ceased to be the sole crop. The freed slaves turned to the cultivation of mace and cocoa and nutmeg, while other islands sank into sugar cane poverty. Grenada has enjoyed a period of remarkable tranquillity—and a dramatic upsurge in tourism —since the invasion of U.S. troops in 1983.

General Information

How To Get There: *By Air:* Grenada Airways and BWIA fly nonstop once a week from New York. Pan Am, American, Eastern, and Air Canada offer Barbados connections with LIAT.
By Sea: A number of cruise ships stop in the lovely harbor of St. George's: Cunard Line, Costa Cruises, North Star Line, Ocean Cruise Line, Windjammer Barefoot Cruises, Sitmar Cruises, Royal Caribbean Cruise Line, Holland America Cruises, Epirotiki Lines, Chandris, Paquet Cruises, Home Line, Sun Line Cruises, Exploration Cruise Lines, Windstar Sail Cruises.

How To Get Around: The buses are cheap, colorful, and go everywhere, but they're spartan. Taxis are plentiful. Self-drive cars and Mini Mokes are available, but the roads are narrow, mountainous, and curved—and left-handed in the British fashion.

Language: English.

Holidays and Festivals: Big event is the carnival on the Monday and Tuesday preceding Ash Wednesday—pageants, steel bands, and a great Mardi Gras parade through the streets of St. George's.

Sports: British. Cricket from January through May; soccer from July through December; horse racing meets at Easter, Whitsuntide in August, and at New Year's. Triathalons take place in November and January. *Swimming.* Excellent, at big Grand Anse and many other good beaches. *Fishing.* Crystal water and plenty of fish make Levera Beach ideal for underwater fishing. Boats can be hired, and the waters around the island abound in game fish. Fresh-water fishing is good in rivers and lakes. *Boating.* Small sailboats or larger craft can be chartered. Motorboats are available. Spice Island Marine Services has made Grenada number one on the yachting scene. For yachting next year, make reservations now through Grenada Yacht Services.

Golf. The Grenada Club has a nine-hole course.

Tennis. Many hotels have courts. Richmond Hill Tennis Club has two courts.

Night Life: The resort hotels have evening shows, dancing and local entertainers. Popular night spots include *The Sugar Mill, BBC Club, Love Boat, Coconut Grove,* and the *Cubby Hole.*

Medical Facilities: Hospitals at St. George's and Grenville, Carriacou.

Additional Information: Grenada Tourist Office, 820 Second Ave., Suite 1100, New York, NY 10017 (212-687-9554); Grenada Tourism Department, The Carenage, St. George's, Grenada, W.I.; Grenada Hotel Reservations Clearing House (in U.S., 800-CALL-GND; in Canada, 800-468-0023).

Where to Stay

Blue Horizons Cottage Hotel,* Grand Anse Beach 5 miles from St. George's, 32 suites. ****The Calabash,* Prickley Bay south of St. Georges, 22 suites, MAP. ****Cinnamon Hill and Beach Club,* 20 suites, Spanish-style village, fantastic views, MAP. ** *Horseshoe Beach Hotel,* 12 rooms, secluded beach and swimming pool, MAP. ***Maffiken Apartments,* 4 rooms, close to Grand Anse Beach. ****Secret Harbour Hotel,* on south coast, 20 rooms, tennis court, swimming pool, and watersports. ***Silver Beach Cottages,* duplex apartments on white sand beach, MAP. **South Winds Holiday Cottages and Apart-*ments,* near Grand Anse Beach, 19 rooms. ****Spice Island Inn,* Grand Anse Beach, 30 rooms, MAP. *** *Twelve Degrees North,* 10 rooms, residential setting at L'Anse Aux Pines. ***Silver Sands,* St. George's, 30 units. ****Ramada Renaissance,* Grand Anse, 186 rooms, watersports, tennis, swimming pool. ***Crescent Inn,* 12 rooms, homey, overlooking yacht basin. There are also a number of very inexpensive cottages which can be rented by the week or month.

Where to Eat

The main restaurants in and around St. George's are the *Nutmeg, Sand Pebbles, Aboo's,* the *Cubby Hole, Ristorante Italia,* and *Rudolph's* on the Carenage; the *Turtle Back* at the entrance to St. George's Harbour; *Crucial Factor, Lucky Heart,* and *Pastry Man* in the Shopping Center; and *Sea Scape* overlooking the harbor. *The Apple, Ross Point Inn,* and *La Belle Creole* feature West Indian fare; *Yin Wo* serves Chinese food. The *Red Crab* at L'Anse Aux Epines features English pub specialties, barbecued chicken, lobster, and steak.

Where to Shop

British imports are good buys. Best native work is palm leaf basket with assortments of Grenada's spices and nutmeg jelly. Also good are hammocks, straw mats, carpets, and carved tortoise shell artifacts. Handicraft and spices at the *Straw Mart,* the *Sea Change Gift Shop, Tikel Arts and Crafts.* Other shops include Grencraft, Spice Island Perfumes, Imagine Souvenirs, Noah's Arkade, and the Poui Art Gallery.

What to See

Grenada is small—only twenty-one miles long and twelve miles wide —but it is rugged and varied, split through the center by a chain of high old volcanic peaks. How you see it depends on how you get there. Point

Salines International Airport is well up on the northeastern shoulder of the island, north of **Grenville,** a busy little town where you can see (and smell) spices being prepared for market and, if you happen to be there on a Saturday morning, enjoy the hubbub and excitement of a fine native market. You can also arrange to visit a farm and learn how mace, nutmeg, cinnamon and chocolate are harvested.

Sixteen miles away is **St. George's,** Grenada's only city (about 30,000), and capital of both the island and of the Windwards Island Colony. The road winds up and over the spiny central ridge past one of the show places of the island—*Grand Etang,* a remarkable mirror lake lying nearly 2,000 feet up in the crater of a volcano. It is in the midst of a forest preserve and bird sanctuary, and its quicksilver surface is burnished blue-green.

On a craggy volcanic peninsula protecting its deep little harbor, St. George's is a picture town—a spectacular splash of white-and-red houses, tropical-green hills, turquoise harbor. The town presses tight to the Careenage, and narrow, almost medieval little streets twist upwards along the cliff between solid old red brick houses. Where the ridge at last becomes too steep for even the terraced streets, a tunnel cuts through the rock to the open town on the other side. Alone on its vantage point is *Fort George,* built in 1705 by the French to guard the harbor and now put to use as the police quarters.

Around the bay just south of the city is *Grand Anse,* a magnificent sweep of two miles or more of sand facing back toward St. George's.

Still further south the island tails out in a long peninsula to *Point Saline* and the lighthouse at its tip. Here the road runs out between two enormous beaches, one of glittering white sand, the other of the blue-black sand scoured from the volcanic rock.

North from St. George's the road hugs the shore in a fine scenic drive that takes you through *Gouyave,* another and smaller spice town, and to the rocky cliffs of *Sauteurs* on the tip of the island. You can drive up to *Le Morne des Sauteurs,* the fierce high point from which the Indians were forced to their deaths on the rocks and in the crashing surf below.

Only a mile or so west, on another tip of land, the island drops off to another superb beach called *Levera.* The sand slopes out gently and great rollers come thundering in past several little islands just offshore.

BARBADOS
(Bar-BAY-dose)

Flying fish and cricket, tropical coral roads and a Trafalgar Square, dazzling beaches—these are just some of this island's attractions.

Only 21 miles long and 14 miles wide, the green island of Barbados has more sunshine, more British color and charm, and more people and sugar cane per square mile than any isle of the Antilles. This island has other distinctions. It was *not* discovered by Columbus, but Washington *did* sleep there the only time he journeyed outside colonial America.

Sitting all by itself 600 miles southeast of Puerto Rico and 90 miles out in the Atlantic, Barbados has beaches of pink and white coral, excellent and comparatively inexpensive hotels, great fishing, good shopping, and cities, harbors, neatly-gardened homes that will remind you of the south of England.

The roads meander like old English lanes, the police bandsmen might be marching in Westminster, and the harbor police could have stepped right off one of Nelson's brigs. Barbados is the most unlikely island in the Caribbean, but if you want to rest, relax, and play amid tropics at their best—this is it.

Discovered in 1536 by a Portuguese navigator, Pedro à Campos, Barbados was not settled until 1627 when the first British settlers landed at a place they called Jamestown, now Holetown, on the lovely west coast. The English and their indentured servants at first grew cotton and tobacco, but with the simultaneous introduction of slaves and sugar cane in the 1630's, Barbados' long, rich years of sugar plantations, slavery, and rum began.

The island needed white settlers and it needed more cheap labor, and for a century Britain continued to send Barbados its most troublesome and rebellious subjects, indentured servants, thieves and cutthroats from the prisons, Royalist captives of Cromwell, religious dissenters, political prisoners, rebellious Scots and Irishmen. Descendants of these involuntary colonists still live in St. Andrew's Parish in the northeast. They are known as "redlegs" (from the old English term for bare-legged, kilted Scotsmen) and their parish is often called "Scotland."

Through the 18th and the first half of the 19th centuries Barbados was rich, buying slaves and producing sugar and the golden rum for which the island is still famous. It was during that time, in 1751, that young George Washington took his brother to the island to recover from tuberculosis. George was enchanted. He wrote in his journal that he and his brother "were perfectly enraptured with the beautiful prospects which on every side presented to our view—the fields of cane, corn, fruit trees, etc., in a delightful green."

Overpopulation and the dependence on the produce of sugar cane alone brought poverty, and though there has been an improvement in recent years, some of it still exists. Barbados gained its independence from Great Britain in 1966. Today tourism is making a most important contribution to the island's economy. Its role seems likely to increase, for every year more people are discovering that with its fine climate, its friendly people, its splendid facilities and colorful customs, Barbados is easily one of the most attractive vacation spots in the Caribbean.

General Information

How To Get There: *By Air:* BWIA, American, Eastern, Pan Am, Air Canada provide service to North America. Air Martinique, British Airways, Caribbean Airways, Cubana, and LIAT also serve the island.
By Sea: Barbados is on many cruise routes.

How To Get Around: The public buses—slow, cheap, and delightful—will take you anywhere on the island. The local color, conversation, and sociability will cost you very little except time.

Taxis are plentiful, rates are fixed and reasonable. Or you can hire a taxi or a chauffeur-driven car by the day at low rates.
Car Rental. Several agencies rent self-drive cars for about $45 a day. Remember, you drive on the left side of the road.

Language: English.

Sports: *Cricket* is the island's great sport, and the Bajans are among the world's best players. The excitement is sky-high in important matches. Three big *horse racing* meets are held in March, August, and September at the Garrison Savannah.

Swimming. The average water temperature is 77°. There are white and pink sand beaches everywhere, and the swimming is as good as anywhere in the Caribbean, with excellent surf on the east coast, calm water on the west. Crane and Bathsheba are the best surf beaches.
Boating. All kinds of launches, sailboats, and yachts are available for hire with professional crews. Ask at your hotel.
Fishing. First class deep-sea fishing boats with adequate equipment are available, and the catch is first rate: marlin, wahoo, tuna, bonito, dolphin, tarpon. Flying fish is the major local specialty. You can hire a power boat or make arrangements to go out with native fishermen in their small motor launches.
Water Skiing. Professional instruction is widely available, and at hotels including the Coral Reef, Paradise, and Hilton Hotel.
Golf. Sandy Lane Golf Club has an 18-hole course. Green fees are reasonable, and visitors are welcome.
Tennis. Hard and lawn courts are available at many hotels.
Horseback Riding. The island has

good trails and good mounts for hire at reasonable rates. You can make arrangements through the hotel.

Night Life: The island has many friendly little bars and enough of the more lively night life to satisfy most visitors. *The Tamarind Cove* in Hastings has local entertainment. The *Carlisle Club* on Bay Street is very popular, as is the *Plantation Garden Restaurant* in Christchurch. An historical dinner-theater show is presented nightly in the open-air courtyard of the Barbados Museum. The larger hotels provide dancing nightly.

Medical Facilities: Many doctors, dentists, and nurses, most of them trained in the United Kingdom, Canada or the United States make up the staff at the Queen Elizabeth Hospital in Bridgetown.

Additional Information: Barbados Tourist Board, 800 Second Avenue, New York, NY 10017 (212-986-6516; 800-221-9831). Barbados Tourist Board, Box 242, Bridgetown, Barbados, W.I. 809-427-2623.

Where to Stay

Furnished homes can be rented for about $300 a week and up.
****Barbados Hilton,* Bridgetown, 188 rooms, on the beach, pool, entertainment. ****Colony Club,* St. James, 75 rooms, a residential club, on the beach, pool, all water sports. ****Coral Reef Club,* St. James, 75 rooms, residential club, luxury beach resort, boating, water sports. ***Royal Pavilion,* St. James, 90 rooms, ocean front, garden. ****Sandy Lane,* St. James. Hotel and cabin facilities on luxurious beach. 112 rooms, 18-hole golf course. ****Tamarind Cove,* St. James. Pool, on the beach. 80 rooms. **Ocean View,* Hastings, 40 rooms, ocean front. **Paradise Villas,* Black Rock, 15 rooms, on nice beach, efficiency apartments. ***Sandpiper Inn,* St. James, on beach. 22 rooms, some apts., pool. ****Marriott's Sam Lord's Castle,* St. Philip, 268 rooms, plantation house, on the sea, tennis. **Windsor,* Hastings, 38 rooms, near beach. ***Southwinds,* St. Lawrence, on beach, pool. 166 rooms. **Rockley Resort,* Rockley, 156 rooms, on the sea. **Sandridge,* St. Peter, 50 rooms on beach, with pool. **Barbados Beach Village,* St. James, 84 rooms. **Inn on the Beach,* beachfront, 20 rooms. ***Settlers Beach,* St. James, 22 cottages, very nice. **Treasure Beach Hotel,* St. James, 24 suites, on beach. ****Southwinds Beach Hotel,* St. Lawrence, 66 rooms. **Super Mare,* Worthing, 24 rooms, on Half Moon Bay. ***Coconut Creek Club,* St. James Beach, on beach, 45 rooms.

There are at least 30 apartment hotels all around the Christ Church St. James Area. You can get a booklet from the tourist board at the airport or write to them for one.

Where to Eat

Basically British, Barbados food is made deliciously different with sea food and local specialties. Flying fish, cooked in every possible way, is one of the great foods of the Caribbean—delicate, moist, succulent.

RESTAURANTS: ***Greensleeves,* excellent continental cuisine, dinner only. Reservations. ***Pelican Village,* for lunch. **Pisces,* St. Lawrence, for seafood. **Bagatelle Great House,* near Sunset Crest. Charming old building. **Germania,* super water vistas. For native Bajan fare: *Brown Sugar,* behind *Island Inn, Josef's, Pisces Restaurant,* and *The Witch Doctor,* at St. Lawrence Gap.

A Bajan fisherman tries his luck

Bajan buffets are served at the *Barbados Hilton, Marriott's Sam Lord's Castle,* and the *Crane, Ocean View,* and *Treasure Beach Hotels.*

Where to Shop

British goods of all kinds are carried at low prices. You can also buy other low-priced imports at in-bond shops in Bridgetown and at the airport.

One of the best buys on the island is tailored clothing. A suit made in three days by these skilled craftsmen will look as though it might have come from Bond Street.

Other good buys in British imports include woolens, cashmere sweaters, china and silver, and antiques. The Bajans make imaginative jewelry from the local raw materials—sea shells, tortoise shell and the like. You will find straw bags, baskets, slippers, and other goods made on Barbados and other West Indian islands. Best of all the best buys is the excellent and inexpensive Barbados rum.

ANTIQUES: *Clarendon Antiques* in Belleville and *Antiquarian* on St. Michael's Row.

CLOTHES: *Cave Shepherd & Co., Ltd.,* Broad Street, Bridgetown; the numerous Bajan boutiques include *Petticoat Lane* in Bridgetown and *Giggles Beach* in St. Peter.

DEPARTMENT STORES: (on Broad Street, Bridgetown) *Cave Shepherd & Co., Ltd.; Da Costa & Musson; C. F. Harrison & Co.*

JEWELERS: *Louis L. Bayley,* Bolton Lane, Bridgetown; *Baldini, Ltd.,* Broad Street, Bridgetown; *Y. De Lima & Co.,* Broad Street, Bridgetown; *Correia's,* Bridgetown.

LIQUORS AND WINES: *Alleyne Arthur & Co.,* High Street, Bridgetown; *J. N. Goddard & Sons, Ltd.,* Fontabelle; *Hanschell Larsen & Co., Ltd.,* Prince William Henry Street, Bridgetown; and in most department stores and supermarkets.

SOUVENIRS AND GIFTS: *India House,* Broad Street, Bridgetown; *Women's Self Help Association,* Broad Street, Bridgetown; *Pelican Village Handicraft and Gift Center,* Hastings and *Best of Barbados,* a chain of six shops located throughout the island.

DUTY-FREE SHOPS: J. Baldini, Louis Bayley & Son, Cave Shepherd & Co., Harrison's, Correia's Jewelry Store, Da Costa & Musson, Y. de Lima's, India House, El Matador, and Knight's.

What to See

Barbados starts at the *Careenage* and the crowded harbor of Bridgetown where inter-island schooners dock with their wares. The harbor has recently been deepened to accommodate big ships. It's a busy little harbor, as colorful and as filled with sights and sounds and smells and sailing ships as it was two hundred or more years ago.

Rowing back and forth among the ships are the *Harbor Police* in the uniform of sailors who served under Nelson—straw skimmers, white middies, and bell-bottom trousers. A tall-masted sailing ship may be careened—pulled over onto its side—so that the crew can scrape and caulk and paint the bottom, an activity which long ago gave the Careenage its name.

In *Trafalgar Square* stands a bronze statue of Lord Nelson, older than the one in London, heroically calm amid the hubbub. Behind the statue are two large, Victorian buildings of gray coral with somewhat incongruous red awnings and green shutters. They house the *House of Assembly* and the *Senate,* next to Bermuda's the oldest legislative body in the New World. Visitors can also watch craftsmen at work in the area called *Pelican Village,* between downtown and Deep Water Harbour.

Just a little off the Square is the native *Fairchild Street Market,* the *IDC* (Industrial Development Corporation) *Handicraft Shop,* and the *West Indies Handicraft Shop* with straw goods from all over the Caribbean.

St. Michael's Cathedral, a coral rock structure beside Queen's Park, was built in 1831. The first cathedral of the Church of England was built in 1665 on this site. Smashed by hurricanes in 1780 and again in 1831, it was replaced by the present structure. George Washington is said to have attended services at this church.

All the activities of Bridgetown center on Broad Street, and all of your shopping and much of your sightseeing will be done here or in the

Modern and historical elements combine in downtown Bridgetown.

side streets with names like Literary Row, Flower Pot Alley, and Amen Alley. It's a colorful crowd—men of business, school girls in neatly washed and pressed uniforms, Bajan policemen in their handsome uniforms, planters rushing to the banks, and housewives with string bags window-shopping their way along the street.

Cricket is played at Queen's Park almost every Sunday. Even if you don't know a bat from a wicket, you will enjoy the Park. It was the headquarters of the British commander in chief of the South Caribbean when Britain was a power in these waters. What is now the *Barbados Yacht Club* was the home of the chief engineer, the *Savannah Club* was the Guard Room, the *Museum* was the military prison, and the red brick buildings that border the Savannah were mess halls, officers' quarters, and hospitals.

On the windward side of the island, the cliffs rise sharply above hidden beaches in coves where the surf pounds in with real force. In places they rise sheer above deep water—at *Crane,* for example, where in colonial days cargo was hoisted by crane from ships directly onto the cliffs. Hence the name. A little further along the coast is famous *Sam Lord's Castle,* now converted into a Marriott hotel without the loss of any of the glamor it must have had when the builder was forced to give up his trade.

Sam was a wrecker. By hanging lights in the trees along the cliffs on dark nights, he was able to deceive pilots into believing they were approaching Bridgetown. When the ships ran aground on the murderous rocks, Sam and his slaves killed off any unfortunate survivors and made off with the cargo. Lord grew rich quickly, hired Italian artisans to build his castle, and furnished it with the finest of everything.

Bathsheba is about halfway up the eastern coast, and if you are wise, you will try to time your trip to arrive here at 2:30 to 3:00 P.M. when the flying fish fleet is usually coming in.

The cross-island road takes you down to the western coast at *Speightstown,* the island's second largest town. There you will have a choice. You can turn north on a good road through one of the less populous parts to *North Point* at the very tip of the island where a sporting resort has been built. There, if the tide is out, you can enter the *Animal Flower Cave,* eerie grottos with strange tidal plants that recoil from the slightest touch. Or you can follow the road south from Speightstown through the lush gold coast of Barbados. All the way back to Bridgetown along the quiet lee side of the island you will be driving past beaches with soft coral sand and gentle seas.

TRINIDAD AND TOBAGO

Trinidad is the cosmopolitan island where everyone dances, where mosques, shrines and churches stand side by side, and where calypso singers puncture every prejudice with witty, earthy ballads based on the news of the day.

Rich in oil, asphalt, and agriculture, Trinidad's polyglot people have built a unique civilization just off the shore of Venezuela. Neither Africans, Syrians, Indians, French, Spanish, Portuguese, Chinese, nor English have lost their identities. Yet they all contribute to the composite picture of a truly fascinating cultural mix—the Trinidadian.

Almost square except for a long peninsula jutting out from the southwest toward the Venezuelan mainland, Trinidad is among the most verdant and charming islands of the Caribbean. It lies in the sea just north of the big Orinoco River Delta with only 7 miles of sea separating its northwest point from Venezuela's Paria Peninsula. The island measures 50 by 38 miles, is a little smaller than the State of Delaware, and slopes up from beaches and lagoons to two big mountain ranges in the interior. It is blessed with oil fields in the southwest and a huge 114-acre Pitch Lake from which comes most of the world's asphalt. Trinidad also supplies all the world's Angostura Bitters.

Trinidad's population of just over a million grows sugar, cocoa, coconuts, and citrus fruits, works in the oil refineries and the Pitch Lake. Only recently has tourism become a major factor economically. It is growing by leaps and bounds, due in part to a marvelously temperate climate, and is now the second largest industry.

Known as *Iere,* Land of the Hummingbird, by the Indians, the island was given its present name by the ubiquitous Columbus for the three peaks sighted on first landfall. The Spanish settled the island early and held it longer than most of their Caribbean empire. Their tenure was by no means peaceful, of course. Sir Walter Raleigh sacked its capital in 1595; it was raided by the French and Dutch, and finally taken by the British in 1797. British possession was legalized in 1802, and the island remained a colony until it gained independence in 1962. But ties to Britain remain strong, and Trinidad is proud of its membership in the British Commonwealth.

Mixed as their backgrounds are, the people of Trinidad seem to have one ancestor in common: music. Nowhere in the world does music so pervade everyday life. It is in the people—and it's irrepressible. You can see it in the way they walk—to an inner beat, moving their arms, snapping their fingers, and humming. This pulsing rhythm has given birth to two new musical forms that began here and are as much a part of Trinidad's life as its mountains and its weather. They are, of course, calypso singing and steel drum bands. Calypso is the older form— sociologists trace its ancestry to the medieval ballad singers and their equivalents in Africa. Wherever it sprang from, calypso is a fascinating and vital musical form. The calypso singer is composer and performer —and sometimes orchestra as well. The songs, set in a strict ritualistic pattern, tell a story—sometimes sad, more often funny, and almost always earthy to the point of being scatological—either of a local happening or an international event. You can hear calypso anywhere in the Caribbean today, but the best, the real article, is heard only in Trinidad.

The same is true of the steel band. They came into being after World War II when a man by the name of Winston Simon evolved a method of marking the cut-off end of an oil drum so that by hitting different areas he could produce varied notes. The tuning process—the drum-end is heated to be shaped—has been refined so that it is possible to make many-toned instruments on which skilled drummers can play not only Caribbean rhythms but Bach and Mozart as well. The music you hear in Trinidad, especially in the months before the pre-Lenten carni-val, is not classical, however. It is pure Caribbean. You hear it all day —and if you are in downtown Port of Spain, all night as well.

At dawn of the Monday before Ash Wednesday, the big jamboree begins. This is the moment the populace has been planning for weeks and months. All work stops, and the crowds in the street swell till traffic comes to a standstill too. Roving bands play here and there, and masked and costumed figures mix with the onlookers. Bars and restau-rants see plenty of action. Henry the Eighth buys a drink for Abraham Lincoln, and then they go back into the street together for a little dancing and shouting. On Monday night there are dances in hotels, clubs and private homes which keep things going all night.

On Tuesday morning, thousands of costumed Trinidadians swarm the streets, steel bands bang and rattle the beat. The whole town goes wild with music, fun-making, and dancing. It lasts throughout the big afternoon competition, getting wilder all the time, and right through the evening. Everybody dances. And then, suddenly, just before mid-night, it stops. Midnight signals the beginning of Lent.

General Information

How To Get There: *By Air:* From New York, Pan Am, American, and BWIA; Cubana, Eastern, Guyana, LIAT, Linea Aero-Postal Venz, and ALM also service Port of Spain from various places.

By Sea: Sunline, Epirotiki, and Ocean Cruise lines call at Port of Spain.

How To Get Around: The island has 2,000 miles of paved roads. Buses are good and cheap, and go to many of the towns. But don't take them if you're sensitive to rough rides, hubbub and crowding.

Taxis are plentiful and good, rates fixed, can be rented by the hour. Late at night, however, settle what the rate's going to be before you step into a cab.

You can hire drive-yourself cars from a number of operators in Port of Spain. The rates run about $35–$40 a day, and your American operator's license will permit you to drive—on the left side of the road.

Language: English—with Trinidad's own peculiar soft accent.

Festivals: Biggest festival of the year is the carnival on the two days before Ash Wednesday. The second big celebration is the two-day Moslem festival of Hosein which takes place shortly after the New Year as recorded by the Moslem calendar. Check with the Trinidad and Tobago Tourist Board in New York or Port of Spain. It can occur almost any time of the year. Al-

though it is mainly celebrated by Trinidad's 50,000 Moslems, everybody wants to join the festivities with drums, music, and parades. There are also two Hindu festivals in late October: Dewali or Festival of Lights, and Phagwah with dancing and singing in the streets, and throwing "abeer," a red liquid with which villagers try to "tag" each other.

Sports: *Cricket* and *horse racing* are the island's two spectator sports. The cricket season runs from January to June. During Christmas holidays and in June you can see horse races at Queens Park Savannah, Port of Spain. April and October meets are held at San Fernando, and May, August, and September meets at Arima Race Club. *Swimming.* There are plenty of good beaches, although most of them are on the rather remote east coast. Maracas Bay on the north coast about 15 miles from Port of Spain is a beach of big, long rollers that are perfect for surf board riding. Swimming is excellent at the small islands in the Gulf of Paria not far from the capital.

Fishing. The sea around the island and the fresh waters inland both abound with fish. Boats can be hired through your hotel.

Boating. You can rent both power and sail-boats through your hotel or a tour operator.

Tennis. There are public courts in Port of Spain and San Fernando.

Golf. St. Andrews Golf Club just a

A carnival parade in Trinidad

few miles from the capital has an excellent 18-hole course with visiting membership available.

Night Life: Dancing, steel bands and calypso singing are available every night. The hotels alternate their floor shows and dinner dancing so there's always some entertainment somewhere in Port of Spain. Generally the schedule provides dancing at the *Bel Air Hotel;* dinner dancing and floor shows at the *Hotel Normandie;* and dancing, floor shows and barbecues at the *Trinidad Hilton Hotel.* Disco dancing is a favorite pastime in Trinidad and some of the most popular discos include the *Atlantis Discotheque* in the West Mall, the *Fortress* on Roundabout Plaza, *Sparkles Entertainment Palace,* and the discos in the *Chaconia Inn* in Maraval, *JB's Restaurant* in the Valpark Shopping Plaza, and the *Waterfront* in the West Mall.

Medical Facilities: There are hospitals throughout the island.

Additional Information: Trinidad & Tobago Tourist Board, 400 Madison Ave., Suite 711, New York, NY 10017 (212-838-7750; 800-232-0082); Trinidad & Tobago Tourist and Trade Center, 200 SE First St., Suite 702, Miami, FL 33131 (305-374-2056; 800-521-0250); Trinidad & Tobago Tourist Board, 122–24 Frederick St., Port of Spain, Trinidad, W.I. (809-623-7405).

Where to Stay

The hotels are adequate, but most of them are in Port of Spain. ******** *Trinidad Hilton,* 442 rooms, air-conditioned, up-side-down hotel where you drive onto the roof and work your way down to your room on the hillside. ******Chaconia Inn, 27 rooms. ******* *Holiday Inn,* 253 rooms, pool. ******* *Normandie,* Port of Spain, 54 rooms, pool, air conditioned. ******Kapok Hotel, 80 rooms, near downtown. ******Bel Air,

Piarco Airport, 53 rooms, pool, good food, music, air conditioning. **Brenfra Haven,* Mayaro, 13 rooms, air conditioned. **Cactus Inn,* San Fernando, 36 rooms. ****Calypso Beach Resort,* 44 rooms, swimming pool. * *Fabienne's Guesthouse,* 6 rooms, air conditioned, swimming pool. **Farrell House Hotel,* 50 rooms, swimming pool, hour from Port of Spain. * *Hillcrest Haven,* 12 rooms, in residential area within walking distance of city. **Monique's Guesthouse,* Mayaro, 8 rooms, on the beach. **Monique's of Maraval,* 7 rooms, air conditioned, walking distance to golf course. * *Poinsettia Guesthouse,* San Juan, 4 rooms. **Queens Beach Hotel,* Mayaro, 37 rooms. **Royal Hotel,* San Fernando, 27 rooms, air conditioned. **Success Inn Guesthouse,* Laventille, 7 rooms. **Villa Maria,* Maraval, 12 rooms, swimming pool. **Zollna House,* Maraval 7 rooms.

Where to Eat

Trinidad's cuisine is as cosmopolitan as its people: British, American, Creole, Indian or Chinese food is available. Armadillo, called *tattoo,* venison, wild duck, pig, and hare often appear on the menu. They're all delicious. Rum, of course, is the national drink, and inasmuch as Trinidad is the home of Angostura Bitters, many a local cocktail gets mixed with more than a touch of bitters.

****Bel Air Hotel,* Piarco Airport, good steaks and chops. ********Normandie Hotel,* 2 Nook Avenue, St. Ann's, good French and Creole cooking. ****** *Mangals* specializes in Trinidadian and Indo/Chinese food. ******Mango Tree, Port of Spain, creole cooking. ****** *Shay Shay Tien,* Chinese. ******The Spaniards' Inn, Spanish. ******The Swiss Chalet, French in two-level mall setting. ******Surf and Turf, Port of Spain.

Where to Shop

Although not a free port, Trinidad

offers bargains in British imports, woolens, sweaters, Liberty silks, silverware, china, leather goods, and, of course, whiskeys and liquors. Oriental goods and silver filigree jewelry are also in good supply. Trinidad has excellent tailors who will make men's and women's clothing to order.

There are excellent shops at King's Wharf and Piarco Airport selling local wooden carvings, ceramics, and straw goods. Most shops are on or near Frederick Street.

DEPARTMENT STORES: Generally good for imports, woolens, silks, china, and silver. Trinidad's main shopping centers are Frederick Street in Port of Spain and High Street in San Fernando. Shopping malls have become very popular; they can be found even in the small towns.

GIFTS: *Stecher's* shops on Frederick Street and at the *Hilton,* and *Bel Air Hotels* and *Piarco Airport* carry nice selections of china, glassware, watches, perfume, jewelry, and imports.

ORIENTAL JEWELRY: Best selections at the bazaars on Western Main Road, at St. James, and in Port of Spain at the *Bombay Bazaar,* Frederick Street, and *Y. De Lima,* Frederick Street, also at *Trinidad Jewelry, Ltd.,* Frederick Street and Mirage Jewelers, Frederick St.

What to See

Simply to say that **Port of Spain** is one of the liveliest, wildest, and most colorful cities in the Caribbean would be understating the case—because it is certainly one of the most fascinating cities in the world. Sit for a while on a bench in *Woodford Square* in the downtown shopping area, and you will see representatives of half the world go by. Port of Spain is a melting pot to end melting pots. Here are Trinidadians wearing the Moslem fez, Trinidadian Buddhist priests in traditional long robes, Trinidadian descendants of African slaves, Trinidadian Indian girls in graceful saris, Trinidadian Chinese women in split skirts, Trinidadian men and women whose facial characteristics tell you they come from Java, Japan, England, the Punjab, and South America.

Look at the buildings throughout the city. The architecture is as varied as the people. A mosque crowds a colonial mansion, a Hindu temple gazes across the street at a building of Moorish design. Where do you start in a crazy quilt city like this; and what do you look for? The best way to see Port of Spain is just to walk through its streets. It doesn't make much difference where you start. Frederick Street, which runs from Queen's Wharf (next to King's Wharf) to the Queen's Park Savannah a dozen long blocks away, is the main drag, and you'll wind up there eventually. The corner of *Frederick Street* and *Independence Square* is Port of Spain's Times Square. Most of the shops are centered around this area, as are the downtown restaurants where you can have lunch.

Facing Frederick Street from the far side of Woodford Square is a

Woodford Square in downtown Port of Spain

building known as the *Red House*—it's the home of the island's government offices. The Anglican *Cathedral* faces onto the Square. Frederick Street, like so many of the main streets of the Caribbean, is built with its sidewalks shaded by an overhanging loggia. These balconies, in turn, are often terraces of second floor restaurants and bars from which you can watch the world go by while you down a cool drink.

At the end of Frederick Street is the 170-acre *Queen's Park Savannah* with its race track and cricket pitches, and its little cemetery where the family, whose sugar plantation it once was, lie resting. On the far side of the Savannah is the *President's residence,* and next to its grounds the fascinating *Botanical Gardens.* The Savannah has always been the "best" part of town, and all around it are houses built by the British civil servants and merchants who ran the island for so many years.

Outside Port of Spain. While the capital is the island's focal point, there is a great deal more to see in Trinidad. A trip to the beach at *Maracas Bay* is doubly rewarding because "getting there is half the fun." The *Skyline Highway* winds up through the hills behind Port of Spain, across the saddle between the mountains, then down again to the northern coast. On a clear day you can get a dramatic glimpse of the Venezuelan mainland to the west and Tobago far to the northeast. The conformation of the reefs around Maracas makes for a Hawaii-like surf. Big rollers break far out and then run in for a hundred yards or more before they crash on the shore. It's just about perfect for surfing. On week ends the beach is busy (but never crowded) with the people of Port of Spain, all happily splashing in the surf.

Interesting as a geological phenomenon—but really less interesting to look at—is Trinidad's famous *Pitch Lake* at La Brea some 60 miles to the south along the west coast. It's 114 acres of grey, natural asphalt that looks something like the hide of an elephant. But it smells worse. This enormous deposit has been supplying a great part of the world's asphalt for centuries. Raleigh stopped here to caulk his ships' bottoms after destroying the Spanish capital at what is now St. Joseph—and it's likely that you've done most of your driving on Trinidadian asphalt.

It has been estimated that Pitch Lake is more than 280 feet deep, and it appears that it's not going to be exhausted for years to come. South of Pitch Lake are the oil fields—unusual for a Caribbean island—but not so unusual for Trinidad, when you realize that it is, in fact, a part of the South American continent. It broke off from Venezuela some milleniums ago, and apparently took its oil reserves with it.

Closer to Port of Spain and prettier by a long shot is the *Caroni Bird Sanctuary* about two-thirds of the way out toward Piarco Airport. You can arrange to go on a conducted tour of the place. Here you will see ibis, parrots of many kinds and other exotic birds in wonderful profusion. It's well worth the trip.

TOBAGO (Toe-BAY-go)

While Trinidad busies itself with asphalt and oil, frantic carnivals and being modern, Tobago, 21 miles to the northeast, is perfectly content to loll in the sun, dressed out in forest green, cooled by a breeze and the sea which laps at the sandy edges of her skirt.

The island is of respectable size, a little narrower than some (7½ miles), somewhat longer than many (26 miles). There is a good harbor and the requisite line of volcanic mountains sheltering rich fields.

Tobago has mementos of the years of wealth and conquest—ruined forts and rows of cannons pointing seaward—but time and tropic scenery have robbed them of their fierceness. Like those who live here and those who only visit, they have been happy to succumb to Tobago's sun-warmed charm.

General Information

How To Get There: *By Air:* BWIA has service from Trinidad.
By Sea: Government ferries connect Scarborough and Port of Spain—an overnight trip apt to be rocky.

How To Get Around: Buses are convenient, modern, and very inexpensive. Taxis, also inexpensive, can be hired by the hour. Bicycles and cars are for rent at reasonable rates.

Language: English.

Sports: There is horse racing in February–March and October–November at Shirvan Park, Scarborough. Tobagonians raise and breed horses. *Swimming,* of course, from some superb beaches—at Store Bay, Man o' War Bay, Crown Point, Pigeon Point, and Milford Bay. A number of hotels have their own beaches. Skin diving and snorkeling are both good. There is *spear-fishing* from the reefs and deep sea trolling; boats, tackle and guides can be hired. (Inquire at your hotel.) *Sail boats* and small power craft are available too. Tobago is criss-crossed with good trails and bridle paths, and there are *horses* for hire. *Tennis courts* are located at the Crown Point Hotel.

Night Life: If you like it noisy, flamboyant, and organized you will have to go back to Trinidad. Some hotels have dances on Saturday evenings, sometimes you'll catch the *bong* of a steel band, and *La Tropicale Night Club* offers floor shows three times a week.

Medical Facilities: There is a hospital at Scarborough.

One of Tobago's beautiful white sandy beaches

Additional Information: Trinidad & Tobago Tourist Board, 400 Madison Ave., Suite 711, New York, NY 10017 (212-838-7750; 800-232-0082); Trinidad & Tobago Tourist and Trade Center, 200 SE First St., Suite 702, Miami, FL 33131 (305-374-2056; 800-521-0250); Trinidad & Tobago Tourist Board, 122–24 Frederick St., Port of Spain, Trinidad, W.I. (809-623-7405).

Where to Stay

***Arnos Vale,* near Plymouth, 24 rooms, private beach, pool, cottages. ****Mt. Irvine Bay Hotel,* 110 rooms, pool. ****Turtle Beach Hotel,* Scarborough, 53 rooms on beach, pool. ***Crown Reef Hotel,* 113 rooms, on the beach at Store Bay. ***Treasure Isle Condotel,* 26 rooms, Bacolet Bay. ****Crown Point on the Bay,* 109 rooms, tennis, water sports. ***Sandy Point Beach Club,* 44 rooms, near Buccoo Reef. ***Coral Reef,* 14 rooms, on Milford Road. ***Della Mira Guest House.* Scarborough, 14 rooms. ***Blue Waters,* Speyside, 11 rooms, beachfront guesthouse with cottages. ***Cocrico Inn,* Plymouth, 33 rooms, game room boutique, pool, dining room and bar. **Glenco Guesthouse,* Scarborough, 7 rooms. **Golden Thistle Hotel,* Crown Point, 14 rooms, swimming pool. ***Kariwak Village,* Crown Point, 18 rooms, excellent cuisine and entertainment. ***Man-O-War Cottages,* Charlotteville, 10 rooms, on the beach. ***Store Bay Holiday Resort,* Crown Point, 14 rooms. **Sunstar Haven Guesthouse,* Scarborough, 14 rooms, swimming pool. ***Tropikist Beach Hotel,* Crown Point. NOTE: The Tourist Board has information about bungalows which may be rented by visitors.

Food is varied and good at the hotels. You can go as Creole as you like.

Where to Shop

The selection is definitely smaller than on Trinidad, but the best buys are about the same—British imports, native goods, and rum.

The best place for native handicrafts is in the recently-opened Scarborough Mall. *Stecher's of Trinidad* has a gift and jewelry shop. *Sports and Games, Ltd.,* and *James A. Scott & Co.* have fishing, snorkeling, and other sports supplies.

What to See

Tobago isn't busy—and it doesn't demand that you be up and doing either. Sightseeing for the most part is about as arduous as lying on a warm beach.

Scarborough, the capital, is a pleasant little city of broad, bright streets and lanes which bravely mount the steep hillside where the houses stay put more by faith than by the old laws of gravity. At the top is retired and ruined *Fort King George* whose guns once protected Scarborough and the harbor. The waterfront market is the busiest place you'll see on Tobago, and there's no great hurry there.

Appearances to the contrary, however, the island's 55,000 people do produce a quantity of cocoa, copra, coconuts, and limes. You'll see some of the island's beautiful plantations if you drive along the southeast coast to *Speyside* and then across the island to *Charlotteville* on the splendid harbor and beach of *Man o' War Bay.*

Another pleasant drive will take you to *Plymouth,* almost directly across the island from Scarborough. *Fort James,* the island's oldest, is worth a visit, as much for its fine view of Great Courland Bay as for its historical associations. Not far away is the excellent beach at *Store Bay* and one of Tobago's show spots, the sea gardens of *Buccoo Reef.* You'll find plenty of guides and boats to take you out to the reef where, equipped with face mask and snorkel (supplied by the guide), you can wade or float through the "garden" of brilliant plants, tropical fish, and coral.

From Store Bay you can walk or climb—it's not a Sunday morning stroll—to "Robinson Crusoe's Cave." There's little point in arguing the authenticity of Tobago's claim to being Crusoe's island. Defoe, who wrote the novel, never visited *any* island, and his book was based on the reports of a South Pacific castaway. Tobagonians will point out, however, that Tobago matches Defoe's descriptions, and that he does mention Trinidad. It's wise and easy to agree that if you're going to be marooned, Tobago is the best place to do it, and then go on to see one of the cases in point, *Bird of Paradise Island.*

Actually, the map name of the island is Little Tobago. It's just off the northeast coast, and you can get there by boat (with guide) from Speyside. At the beginning of the century, Sir William Ingram brought several pairs of Birds of Paradise from New Guinea and made a haven for them on his island, Little Tobago. The birds flourished, and Ingram's heirs gave the island to the government on the condition that it be maintained as a bird sanctuary. Many other sorts of tropical birds inhabit Little Tobago today. You'll have to tread softly if you want to see the Birds of Paradise, for they're shy despite their gilded plumage. Perhaps they've learned, as you will if you linger long enough on Tobago, that sun and solitude are the island's greatest gifts.

THE NETHERLANDS ANTILLES

Clean, prosperous, and Dutch as an old wooden shoe, the Netherlands Antilles are the Cinderella islands of the Caribbean—spotless, sparkling pockets of old world charm in an oil-rich new world.

Having come out of the Caribbean struggle for power and position with next to nothing—five and a half tiny specks of land so arid or inconsequential that none of the other powers cared to keep fighting for them —the Dutch (being Dutch) have turned their ugly-duckling holdings into some of the most attractive, valuable, and prosperous possessions in the whole area.

Geographically, the Netherlands Antilles are split into two clusters of islands. The smaller group lies in the Lesser Antilles between the Virgin Islands and Guadeloupe and includes Saba and St. Eustatius, and half of a third called Sint Maarten by the Dutch and St. Martin by the French owners of the other half. Sint Maarten has developed tourist accommodations, but the other two are still for the adventurous who want sun and sky and hills, and are willing to sacrifice luxury for such strange sights as Saba's capital, The Bottom, on the side of an extinct volcano.

More than 500 miles southwest, just off the northern coast of Venezuela, is the so-called ABC group—Aruba, Bonaire, and Curaçao. Politically, Aruba is no longer part of the Netherlands Antilles, having gained its independence in 1986.

CURACAO (Koor-ah-saoh)

Only 38 miles off the coast of Venezuela, Curaçao was no gem when the Dutch first settled there. It was a dry, uninteresting piece of real estate 37 miles long and seven to two and a half miles wide with only its cactus, its harbor, and its location to recommend it. But good fortune favors those who work for it, and it has greatly favored the industrious Dutch.

Curaçao's prosperity depends on the huge refinery in the inner harbor. Except when the trade winds shift, it is only noticed as a glow in the night sky. Usually the trades keep the heat to an average 81 degrees Fahrenheit, cool the nights for comfortable sleeping, and, more importantly, sweep the smell of petroleum away from the city and out to the sea.

Amerigo Vespucci and Alonso de Ojeda discovered Curaçao's land-locked harbor in 1499, and the Spanish colony lasted until 1634, and then the Spanish were thrown out by the powerful Dutch West India Company. Nine years later Peter Stuyvesant arrived to rule the island, which had already become a flourishing depot for the slave trade.

The Dutch held on to Curaçao, but with the end of the slave trade the island lapsed into poverty until the discovery of oil in nearby Venezuela in 1916 and the building of refinery facilities by a subsidiary of Royal Dutch Shell. Since then, however, the island has drawn people from all over the world—Dutch, Spanish, Portuguese, Chinese, East Indians. Under their present autonomy, the 163,000 inhabitants have mingled, flourished, devised their own language, Papiamento, and given the island the most cosmopolitan air in the Caribbean.

General Information

How To Get There: By Air: American, Eastern, and ALM fly from New York and Miami. Aero-Postal, Avianca, BWIA, Dominicana, KLM, Linea, Surinam, Venz, and VIASA also serve Curaçao.

By Sea: Most Caribbean cruise ships stop at Curaçao. Costa Lines has year round cruises and the Royal Caribbean sails regularly from N.Y. Cruise ships also sail from Miami, New Orleans and West Coast ports.

How To Get Around: Willemstad is small and best toured on foot. Most of the sights and shops are in the Punda section east of the channel. The "other side" is called the Otrabanda.

Good modern buses go everywhere on the island from terminals at De Ruyterkade on the Punda side and Brion Square in the Otrabanda. Taxis are available almost anywhere in town, and the drivers carry official tariff charts. You can rent drive-yourself cars from $25–$35 daily or $125–$150 weekly. Sightseeing tours are conducted by Taber Tours (76-637) and Daltino Tours (625621).

Language: Dutch is the official language. Spanish, English, and one of the world's comparatively new languages, Papiamento, are all widely spoken. Papiamento has evolved over the last 300 years as the people borrowed and battered each other's words. So far, it has no official grammar or pronunciation, and if you can't remember a Papiamento word, you simply use one from your own language.

Festivals: The Netherlands Antilles all have big holidays on New Year's Day, which is celebrated with parades, fireworks, dancing and music in the streets; during Carnival week just before Lent; on the Queen's Birthday, April 30, when the festivities include parades and fireworks; on Sint Nicholaas Eve, December 5, when Sinterklaas parades in the streets, and on December 15, when Autonomy Day is celebrated.

Sports: *Swimming.* Best beaches are at Knip Bay, Santa Barbara, Blauw Beach, and Santa Cruz. You can also swim at West Point and Jan Thiel.

You may have to wear shoes on some of the beaches because of the coral bottom.

Fishing. Spanish Water and Knip Bay are best for either a hook and line or the spear.

Boating: Motor- and sailboats can be rented at the Piscadera Watersports Center at the Curacao Caribbean Marina. Charter boats can be rented through Curacao Sightseeing, Bon Bini Tours, Daltino Tours, Taber Tours, or your hotel.

Golf: The Shell Golf Club has a nine-hole course and you can play if you are registered at a hotel.

Tennis: Curacao Caribbean, Las Palmas Hotel, Holiday Beach, Princess Beach, and Coral Cliff have courts. Inquire at your hotel.

Night Life: The *Hotel Curacao Plaza* offers a floor show and nightly dancing in its unique disco. The *Holiday Beach* also has nightly floor shows and dancing. The *Kini-Kini Bar* is a favorite spa and the *Gambling Casino* is a handsome playground. The *Avila Beach* presents folk dancing programs and you can dance to local combos at the *Princess Beach* and *Trupial Inn.* The *Curacao Caribbean* has a cocktail lounge, night club, and casino. The *Festival of Arts Theater* presents concerts, ballet, opera, and plays.

Additional Information: *Curacao Tourist Board,* 400 Madison Ave., New York, NY 10017 (212-751-8266); *Curacao Tourist Bureau,* Plaza Piar, Willemstad (613397 or 611967).

Where to Stay

HOTELS: ***Avila Beach Hotel,* on ocean just outside Willemstad, 45 rooms, air conditioned, old Dutch decor, MAP. **Coral Cliff Hotel,* 35 rooms, panoramic vistas, 35 minutes from Willemstad, MAP. ***Curacao Caribbean Hotel & Casino,* 200 rooms with balconies, air conditioned, salt-water swimming area, casino, shops, MAP. ***Curacao Plaza,* 250 rooms, air conditioned, view of harbor entrance, MAP. ***Holiday Beach & Casino,* 200 rooms with balconies, swimming pool, MAP. ***Las Palmas Hotel & Vacation Village,* Piscadera Bay, 100 rooms & 94 cottages, lighted tennis courts, MAP. ***Princess Beach Hotel & Casino,* 140 rooms, saltwater pool, water sports, MAP. **Trupial Inn,* 72 rooms, recently renovated and refurbished, MAP. *Hotel Holland,* 20 rooms. * Park Hotel,* 81 rooms.

The Dutch are the trenchermen of the tropics, and on Curaçao the Dutch cuisine is made heavier and hotter with Indonesian complements. But

A striking aerial view of Willemstad with its many bridges

the island cooking is also cosmopolitan. Many restaurants serve fine French, Italian, Chinese, and American foods.

RESTAURANTS: ***Curaçao Plaza, American, Dutch and international food. ***La Iströelle, French dining on a pier in Caracas Bay, just outside Willemstad. ***Princess Beach, good food and ocean view. ***Fort Nassau, international with excellent desserts, panoramic view of the harbor. ** Rijsttafel Restaurant Indonesia, Indonesian food overlooking colorful Santa Ana Bay. **Avila Beach, dine under parasols. Chunking, Lam Yuen, Rose Garden and The Great Wall have excellent Chinese food; San Marco has a good Italian kitchen; and Zuikertuintje offers late snacks on the patio of the landhouse. All are very moderately priced.

Where to Shop

The Dutch ABC islands are semi-free ports—and the shops in Willemstad are stocked with luxury goods from all over the world.

Best buys are Dutch products—gin, Curaçao liqueur made from the essence of the island's bitter orange, and famous Delft pottery. But shops, from the smallest to the most elegant, also feature bargains in French perfumes, British sweaters, woolens, German and Japanese photographic equipment, and Swiss watches.

DEPARTMENT STORES: M. Dialdas & Sons carries more than a thousand different items in an air conditioned emporium in the middle of the shopping district. Cosmopolitan, four floors of fine European clothes, shoes and leather goods. Julius L. Penha & Sons, Inc., at Queen Emma Bridge, sells dolls, sweaters, fine French perfumes, leather goods, and men's wear.

IMPORTED HANDICRAFTS: La Estrella features Dutch costumes and wooden shoes, gifts from Israel, fabrics from Mexico and Guatemala. Palais Oriental is well stocked with Chinese curios, linens, and handbags. Oriental Art Palace features fine oriental goods from India and China.

JEWELRY, GIFTS: El Continental carries gifts, jewelry, silver, watches from all over the world. The Beehive for fine jewelry and gems. Master goldsmiths in the store can execute your own designs. Spritzer and Fuhrmann Ltd. is the Tiffany of the Caribbean, five air-conditioned floors are stocked with everything from dollar gifts to rare pearls and oversized diamonds. Aquarius, a boutique with the newest French look and labels.

PERFUMES, CHINA, LINENS: Vendôme for an extensive array of both linens and perfumes. The New Amsterdam Store carries linen, lace, gloves, jade, and Japanese cultured pearls. The Yellow House (La Casa Amarilla) is replete with the French perfumes, cosmetics, and liquor that have pleased shoppers since before the turn of the century.

What to See

The sights that make Curaçao worth coming a long way to visit are in **Willemstad,** the most lovely and unusual capital of the Caribbean. The city is busy, bright, and easy to walk around in.

First of things to see and focal point of the city is the famous Queen Emma, the bridge that floats on pontoons and connects the Punda and Otrabanda sections of the city. In 1974 the Queen Juliana Bridge, with a four lane highway, was opened at St. Anna Bay. Thus, Queen Emma was closed to vehicular traffic and became a giant floating sidewalk for pedestrians.

Within a short walking distance are two of Willemstad's most beautiful buildings, the old *Dutch Reformed Church* built in 1763, with an English cannonball of 1804 in its wall; and the *Mikve Israel Synagogue*, the oldest in the New World. Built in 1732, it is still used by descendants of Jews who settled here more than 300 years ago. Also, *Temple Emanuel*, a restored landmark building, now houses a new multimedia show, "Bon Bini Curaçao" (Welcome to Curaçao) which introduces visitors to the cultures of the island's many peoples.

Near St. Anna Channel are old *Fort Amsterdam,* the *Government House,* the *Legislative Council Building,* and the *Court House* with an impressive statute of Queen Wilhelmina.

When you cross to Otrabanda, you will come face to face with the statue of Curaçao's best known hero, Pedro Luis Brion, to whom the nation of Colombia, in the words of Simón Bolívar, "owes half her blessings." Further out in Otrabanda is the *Curaçao Museum,* well worth visiting as an example of early Dutch architecture. The museum has many rare relics of the early days, and its gardens are handsomely planted with the island's flora.

For a sweeping view of the harbor and city, you should visit *Ararat Hill* just beyond the edge of town on the Punda side. On the summit is an exquisite white statue of the Madonna. Not far away are the new *Venezuelan Consulate* and the handsome *American Consulate,* which the Dutch called Roosevelt House.

A tour of the island will take you to *Caracas Bay* and old *Fort Beekenburg;* the bunkering station; *Spanish Water Bay* and *Boca Beach.* If you want to see how the colonials lived in the old days, there is a magnificently restored 18-century plantation house at *Brievengat.* With a guide, or one of the Curaçao Sightseeing, Bon Bini, Daltino Tours, or Taber Tours to the far reaches of the island, you can visit *Boca Tabla,* where the sea has carved a huge grotto. At the end of the island is *West Point* with a bay, old slave quarters, a fishing village, a nice beach, and restaurant. A new Seaquarium with 75 open-air aquariums, a shipwreck, and a coral reef opened in 1986. The 12.5-mile Curaçao Underwater Park is one of the largest dive operations in the Caribbean.

ARUBA

Until this century, Aruba actually was a desert isle. So dry, so rocky, and so unfruitful was it that even the Dutch were unable to make it produce more than a meager crop of cactus-like aloes. Then came the oil. Within a generation this barren little strip of land, 50 miles west of Curaçao and half that distance from the coast of South America, has become one of the most prosperous islands of the Caribbean.

In 1929, the Lago Oil and Transport Company, a subsidiary of

The stately colonial Government Palace in Fort Amsterdam

Standard Oil of New Jersey, built a huge refinery at the southeast tip of the island. After operating for nearly 50 years, the refinery recently closed but, in the meantime, Aruba had had time to develop its pristine beaches and other tourist resources.

In 1986, Aruba attained separate status within the Kingdom of the Netherlands and no longer belongs to the political entity known as the Netherlands Antilles. The change enables Aruba to maintain direct ties with the Netherlands.

General Information

How To Get There: *By Air:* American and ALM (Antillean Airlines) provide service from New York, and Eastern and ALM provide service from Miami.
By Sea: Many cruise ships now call at Aruba including Royal Caribbean, Home Lines, and Sitmar.

How To Get Around: The tidy town of Oranjestad is easily explored on foot. Buses and taxis are readily available. Roads are good, and you can make arrangements for taxis or for rental cars in Oranjestad or at your hotel.

Language: The official language is Dutch, but, as in Curaçao, most of the people speak Papiamento, English, and Spanish.

Festivals: Aruba's Carnival during the week before Lent is the greatest.

Sports: *Swimming.* Aruba's beaches provide excellent swimming with no need to worry about a chill. Palm Beach has a safe, gradual slope and quiet water, but surf bathers should avoid beaches on the northern coast.
Fishing. The fish are there. You can try your luck with bonita, tuna, and dolphin fish. Fishing boats are available for rental at all hotels.
Boating: Windsurfing, Sunfish and Minifish sailing is available. Sailing trips on catamarans, trimarans and ketches are available from De Pal Tours (24400 or 24545).
Water Skiing: The smooth seas of the south and west coast are perfect for both beginners and experienced skiers.
Tennis: Most leading hotels have tennis courts and tennis instructors and many private clubs welcome visitors.

Night Life: You can gamble at the

casinos, dance or watch the nightly floor show at the Aruba Caribbean, Sheraton, or Holiday Inn on Palm Beach. Dancing at Talk of the Town, which overlooks the Caribbean, midway between the airport and Oranjestad. All hotels have live entertainment nightly.

Medical Facilities: Horacio Oduber Hospital has excellent medical and dental facilities.

Additional Information: Aruba Tourist Bureau, 1270 Avenue of the Americas, Suite 2212, New York, NY 10020 (212-246-3030); Aruba Tourist Bureau, 2-A Schuttestraat, Oranjestad, Aruba (23777).

Where to Stay
***Americana Aruba,* 206 rooms, beachfront location. ***Aruba Beach Club,* 131 rooms, Spanish-style decor, MAP. *****Aruba Concorde Hotel & Casino,* 500 rooms, recently refurbished, MAP. *****Aruba Palm Beach Hotel & Casino,* 200 rooms, MAP. ***Atlantis Apartahotels & Villas,* 80 rooms, motel-style 10 minutes from town. ***Best Western/Manchebo Beach,* 71 rooms, congenial beachfront setting, MAP. ***Best Western /Talk of the Town,* 64 rooms, sophisticated European style, MAP. ***Bushiri Beach Hotel,* 150 rooms, casual low-rise with pool, MAP. *****Divi Divi Beach Hotel,* 200 rooms, elegant, MAP. *****Dutch Village,* 28 rooms, luxury apartments, pool and beach, MAP. *****Holiday Inn Aruba,* 387 rooms, complete resort facilities, MAP. ***Playa Linda Beach Resort,* 60 suites, elegant, recently expanded. *****Tamarijn Beach Hotel,* 204 rooms, swimming pool and tennis courts, MAP.

What to See

Where to Eat
****Bali,* on a houseboat moored in the harbor at Oranjestad, East Indian decor, Javanese rijsttafel ("rice table") cuisine. ****De Old Molen,* Palm Beach, Dutch windmill with specialties like wild boar, venison, and snipe. ****La Serre,* Aruba Concorde Hotel, Continental cuisine. ****Red Parrot,* Divi Divi Beach Hotel, outdoor terrace with French and American cuisine. ****El Gaucho,* Argentinean specialties. ***Papagayo,* overlooking schooner harbor, seafood, steaks, Italian specialties. **Astoria,* Sint Nicolaas, Chinese. **Hong Kong,* Oranjestad, Chinese.

Where to Shop
Aruba specialties include attractively priced crystal, china, table linens, perfumes, as well as jewelry and designer fashions.

Shops in Oranjestad include the *Aruba Trading Company, Ecco, Bon Bini Bazaar,* and the *New Amsterdam* featuring perfume, fashions, and Delftware. Other shops include *Spritzer & Fuhrman* locations on Nassaustraat and in the shopping arcades of major hotels such as Holiday Inn, the Concorde, and the Divi-Divi. *I. Kan* carries jewelry and baubles from the Netherlands. The new *Boulevard Shopping Center* has many small boutiques carrying mementos, jewelry, fashions, children's items, and sporting goods. The *Aruba Peasant Shop* has lovely dolls and goods from Spain, Hong Kong, and 40 different nations. *Aruba Trading* and *I. Kan* carry attractively priced equipment from Germany and Japan. The shop at Beatrix Airport carries gifts of all kinds and Dutch ceramics.

Shank's mare and a leisurely hour or so are all you need to see the bright delights of Oranjestad with its blend of Dutch colonial, Spanish, and modern architecture, and the spacious parks and meandering streets that give the city the air of a well-scrubbed suburb.

Off the deep-water harbor is Paarden Baai, where the fishing boats and native schooners tie up to display glistening fish and fruits, vegetables, and goods from Venezuela and the islands. A short walk along Lloyd Smith Boulevard, past the colorful Bali restaurant houseboat, will bring you to the government buildings and then to the magnificent *Statue of Queen Wilhelmina* in the city's newest park. Sculptured in white marble by Arnoldo Lualdi, the statue was unveiled by Queen Juliana and Prince Bernhard when they visited the island in 1955.

The beauty spot of Aruba, and the one the people are proudest of, is Palm Beach, a short ride out along the coast from the city. It is a magnificent curving stretch of brilliant white sand shaded by a row of tall coconut palms. Free of the coral and nettles that mar some Caribbean beaches, it is one of the finest and most attractive swimming spots in the West Indies.

The interior of the island is called the *cunucu.* Except for its brightly painted houses, many with "hex" signs, and strange horizontal *divi-divi* trees, you could be in Arizona.

Giant stone monoliths, put there by some unknown force, are strewn about parts of the interior, particularly at Ayo. Many of them are smoothly scooped out on the side away from the wind, and nobody has yet explained their origin or how these huge boulders were piled so precariously on one another.

Also worth seeing is the rugged windward coast, with its coves, grottoes and natural bridges that have been carved by the sea.

BONAIRE

About 50 miles east of Curaçao, Bonaire is the least visited of the ABC islands—a haven for bird watchers, underwater buffs, fishermen, and escapists.

The sun is brilliant and tanning. The water is a scuba diver's and snorkler's dream—so clear that you can see coral 65 to 120 feet down in reef-protected Lac Bay. Bonaire is ranked among the top three diving spots in the Caribbean by diving experts. And you can walk for miles along dazzling white beaches that you share only with the birds.

About two-thirds the size of Curaçao and larger than Aruba, Bonaire is as dry as its neighbors, flat in the south and hilly in the north. Island life centers around Kralendijk, a doll-house town of 2,000 people, with neat, vari-colored Dutch colonial houses, a church, and an old fort.

Most famous of Bonaire's attractions are the enormous flocks of flamingoes that breed along the salt pans at the southern end of the island. The algae which flourishes in the salt pans gives them their extraordinary rosy-pink color, the most brilliant in the world. The whole island is a kind of natural sanctuary visited by an immense variety of brilliant tropical birds—bright green parrots, parakeets, big-billed pelicans, snipes, terns, herons, and even hummingbirds. For lovers of marine life, the island's coral reefs are thick with the rainbow-hued fish of the tropics, and from September to February the deeper waters abound in bonito, sailfish, tuna, wahoo, and kingfish.

General Information

How To Get There: *By Air:* American Airlines and Eastern from New York to Curaçao with connecting service via ALM. Eastern and ALM have service from Miami with connections in Curaçao or Aruba.

How To Get Around: The roads are good, and you can arrange for cars with or without drivers through the hotel or the Tourist Bureau.

Language: Dutch, Spanish, native Papiamento, and English.

Festivals: The same as Curaçao and Aruba.

Sports: Besides bird watching, the sports are confined to the water variety. Swimming and scuba diving are excellent. Favored beaches are at Lac Bay, Bachelor's Beach and at the hotels. Sailboats and outboards are available at the Flamingo Beach and Hotel Bonaire. Fishing boats are also available for deep-sea fishing.

Medical Facilities: The island has a hospital, and you can reach Curaçao within an hour in an emergency.

Additional Information: The Bonaire Tourist Bureau, 275 Seventh Ave., New York, NY 10001-6708 (212-242-0000); Bonaire Tourist Bureau, Kaya Grandi, Kralendijk, Bonaire (8322/8649).

Where to Stay

HOTELS: ****Bonaire Beach Hotel & Casino,* 145 rooms, MAP. ****Flamingo Beach Hotel & Casino,* 150 rooms, dive center overlooking Calabras Reef, MAP. ****Habitat,* 19 rooms, oceanfront villas, MAP. ** *Hotel Rochaline,* central Kralendijk, 35 rooms, air conditioned. **Sorobon Beach Resort,* 16 rooms, clothes optional resort on Lac Bay.

Where to Shop

Bonaire's two main shops sell goods at the usual low, almost freeport prices. *Spritzer & Fuhrmann* and *Littmann Jewelers* carry all kinds of goods, Delft ware, jewelry and features souvenirs made from large conch shells. Skindiving gear is available at *Habitat, Bonaire Scuba Center, Dive Bonaire, Carib Inn,* and *Sand Dollar.*

What to See

If you're coming to Bonaire chiefly for the flamingoes, you will want to be there in the spring. The birds are usually nesting and tending their young in March, April, or May, and at that time you will be able to see the chicks downed in their first plumage, an appropriate baby blue.

Take your binoculars. The birds are flighty, and the government doesn't like them to be disturbed.

The salt pans here were once worked by slaves, and you will see the shockingly primitive stone huts, bare shelters little more than waist high, where they were forced to live. Nearby are the three 30-foot

Bonaire's graceful flamingoes on their nests in the salt lake

obelisks, one red, one white, and one blue, that guided early salt ships to their moorings.

Kralendijk is so small that it is difficult to miss its sights. But while you are strolling be sure to stop for the lovely stained-glass windows of *St. Bernard's Church* and see *Fort Oranje* with its cannon from the days of Napoleon. Perhaps the liveliest and best sight in town is the *Fish Market* on the water front. It's worth the effort of getting up early just to see the boats in the little harbor, to watch the fishermen handling the amazing variety of strange and brilliantly colored fish, to experience the little splash of excitement with which the town begins its sleepy day. A trip through the hilly northern part of Bonaire provides a stunning view of Bonaire's inland lake where flamingoes feed and of the sea crashing against spectacular coral rock formations.

SINT MAARTEN (Sint MAHR-ten)

St. Maarten is the delight of the Dutch Windwards, a little half-island that only in the last few years has begun to develop its superb beaches, its quiet bays and wooded hills.

Northernmost of the Netherlands Antilles and some 150 miles southeast of Puerto Rico, St. Maarten is a lush little island of only 37 square miles, rimmed with bays and beaches and pampered with a year-round average temperature of 80°. The island, however, isn't all Dutch. The northern part, called Saint Martin, is French, and the Dutch control only the 17 square miles across the southern end. For more than 300 years the two countries have shared this little spot of land with unruffled amiability. The 20,000 French citizens and the 20,000 Dutch—both groups largely black or mulatto—travel back and forth from Dutch Philipsburg in the south to the French capital of Marigot in the north.

The favorite local legend is the tale of how the island was divided. In 1648 when both the Dutch and the French claimed sovereignty, the dispute was settled by a walking contest. A Frenchman and a Dutchman started from the same spot and walked around the island in opposite directions until they met. The fast-walking Frenchman claimed the larger northern part, but the Dutchman was luckier. His half included the salt pans near Philipsburg that for a century made Sint Maarten the most valuable property of the Netherlands West India Company.

General Information

How To Get There: *By air:* American and Pan Am fly from the Northeast; American from Dallas and the Southeast; Eastern and Pan Am from Miami. Prinair, ALM, LIAT, WIN-AIR, and BWIA provide inter-island service.

By sea: Major cruise lines serve St. Maarten; the Explorer Starship and the Vacationer serve Saba. The Alisur Amarillo provides weekly ferry service from St. Maarten to Saba. The Windjammer ship Polynesia II, based in St. Maarten, calls at St. Eustatius.

How To Get Around: You can walk around Philipsburg with ease. There are plenty of taxi cabs, all carrying the letter "H" on their windshields, and you can rent drive-yourself cars.

Language: Officially Dutch, but everyone speaks English.

Sports: *Swimming.* Excellent beaches all over the island, as well as right at Philipsburg.
Fishing and Sailing. Game fish, particularly tarpon and bonefish, are plentiful. You can rent sailboats with crews.
Water Skiing and Spear Fishing. Equipment for rent in Philipsburg.

Additional Information: St. Maarten Tourist Bureau, 275 Seventh Avenue, New York, NY 10001-6708 (212-989-0000).

Where to Stay

HOTELS: (Some hotels levy a 5 per cent service charge; other ask a 10 per cent energy surcharge.) ***Bel Air Beach Hotel,* Little Bay Beach, 72 rooms. ***Caravanserai,* on beach at Maho Bay, 63 rooms. **Cupecoy Beach Resort,* Cupecoy Bay, 251 rooms, three swimming pools, casino. ***Dawn Beach,* at Dawn Beach Oyster Pond, 155 rooms, MAP. ***Great Bay Beach Hotel,* edge of Philipsburg, 225 rooms, air conditioned, MAP. ** Holland House Beach Hotel,* on Great Bay Beach in Philipsburg, 43 rooms. ***Little Bay Beach Hotel,* on beach near Philipsburg, 120 rooms, MAP. ***Maho Beach Hotel & Casino,* 247 rooms, tennis courts, air conditioned, MAP. ***Mary's Fancy Plantation,* 11 rooms, on grounds of 18th century sugar plantation, MAP. ***Mullet Bay Resort,* 597 rooms, 18-hole championships golf course, fresh- and saltwater pools, 16 tennis courts, MAP. **Pasanggrahan Royal Guesthouse,* 21 rooms, formerly a royal residence on Great Bay Beach in Philipsburg. ***Pelican Resort Club,* Simpson Bay, 168 rooms, tennis courts, swimming pools, two beaches. **Seaview Hotel,* 45 rooms, air conditioned, water sports available. ***St. Maarten Beach Club & Casino,* Philipsburg beachfront, 75 rooms. ***Summit Hotel,* Simpson Bay Bluff, 61 rooms, close to beach, MAP. ***The Oyster Pond Yacht Club,* 20 rooms, marina, boating, fishing, and water sports. **Horny Toad Guesthouse,* Simpson Bay Beach, 8 units. **Golden Tulip Apartment Hotel,* 15 units at edge of Philipsburg, near marinas. **Mary's Boon,* 12 units on beach at Simpson Bay. **St. Maarten Sea Palace,* Great Bay Beach in Philipsburg, 58 rooms.

***Beachside Villas,* 24 rooms. *
Caribbean, 34 rooms.

Where to Shop

Both Dutch and French capitals are free ports and, although their shops are not lavishly stocked for tourists, they carry goods at bargain prices. On Front Street, *Penha* and *Yellow House* carry perfume, cameras, and cashmere items. *Around the Bend, the Shipwreck Shop,* and *Impressions* in the Promenade Arcade have authentic handcrafts. *Little Switzerland* carries luxury items such as fine watches and Delft ware. *Spritzer and Fuhrmann* has shops at Mullet Bay and the airport.

What to See

Philipsburg, neat and attractive, lies on a sand bar with the Great Salt Bay behind it and Great Bay and the Caribbean Sea in front. Two streets run the length of the town, Front Street and Back Street. On either side of Philipsburg and the bays are mountains, and on the peninsula that juts out between Great and Little Bays you will find the remains of Fort Amsterdam, the 17th-century fort that guarded the harbor and the rich salt trade. To the west are Simpson Bay Lagoon, a huge, lovely land-locked bay, a small village devoted to fishing, the airport, and a deluxe resort complex.

Historic post office in Philipsburg, St. Maarten—one of the island's only "monuments."

SINT EUSTATIUS (SINT U-STAY-she-us) and SABA

Sint Eustatius, once one of the busiest ports of the Caribbean, today exists in quiet ruins, its harbor unused, and its 1,600 people mostly engaged in growing yams and sweet potatoes for Curaçao. Yet less than 200 years ago, scores and even hundreds of ships crowded the harbor of "Statia," its plantations produced sugar, tobacco, and other crops, and 8,000 people lived there in comparative prosperity.

Fort Oranje, which guards the harbor, fired the first salute by any foreign power to the flag of the United States of America on November 16, 1776. The flag was flying from the U.S. brig *Andrew Doria.* Statia became the main trans-shipment point for food, arms, and clothing for the blockaded American colonies.

Four years after Fort Oranje's salute, the British took their revenge. Admiral Rodney and his fleet attacked and captured the harbor. The Admiral kept the Dutch flag flying to bring in unsuspecting cargo ships, and his prize goods brought $3,000,000 at auction. Before he left, he looted and burned so well that Sint Eustatius has never recovered.

The main sights on the island today are the recently restored fort, the *Dutch Reformed Church* and the old *Jewish Synagogue.* Along the narrow beach you will find the remains of the big warehouses that were once such an important part of Statia's economy. At Fort Oranje are the government houses and the police station.

You can explore the whole island within a day or two and still have time to sample the native grog, a heritage of the good old days, called "Miss Blyden." Shopping is limited to some lace, a few baskets and wooden articles made by the Golden Rock Artisans foundation.

Saba (population: 1,000) is an extinct volcano that sticks straight up out of the sea to a peak 2,900 feet high. The views are striking and orchids grow in profusion. There are no real beaches.

On this jagged 5 square miles of volcanic rock the indomitable Dutch have been able to perform their usual tidy miracle since they settled there in the mid-1600's. On the only level bit of ground on the island, 800 feet above the sea, they built the island's main village, *The Bottom.*

A new pier was built in 1973 which allows boats and tenders to land. One road connects the pier, four villages and the airport.

Tours of the island by taxi cost $25 per car load from either the airport or pier. The energetic can hike 3,000 feet up Mt. Scenery or hike down Ladder Bay. There are several small gift shops where "Saba lace" is sold, as well as hand-drawn threadwork on aprons, linens, etc. Also available is Saba spice, a sweet but potent liqueur. The Saba Artisan's Foundation prints fabrics and makes clothes which are sold in the gallery/museum, *Captain's Quarters.* And there is a new scuba diving operation, Saba Scuba Safari.

One of the cannon which fired the fateful first salute to the U.S. Navy

General Information

How To Get There: Windward Islands Airways has daily flights from St. Martin to Saba; small twin-engine planes can be chartered in St. Thomas or St. Martin to Saba. Service to St. Eustatius is via LIAT through Antigua and St. Kitts.

Language: Officially Dutch but everyone speaks English.

Additional Information: *Saba & St. Eustatius Tourist Bureau,* 275 Seventh Ave., New York, NY 10001-6708 (989-0000).

Where to Stay

St. Eustatius: ***The Old Gin House,* Lower Town, 20 rooms, swimming pool. **Golden Era,* in Lower Town on Oranje Bay beach, 20 rooms. **La Maison Sur La Plage,* Zeelandia, 10 rooms, on two-mile stretch of beach.

Saba: ***Captain's Quarters,* Windwardside, 10 rooms, excellent views, MAP. **Cranston's Antique Inn,* 6 rooms, former government guesthouse in capital city. **Scout's Place,* Windwardside, 5 rooms, open-air dining terrace and bar.

JAMAICA

Sun and sand, luxurious hotels, and mile-high mountains on a tropical island where buccaneers once ruled in "the wickedest city on earth."

Jamaica, an island of mountains and rivers that was once notorious for its cutthroat buccaneers and its slave-worked plantations, is today famous for its enormous bright beaches, its luxurious hotels, and the international set that has made its north shore the Riviera of the Caribbean.

Almost 600 miles southeast of Miami and ninety miles south of Cuba, Jamaica packs 2.1 million people and a range of towering mountains into a space 150 by 50 miles, an area a bit smaller than Connecticut. The highest peak, Blue Mountain, reaches 7,402 feet into the sky. The island's beaches are brilliant, its water blue and warm, and along the hundred rivers that flow down from the mountains it has all of the lush green vegetation of the tropics. Spread for miles along the Gold Coast on the northern shore are the seaside resorts of Port Antonio, Ocho Rios, and the elegant Montego Bay. On the south side is Kingston, the capital, and up in the hills is Mandeville, the old British "summer capital," with its cool breezes, English atmosphere, lovely countryside, and tennis, golf, and tea. At the westernmost point of Jamaica is Negril, where no building can be taller than a palm tree.

The people of Jamaica are mostly black, and their motto, "Out of many, one people," is evident. There are large groups of African, Chinese, Spanish, British and Indian people who have become integrated over the years. The language and customs of Britain, so long the ruler, are still obvious, especially in the government operation. But there are many customs and arts that are uniquely Jamaican—especially dance and music—and others that have African and Latin influence. The *reggae* music popularized by Bob Marley is unique to Jamaica, and the National Dance Theater Company tours internationally.

Columbus touched the northern shore of Jamaica in May, 1494, on the second of his Caribbean rambles, and ten years later spent one of his most unhappy years in St. Ann's Bay. For twelve months the Admiral fought disease, mutiny, and the dangers of native attacks before he was at last able to sail back to Spain. His son, Diego, and those who followed him, colonized the island in the usual Spanish fashion, wiping out the Arawak Indians. Only a few were left when Admiral William Penn, father of Pennsylvania's founder, took the island for England in 1655. But within a few years, Port Royal, on the tip of the peninsula that encloses Kingston harbor, had become a capital for privateers, buccaneers, and pirates. Rum soaked and wicked, the town for years glittered with riches taken by sword and seamanship.

From here young Henry Morgan led his unruly pirates on forays to plunder treasure cities all along the Spanish Main. But even piratical thieves fall out, and Morgan was at length shipped to England to answer charges of piracy. He was convicted, but the fabulous wealth he had stolen not only saved him from the gallows, but earned him a knighthood. He returned to Jamaica as Sir Henry Morgan, Lieutenant Governor, subdued the remaining pirates, and years later died in his bed. Shortly after his death an earthquake dropped two-thirds of wicked Port Royal into the sea and killed some 2,000 people.

After the pirates had been wiped out, the island turned from buccaneering to sugar cane and slavery. In 1807 the slave trade was forbidden, and in 1838, emancipation was declared. By then Jamaica's population was overwhelmingly black.

With the end of slave labor, the fabulously rich plantations began a slow decline that was hastened in the 19th century by the development of the beet sugar industry and increasing competition from other islands. In this century bauxite, tourism, sugar, and rum have helped to keep the island's books in balance.

In 1958 the Federation of the West Indies was established with Jamaica as a member, however, by referendum in 1961 Jamaica seceded from the Federation. On August 2, 1962, after more than 300 years of British rule, the island became independent, a dominion in the British Commonwealth, and a member of the United Nations.

General Information

How To Get There: *By Air:* Air Jamaica has flights from Atlanta, Baltimore, Los Angeles, Miami, New York, Philadelphia, Tampa, and Toronto; American flies daily out of New York and Boston; Challenge International Air flies twice daily from Miami, and Eastern flies from Atlanta and Miami. Air Canada has weekly service from Halifax, Montreal, Toronto, and Winnipeg. Air Jamaica has also recently begun weekly Concorde service from New York December to March.

By Sea: Kingston, Montego Bay, Ocho Rios and Port Antonio are regular stops for more than a dozen cruise ships.

How To Get Around: Transfer service in mini-buses offers good transportation to hotels. Most taxis are called "contract carriages" and have predetermined rates to most destinations.

You can rent cars from Hertz, Avis and many local rental agencies. Once you learn to keep to the left, driving is no problem. The roads are good, but narrow in some parts.

You can cross the island between the major cities by transfer (mini-bus) companies, train, or Trans-Jamaica, the local airline which has several flights daily and which provides a breathtaking view of the countryside.

Travel agencies operate numerous tours of the cities, resorts, or the island that last a few hours, a day, a week, or longer.

Language: English with a rather fascinating accent.

Sports: You can watch cricket or polo on Saturday and Sunday in most large towns. International soccer meets are often held in Kingston. A well-attended race track is located outside Kingston, at Caymanas Park.

Swimming. Many hotels have pools, and the resort establishments not on the shore provide transportation to the beaches—which some aficionados claim are the world's best. Skin diving is popular along the north coast.

Boating. Boats can be obtained through the hotels, many of which have their own docks.

Water Skiing. Centers are Negril, Montego Bay and Ocho Rios. Facilities at most hotels.

Rafting. One of Jamaica's most famous trips for visitors is the seven-mile run down the Rio Grande at Port Antonio. Rafting is also good on the Martha Brae in Falmouth.

Fishing. Marinas and deep sea fishing boats can be chartered for a half or full day in Montego Bay, Ocho Rios and Port Antonio. Make arrangements through your hotel.

Golf. Clubs at Kingston, Ocho Rios, Montego Bay and Runaway Bay have

18-hole championship courses. Mandeville has a 9-hole course.

Tennis. Most of the large hotels have courts.

Horseback Riding. You can arrange through your hotel to rent hacks at such places as the Good Hope Hotel in Falmouth, the Circle V Ranch in Montego Bay, Hedonism II, Trelawny Beach Club and Couples in Ocho Rios. Also near Ocho Rios is the new Chukka Cove Farm, a full-scale equestrian center offering instruction in riding, jumping, dressage, and polo.

Night Life: There are many nightclubs. In KINGSTON, the "in" places are *Jonkanoo Lounge, Toppsi's, Exodus, Mingles, Epiphany,* and others. *MONTEGO BAY* has *Sir Winston's Reggae Night Club, Fantasy, Disco Inferno,* the *Hellfire Club,* and *Witch's Hideaway.* In *OCHO RIOS* it's *The Ruins* and *Silks;* In *NEGRIL, Rick's Cafe* and *Hedonism II.*

Medical Facilities: Doctors are good. The island has private and public hospitals.

Additional Information: The Jamaica Tourist Board, 866 Second Avenue, New York, NY 10017 (212-688-7650); 36 S. Wabash Ave., Suite 1210, Chicago, IL 60603 (312-346-1546); 1320 S. Dixie Highway, Suite 1100, Coral Gables, FL 33146 (305-665-0557); 3440 Wilshire Blvd. Suite 1207, Los Angeles, CA 90010 (213-384-1123); 21 Dominica Drive, New Kingston, Jamaica (809-922-0131).

Where to Stay

Kingston and St. Andrew: *** *Jamaica Pegasus,* 350 rooms, view, good food and service. ****Wyndham New Kingston,* 385 rooms, pool, resort shops. ****Hotel Oceana,* 250 rooms, recently renovated. ****Terra Nova,* 34 rooms, pool, fine cuisine. ***Courtleigh Hotel,* 42 rooms, pool, night-

Fort Charles at Port Royal, once commanded by Horatio Nelson

club. **Morgan's Harbour,** in Port Royal, 20 rooms, private beach, fishing. **Hotel Four Seasons,** 35 rooms, restaurant. *Medallion Hall, 8 rooms, good value. **Mayfair Hotel, 30 rooms, pool. *Indies Hotel, 14 rooms, restaurant. **Sutton Place, 53 rooms, pool.

Ocho Rios Area: ****Plantation Inn, 79 rooms, cottages, beach, water sports. ****Sans Souci Hotel, 78 rooms, water sports, horseback riding. ****Jamaica Inn, 45 rooms, private beach, sailing. ***Couples, 152 rooms, all-inclusive resort for couples only. ***Eden II, 263 rooms, another everything-included resort, nightclub, golf, water sports. ***Shaw Park Beach Hotel, 118 rooms, beach, scuba, horseback riding. ***Americana Hotel, 325 rooms, water sports, nightclub. ***Turtle Beach Towers, 123 rooms, jet skiing and other water sports. **Arawak Inn, 15 rooms, pool, nightclub. **Casa Maria, 16 rooms, pool, private beach. *Hibiscus Lodge, 19 rooms, on the sea, excellent value. *Pineapple Penthouse, 23 rooms, pool.

Montego Bay: ****Wyndham Rose Hall, 480 rooms, on the site of famous plantation, golf, beach, water sports. ****Half Moon Club, 197 rooms, cottages, beach, water sports, horseback riding. ***Sandals Royal Caribbean, 167 rooms, pool, beach, nightclub, water sports. ***Sandals, 225 rooms, all-inclusive, cottages, squash courts, scuba. ***Jack Tar Village-Montego Beach, 128 rooms, also all-inclusive, sailing, resort shops. ***Richmond Hill Inn, 18 rooms, fishing, sailing, pool. ***Casa Montego Hotel, 129 rooms, all-inclusive, jet skiing and other water sports. ***Doctor's Cave Beach Hotel, 77 rooms, pool, nightclub. **Winged Victory, 16 rooms, pool, restaurant, intimate. ***Holiday Inn, 516 rooms, pool, beach, horseback riding. ***Seawind Beach Resort, 428 rooms, beach, cottages, sailing. **Carlyle Beach, 52 rooms, fishing, horseback riding. **Wexford Court, 36 rooms, pool. *La Mirage, 15 rooms, pool. *Chalet Caribe, 28 rooms, beach.

Port Antonio and East Coast: ****Trident Villas and Hotel, 27 units. Beach, pool, the only "white-glove" service on the island. ***Frenchman's

Cove, 26 rooms, private beach, all the facilities. **Bonnie View,* 23 rooms, on a hill, panoramic view, pool.

Mandeville: ***Mandeville Hotel,* 66 rooms. ***Hotel Pontio,* 12 rooms, *** The Astra,* 18 rooms.

Falmouth: ****Trelawny Beach Club,* 350 rooms, on beach, sports, tennis, pool.

Negril: ****Hedonism II,* 280 rooms, all-inclusive. ****T-Water Beach Hotel,* 61 rooms, fishing, private beach. ****Charela Inn,* 26 rooms, beach. ***Sundowner,* 25 rooms, private beach. ***Negril Beach Club,* 85 rooms, horseback riding, water sports. ***The Villas Negril,* 60 rooms, pool resort shops. ***Foote Prints On The Sand,* 12 rooms, fishing, beach.

Runaway Bay: ****Jamaica, Jamaica* 152 rooms, all-inclusive, golf, beach. ****Club Caribbean,* 110 rooms, cottages, water sports. ***Ambiance Jamaica,* 73 rooms, pool, fishing. ** Caribbean Isle,* 14 rooms, pool.

Where to Eat

Most resorts run on the American plan. The highly-spiced native dishes may tempt your taste. Most famous is Jamaica Pepperpot, a dish of kalalu (kale), diced pork and spices, and curried goat. Salt fish cooked with ackee (a fruit) is the national dish. The festive dish is stuffed roast suckling pig.

RESTAURANTS: **Kingston:** The rooftop restaurants at ***Jamaican Pegasus* and ***Wyndham New Kingston* offer Jamaican cuisine and breathtaking views of the city. Other places to try Jamaican fare are the ***Courtleigh* and ***Devon House,* also known for its fine ice cream. ***Terra Nova* serves international cuisine; the ***Four Seasons* features German food. Try the ** Indies Pub* for fish and chips.

Montego Bay: *Sign Great House,* the place to try native curried goat and pumpkin soup. ***Town House,* built as a private home, and ***Richmond Hill Inn* serve continental cuisine in an elegant atmosphere. **Ocho Rios:** *** The Ruins* is famous for its 40-foot waterfall as well as its international cuisine. ***Moxons,* in nearby Boscobel, requires reservations. For Jamaican food try ***The Almond Tree* or *** Honeycomb Village.*

Port Antonio: The ****Trident* has white glove service and continental cuisine. Try ***DeMontvin* for Jamaican fare. The proprietor's wife was Errol Flynn's cook.

Where to Shop

Jamaica has free port prices for visitors. The "in bond" shops display merchandise at prices often one-third or one-half lower than you would pay in the United States, and deliver your purchases to customs when you leave. Kingston, Port Antonio, Ocho Rios, and Montego Bay all have "in bond" shops.

Imports from Great Britain are best buys: silver, china, sweaters, woolens, leather goods, Liberty silks and cottons, glassware. The shops also feature watches, clocks, cameras, perfumes, liquors, and brandies at low prices.

Well-tailored, attractive sport clothes are available at many local fashion shops. Shops in Kingston and on the north coast carry excellent native straw goods, wood crafts, and jewelry. Look for the *Things Jamaican* label and shops.

Other local buys are the rum, which is world famous, Blue Mountain coffee, and Tia Maria coffee liqueur.

DEPARTMENT AND FREE PORT STORES: **Kingston:** *Devon House* shopping arcade, *Hemisphere,* at the Wyndham New Kingston, *Carousel,* 24 King St, *India House,* 60 King St. *Swiss Stores,* Harbour and The Mall.

Montego Bay: *Casa de Oro,* Holiday Village, *Holiday Duty Free Gift Shop,* Holiday Inn, *Chulani,* City Centre.

Ocho Rios: *Pineapple Place* shopping arcade, *Coconut Grove, Mingles* at Couples Hotel.

JEWELERS: **Kingston:** *Bijoux, Italcraft, Blue Mountain Gems.*

Montego Bay: *Blue Mountain Gems.*

Ocho Rios: *Americana Shops.*

LEATHER GOODS: **Montego Bay:** *Issa's,* Montego Inn.

PHOTOGRAPHIC EQUIPMENT: **Montego Bay:** *Chulani, La Belle Creole.*

Ocho Rios: *Geeta, Soni's* and *Mohans.*

SOUVENIR AND GIFT SHOPS: **Kingston:** *Victoria Crafts Market,* foot of King Street. **Montego Bay:** *Montego Bay Crafts Market, Shops of Sasha,* Tryall. **Ocho Rios:** Satnam Unique Gifts.

WINES AND SPIRITS: Every hotel in the major towns has an in-bond shop for liquor.

WOMEN'S READY-TO-WEAR: *Boutiques* are numerous at hotels and in Montego Bay and Ocho Rios.

What to See

Kingston Area. Kingston, the capital, is the largest English-speaking city south of Miami, with 700,000 people. It isn't quaint, and you're not likely to go around snapping pictures of the official buildings or the civic center or the Parade Grounds. But it does have sights and sections that you will want to see. The *Crafts Market* with its vast and jumbled collection of straw products and other native handicrafts is one of the most fascinating. It is located at Pier One, handy to cruise ships. *Devon House,* on Hope Road, a restored 19th century planter's mansion, and the cluster of shops around it offer antiques, accurate reproductions, and contemporary crafts, all in a picturesque and historic setting. You will also want to visit the *Institute of Jamaica* on East Street. It is the home of the *National Library,* one of the world's largest collections of books and other material devoted to the West Indies.

The 19th-century home where singer *Bob Marley* lived with his wife and children has been turned into a museum of reggae memorabilia, at 56 Hope Road.

One of the most remarkable sights of the island is the *Hope Gardens,* only five or six miles from the center of the city. They are imaginatively planned, and in their 200 acres are hundreds of varieties of tropical trees, plants, and flowers.

Most interesting of the historical spots is old *Port Royal,* now a fishing village, which you can reach by car or by launch which crosses the busy harbor to the tip of the peninsula. Part of the crumbling ruins are visible, much more lies underwater where it was dumped by the earthquake of 1692. Enough of *Fort Charles* survived for you to see the ramparts that Horatio Nelson walked. Nearby is *St. Peter's Church,* built in 1725 at the insistence of a grateful survivor of the earthquake. Morgan's Harbour Beach Club is the center for yachting, water-skiing, fishing, and for underwater explorers who want to take a look at the sections of Port Royal now beneath the sea.

Ten miles west of Kingston is **Spanish Town,** the island's original capital, founded by Diego Columbus as Villa de la Vega. Today it has the unmistakable stamp of Britain. Government Square, with its statue of Admiral Rodney, has been restored, and around the square are the old *House of Assembly* and *Old King's House,* the residence of the early governors. Not far from the square is the oldest Anglican Church in the West Indies, the *Cathedral of St. James.*

Mandeville. The old British "summer capital," another 40 miles west, is further up in the hills. Mandeville is a bit of old England trans- planted, with its village green, the parish church whose steeple might be poking up over rolling English hills, and the Georgian houses. Although it is Jamaica's fifth-largest city, Mandeville has long been a mecca for birdwatchers and naturalists. A favorite spot is *Marshall's Pen,* a former coffee farm and now a working plantation with several hundred acres of woods for hiking and a wildlife sanctuary. Its 200 year-old Great House, filled with antiques, is open for special tours. The *Pioneer Chocolate* and *High Mountain Coffee* plants also offer tours.

Negril. This resort, a gathering place for flower children in the 1960's, still has a reputation as a free-and-easy vacation spot. Many beaches are "clothing optional." There are several hotels, but no highrises to spoil the skyline.

Montego Bay. Known as Mo' Bay, Jamaica's most popular resort area stretches over a distance of 50 miles along the northwest coast. It is a historic city, but today its sights are the beaches and blue water, the luxurious hotels, clubs, and shops that serve the tourists. Montego Bay has long been one of the most fashionable resorts in the Western Hemisphere. It has its own international airport, literally dozens of the most elegant and luxurious hotels, unbeatable facilities for sailing, tennis, golf, fishing, and of course, beaches strung out along the bay. On the coast just east of Montego Bay is Rose Hall, the completely restored "Great House" of one of Jamaica's famous old plantations. It is said to be haunted by its former mistress, who reputedly murdered three husbands before being killed by her slaves.

About 15 miles inland from the gold coast of Montego Bay is the wild, primitive land of the Maroons, the **Cockpit Country.** Here during the 18th century escaped slaves fought the British so viciously from the hills that their country became known as the "Land of Look Behind" where no stranger's life was safe. Today hundreds of Maroons still live here in tribal semi-independence.

Ocho Rios. Newer but on its way to overtaking Montego Bay is Ocho Rios with its fabulous resort hotels on the north central coast. It covers an area of more than 40 miles from Discovery Bay in the west through the town of Ocho Rios to Port Maria on the east. Discovery Bay was Columbus' landing point in 1494, and St. Ann's Bay is the site of the first Spanish colony, Sevilla Nueva.

If you drive across the island from Spanish Town, you will come down to Ocho Rios through *Fern Gully,* three extraordinary miles of an old river bed between steep cliffs where only dappled sunlight penetrates through the mahogany trees and ferns. A few miles east of St. Ann's Bay is *Dunn's River Falls,* where a mountain stream tumbles down natural rock steps at the edge of the Caribbean.

Thirteen miles east of Ocho Rios is **Oracabessa,** which lured two of Britain's best-known writers to Jamaica. Noel Coward and Ian Fleming both had homes on the water. Coward later moved to a mountain retreat called *Firefly,* which is now a museum. Fleming's home, *Goldeneye,* is privately owned but can be rented.

Port Antonio. Jamaica's chief banana port with its deep harbor and handsome landlocked bay on the northeast coast is also enjoying something of a boom. Movie idol Errol Flynn is credited with popularizing rafting down the Rio Grande. His widow, Patrice Wymore Flynn, still gives tours of their *Priestman's River Plantation.*

The rafting trip down the *Rio Grande* starts at the village of *Berrydale* near Port Antonio. A licensed boatman poles the bamboo raft between jungle-covered banks, and you can make stops to swim in quiet pools or picnic in the shade. You shoot through the rapids and end the trip about three hours later at a fishing village on *St. Margaret's Bay.*

Port Antonio, where a steady breeze keeps sails almost always evenly filled in the harbor, is famed for its sailing. Blue water is unusually close in, and only half a mile offshore deep sea fishermen take marlin, tuna, kingfish, dolphin. Seven miles east of the port is colorful *Blue Lagoon,* with its dark blue water and white sand against a backdrop of green jungle—the vivid colors of a vivid island.

CAYMAN ISLANDS

The three Cayman islands, which together form a British dependency 500 miles south of Miami, are far enough off the tourist track to be vacation bargains for escapists who never get enough scuba diving, fishing, or lazing in the sun.

The islands are peopled mainly by descendants of Cromwell's soldiers, and a mixture of other whites who arrived with the buccaneers or as marooned sailors. The men were formerly merchant mariners or fishermen, many of them making a living by hunting turtles in Nicaraguan waters, but today the island's chief industry is tourism.

Grand Cayman, with its *Seven Mile Beach* lined with dozens of hotels, resorts, and condominiums, is the largest of the three and the tourist hub. Cayman Brac is known for a spectacular 140-foot bluff topped by a lighthouse, and easily accessible caves. Little Cayman, relatively unchanged since it was discovered by Columbus, is the place to play Robinson Crusoe.

Diving reigns supreme in the Caymans, with remarkable coral reefs and wrecks just offshore, but landlubbers can visit *The Turtle Farm,* the only such breeding ground in the world, or *Hell Post Office,* where you can mail a postcard to friends saying you've been to Hell and back. Both are on Grand Cayman.

General Information

How To Get There: *By Air:* Cayman Airlines flies twice-daily from Miami and twice-weekly from Houston. Air Jamaica comes in from Kingston three times a week.

How To Get Around: Bicycles and motor scooters are popular, but you can rent cars.

Language: English.

Special Events: Million Dollar Month, an international fishing tournament held every June, is one of the island's biggest draws. Pirates' Week in October has parades and harbor activities.

Sports: Diving has become such a big business that it has spawned operations specializing in deep water dives for the experienced, beginners' courses, programs for the handicapped, and underwater photography. Introductory resort courses cost about $75 and a full certification course with equipment about $300.

Snorkeling is also popular, and the deep sea fishing season runs from November to June.

Golf: An 18-hole course designed by Jack Nicklaus is at Britannia Beach Resort.

Night Life: Most hotels have live music. *Tiffany's* and the *Cayman Islander Night Club* are two hot spots.

Medical Facilities: George Town, capital of Grand Cayman, has a hospital.

Additional Information: Cayman Islands Department of Tourism, 420 Lexington Ave., New York, NY 10017 (212-682-5582); 250 Catalonia Ave., Coral Gables, FL 33134 (305-444-6551); P.O. Box 67 George Town, Grand Cayman, B.W.I. (809-949-7999).

Where to Stay and Where to Eat

HOTELS: ***Hyatt Regency Grand Cayman,* 240 rooms, beach, pool, scuba, golf. ***Treasure Island Resort,* 290 rooms, beach, scuba, nightclub. ***Holiday Inn Grand Cayman,* 215 rooms, beach, sailing, water sports, nightclub. **Buccaneer's Inn,* 36 rooms, on beach, popular. **Brac Reef Beach Resort,* 40 rooms, on Cayman Brac. **Cayman Islander Hotel,* new, 69 rooms, with entertainment complex. *Ambassador's Inn Diving Resort,* near beach. *Island House Resort,* 11 rooms, pool, scuba. On Little Cayman there's ***Sam McCoy's Diving and Fishing Lodge,* which includes meals, diving and transportation charges in its package.

George Town has a growing freeport shopping street and several restaurants. *Grand Old House, Cayman Arms, Lobster Pot, Pedro Castle Inn, Almond Tree* and the *Cracked Conch* offer everything from local seafood and turtle steaks to elegant, fullcourse meals.

SAN ANDRES
(San On-DRACE)

Located on the "far side" of the Caribbean, 950 miles south of Miami and 150 miles east of Nicaragua, is the verdant Colombian island, San Andrés. Eight miles long and almost two miles wide, this tiny tropical paradise has a population of 18,000, one town, one harbor, and what is thought to be the greatest pirate treasure buried anywhere in the Western Hemisphere.

The island has belonged to the English, Dutch, Spanish, and French respectively since the early 1600's. In 1822, Simon Bolivar claimed San Andrés for Colombia. Coconut plantations flourished and in 1953, Colombia established a free port to encourage tourism and began to develop the island's potential as a resort area.

The islanders make their living by fishing, tending the plantations, and processing coconut lard.

San Andrés' most exciting claim is that there is a 35 million dollar treasure buried somewhere in her soil. In 1671, Captain Henry Morgan, the British buccaneer, plundered Old Panama, and it is believed, hid 35 million dollars in gold and silver on the island while en route to Jamaica. Countless other treasures lie sunken off her shores today.

Just off the island is *Johnny Cay,* ten acres of white sand beach ideal for an afternoon swim or picnic. Nearby *Haines Cay,* with its natural seaquarium, is an open invitation for underwater exploring. You can hire fishermen to take you to the cays and guides are available and eager to show you through the beautiful coral gardens and reefs.

With only one cinema and two small casinos, San Andrés has little

to offer in the way of nightlife. It's an ideal spot for those who really want to rest on their vacation.

How To Get There: *By Air:* Avianca flies twice weekly from Miami.

General Information

Entry Requirements: A valid passport, a round trip ticket and a visa or tourist card are required of U.S. and Canadian citizens.

How To Get Around: Taxis and tour guides are available for hire but there is no public transportation.

Sports: Bahia Marina resort rents boats for waterskiing, fishing, scuba diving and snorkeling at rates from $5 an hour to $110 a day.

Night Life: The Royal Abacoa and the Hotel Eldorado have casinos. Stakes are low but betting is spirited.

Medical Facilities: There is a hospital staffed by Colombian doctors and nurses.

Additional Information: The Colombian Tourist Board, 140 East 57 Street, New York, NY 10022 (212-688-0151). The average double room rate for a San Andrés hotel is about $65 a day. Most of the hotels are on the European Plan. Hotels are modern.

Where to Stay

HOTELS: **Abacoa Hotel,* 38 rooms. ***Aquarium Hotel,* 67 rooms deluxe. **Hotel Capri,* 84 rooms, near town. ***Grand Hotel International,* 124 rooms, three blocks from beach. ****Hotel El Dorado,* 61 rooms, ocean-front. **Royal Abacoa Inn,* 74 rooms, air-conditioned. **Natania,* 33 rooms, air-conditioning, suites available. **Casablanca,* 32 rooms, 12 cottages, air-conditioned, pool. **Hotel Mediterraneo,* 36 rooms, restaurant.

Where to Eat

Try *Bahia, La Bruja,* and *El Oasis* for seafood and *La Fonda Antiquana* and *Los Recuerdos* for mainland Colombian fare.

What to See

San Andrés is a free port. China, perfumes, imported fabrics, cameras, and liquor are the best buys.

INDEX

Abaco, 37, 41
Admiral's House, 100
Aguada, 64
Aguadilla, 64
Airplanes, 22–24. *See also* each island
American Consulate (Willemstad), 133
American Embassy (Port-au-Prince), 50
Andros, 37–38, 41
Anegada, 80, 82
Anguilla, 9, 87
Animal Flower Cave, 119
Antigua, 9, 98–101
Ararat Hill, 133
Arawaks, 14, 15, 80
Aruba, 9, 133–136

Bahamas, 8, 13–14, 33–42
Barbados, 9, 10, 31, 114–119
Barbuda, 101
Bass Terra (Guadeloupe), 88–92
Basseterre (St. Kitts), 84–85
Bath House, 86
Bathsheba, 119
Bequia, 110
Beretta Center, 76
Berry Islands, 38, 41
Berrydale, 150
Bimini, 38, 42
Bird of Paradise Island, 128
Blackbeard, 41, 80
Bligh, William, 11, 109
Block House, 100
Blue Lagoon, 150
Blue Mountain, 143
Bluebeard's Castle Tower, 77
Boca Tabla, 133
Bois, Chevalier de, 67
Bonaire, 9, 136–138
Botanical Gardens, Kingstown, 109
Port of Spain, 125

Boutillier, 51
Bridgetown, 118–119
Brievengat, 133
British, the. *See* England and the English; specific islands and groups
Buccaneers, 15–16
Buccoo Reef, 128

Cabo Rojo, 65
Cabras Island, 62
Caneel Bay Plantation, 78
Cap Haitien, 43, 48, 51–52
Caracas Bay, 133
Careenage (Barbados), 118
Caribbean National Forest, 63
Caribs, 14, 15. *See also* each island
Carolina, 63
Caroni Bird Sanctuary, 126
Carriacou, 110
Cars, 32
Casa Blanca, 61
Castries, 106–107
Catano, 64
Cayman Brac, 151
Cayman Islands, 151–152
Charlestown, 85, 86–87
Charlotte Amalie, 72ff., 76–77
Charlotteville, 128
Christiansted, 67ff., 71–72
Christophe, Henri, 44, 51–52, 84–85
Churches and chapels, Capilla del Cristo (San Juan), 62
Dutch Reformed (Charlotte Amalie), 76
Dutch Reformed (St. Eustatius), 141

Churches *(contd.)*
Dutch Reformed (Willemstad), 133
Fig Tree (Nevis), 87
Frederick Evangelical Lutheran (Charlotte Amalie), 77
Holy Trinity (Port-au-Prince), 51
Methodist (Kingstown), 109
Nisky Moravian Mission (Charlotte Amalie), 76
Old Catholic (Port-au-Prince), 51
Our Lady of Guadalupe (Ponce), 65
Port of Spain Cathedral, 125
Porta Coeli (San German), 64–65
St. Bernard's (Kralendijk), 138
St. George's (Kingstown), 109
St. James (Spanish Town), 149
St. Mary's (Kingstown), 109
St. Michael's (Bridgetown), 118
St. Peter's (Port Royal), 149
St. Thomas (Sandy Point), 85
San José (San Juan), 61
San Juan Cathedral, 62
Citadelle Laferrière, 44, 52
Citizenship, proof of, 20
Clarence House, 100
Climate, 9–10, 19, 20–21
Clothing, 20–21
Cockpit Country, 149–150
Columbus, Christopher, 13–15, 64, 83, 89, 143–144

Coral Bay, 77ff.
Costs, 20
Cotton Ground, 87
Crafts Market
    (Kingston), 148
Crane, 119
Crusoe, Robinson, 11,
    128
Cruz Bay, 77ff.
Cuba, 8, 10, 18
Curaçao, 9, 129–133
Customs House
    (Christionsted), 71

Danish Consulate
    (Charlotte Amalie), 76
Danish Post Office, 71
Dead Man's Chest, 80
Denmark; Danish
    islands, 17, 18. See
    also Virgin Islands
Désirade, 88, 91
Dessalines, Jean
    Jacques, 17, 44
Devil's Bridge, 101
Discovery Bay, 150
Dominica, 9, 103–104
Dominican Convent, 61
Dominican Republic, 9
Don Q Rum Distillery,
    65
Drake, Francis, 16, 77
Drake's Seat, 77
Drink, 29
Dunn's River Falls, 150
Dutch islands and the
    Dutch, 17, 18, 31,
    129–142. See also
    each island
Duvalier, "Papa Doc"
    and Jean Claude, 44

Eleuthera, 33ff., 42
Elizabeth I, 15, 16
Emancipation Park, 76
England and the English
    (the British), 15–16,
    17, 18, 31, 103–113.
    See also Virgin
    Islands; specific
    islands

English Harbour, 100
Estate Whim, 72
Exposition Grounds
    (Port-au-Prince), 50
Exuma, 42

Fajardo, 63
Fern Gully, 50
Festivals. See Special
    events; specific islands
Fig Tree Drive, 100–101
Fontaine Lumineuse, 50
Food, 27–28. See also
    each island
Fort de France, 96
Forts,
    Amsterdam
    (Philipsburg), 140
    Beekenburg (Curaçao),
        133
    Brimstone Hill (St.
        Kitts), 84
    Canuelo, El (San
        Juan), 62
    Charles (Port Royal),
        149
    Charlotte (Nassau), 41
    Charlotte (St.
        Vincent), 109
    Christian (Charlotte
        Amalie), 76
    Christiansvaern
        (Christiansted), 71
    Citadelle Laferrière
        (Haiti), 44, 52
    Fincastle (Nassau), 41
    Fortaleza, La (San
        Juan), 61–62
    George (St. George's),
        113
    James (St. John's),
        100
    James (Tobago), 128
    King George
        (Scarborough), 128
    Little Fort (Roseau),
        104
    Montagu (Nassau),
        41
    Morro, El (San Juan),
        60

Forts (contd.)
    Old Danish
        (Frederiksted), 71
    Oranje (Bonaire), 138
    Oranje (St. Eustatius),
        141
    San Cristobal (San
        Juan), 61
    Vieux Fort (St. Lucia),
        107
France; the French, 17,
    18, 31, 88–97. See also
    each island
Frederiksted, 67ff., 71
Freeport, 39ff.
Furcy, 51

Gaguere Cockpit, 50
Gonaïves, 52
Gonave Island, 52
Gosier, 91
Gouyave, 113
Government House,
    Charlotte Amalie, 76
    Christiansted, 71
    Nassau, 41
    Plymouth, 102
    Port of Spain, 124–125
Grand Anse, 113
Grand Bahama, 37ff., 42
Grand Cayman, 151ff.
Grand Etang, 113
Grand Hotel (Charlotte
    Amalie), 76
Grande Terre, 88ff.
Grant's Town (Nassau), 41
Great Inagua. See
    Inagua
Greater Antilles, 8–9.
    See also Cuba;
    Hispaniola; Jamaica;
    Puerto Rico
Grenada, 9, 110–113
Grenadines, the, 9,
    109–110
Grenville, 113
Gros Islet, 106
Gros Piton, 106
Guadeloupe, 9, 31,
    88–92
Gustavia, 93

Haines Cay, 153
Haiti, 9, 10, 17, 18, 31,
    43–52
Half-Way Tree, 85
Hamilton, Alexander, 85
Harbor Police
    (Barbados), 118
Harbour Island, 42
Hawkins, John, 15–16
Hispaniola, 8–9, 14. *See
    also* Haiti
Hog Island, 41
Holetown, 114
Holidays, 31–32. *See
    also* each island
Holland. *See* Dutch
    islands and the Dutch
Hope Gardens, 148
Hotels, 26–27. *See also*
    each island
House of Assembly,
    Nassau, 40
    Spanish Town, 149
Houses, Great, 71–72,
    149
Hurricanes, 19

Île de la Tortue
    (Tortuga), 16, 52
Îles des Saintes, 88, 92
Inagua, 42
Ingram, Sir William, 128
Inoculations, 20
Institute of Jamaica, 148
Inter-American
    University, 65
Iron Market, 51–52
Isabela, 14, 64

Jacmel, 52
Jamaica, 8, 16, 31,
    143–150
Jérémie; 52
Johny Cay, 153
Josephine, Empress, 17,
    96
Jost Van Dyke, 80

Kenscoff, 51
King's House (Spanish
    Town), 149

Kingston, 144ff.,
    149–150
Kingstown, 109
Kralendijk, 136, 138

La Navidad (settlement),
    14
Lac Bay, 136
Language. *See* each
    island
Las Croabas (town), 63
Law Courts (Nassau), 40
Le Diamant (town), 97
Leeward Islands, 9. *See
    also* each island
Legislative Council and
    Assembly
    (Bridgetown), 118
Les Cayes (town), 52
Les Trois Islets (town),
    96
Lesser Antilles, 9. *See
    also* Barbados;
    Leeward Islands;
    Netherlands Antilles;
    Trinidad; Windward
    Islands
Levera, 113
Little Dix Bay, 80
Little Tobago, 128
Lodgings, 26–27. *See
    also* each island
Loiza, 63
Long Island, 38, 42
Lord, Sam, 119
Lualdi, Arnoldo, 136
Luquillo Beach, 63
Lutheran Parsonage
    (Charlotte Amalie),
    76

Magazines, 32
Magen's Bay, 77
Mail, 32
Man O' War Bay, 128
Mandeville, 143, 149
Mansions, 71–72, 149
Maracas Bay, 125
Marie Galante, 88, 93
Marigot, 138
Maroons, 149–150

Martinique, 9, 10, 31,
    88, 94–97
Mayagüez, 64
Medical facilities, 32.
    See also each island
Mesopotamia Valley,
    109
Milot, 51
Misery Mountain, 85
Money, 25–26
    costs, 20
Montego Bay, 143ff.,
    149–150
Montserrat, 101–102
Morgan, Sir Henry, 16,
    144, 153
Morne Diablotin, 104
Morne Fortune, 107
Morne des Sauteurs,
    111, 113
Morro, El, 60
Moule, Le (beach), 91
Mountains. *See* by name
Museums,
    Barbados, 119
    Casa del Libro (San
        Juan), 62
    Curaçao, 133
    Library and Museum
        (Nassau), 39
    National
        (Port-au-Prince), 51
    St. Croix, 71

Nassau, 33ff., 38–39
Nelson, Horatio, 85–86,
    87, 98, 100
Netherlands Antilles,
    129–142. *See also*
    Dutch islands and the
    Dutch
Nevis, 9, 85–87
Nevis Peak, 85
New Providence, 16
Newcastle, 85ff.
Newspapers, 32
Night life. *See* specific
    islands
Nisbet Estate, 87
Nisky Moravian Mission,
    76

Norman Island, 11, 80
North Point, 119

Ocho Rios, 143ff., 150
Old Road, 85
Old Town Square
    (Christiansted), 71
Oranjestad, 135–136
Out Islands, 14, 33,
    37–38, 41–42

Paarden Baai, 136
Palais National
    (Port-au-Prince), 51
Palm Beach (Aruba),
    136
Paradise Beach, 41
Parguera, 65
Parque de Bombas, 65
Pelée, Mt., 97
Pétion, Alexandre, 44
Pétionville, 48, 51
Petit Piton, 107
Philipsburg, 138, 139,
    140
Phosphorescent Bay, 65
Pigeon Point, 107
Pinney's Beach, 87
Pirates, 15–16. See also
    specific men
Pitch Lake, 120,
    125–126
Planning trip, 19–25
Plymouth (Montserrat),
    102
Plymouth (Tobago), 128
Point des Châteaux, 91
Point Saline, 112–113
Point Salines
    International Airport,
    112–113
Pointe-à-Pitre, 89, 91
Ponce, 65
Ponce de León, Juan,
    61
Port Antonio, 12ff., 150
Port de Paix, 52
Port-au-Prince, 46ff.,
    50–51
Port Royal, 16, 144,
    148–149

Port of Spain, 120ff.,
    124–125
Portsmouth, 104
Pottery Market, 118
Privateers, 15–16
Puerto Rico, 9, 18, 30,
    53–65

Quarters B, 76
Queen Emma Bridge,
    132–133
Queen's Park Savannah,
    125
Queen's Staircase, 41

Rawson Square (Nassau),
    40
Red Hook, 77
Red House, 124–125
Reservations, 20
Restaurants, 26–29. See
    also each island
Rio Grande (Jamaica),
    150
Rio Grande (Puerto
    Rico), 63
Rio Piedras, 63
Rivière Salée, 88
Rocher du Diamant, 97
Rockefeller, Lawrence,
    64, 77
Rodney, George, 141
Rose Hall, 149
Roseau, 103
Rum, 29. See also each
    island

Saba, 9, 141
St. Andrew, 145–146
St. Ann's Bay, 150
St. Barthélémy, 88, 93
St. Christopher, 9, 83–85
St. Claude, 92
St. Croix, 66, 67–68
St. Eustatius. See Sint
    Eustatius
St. François, 91
St. George's, 113
St. John, 66, 67, 77–80
St. John's, 100
St. Kitts, 9, 83–85

St. Lucia, 9, 105–107
St. Maarten. See Sint
    Maarten
St. Margaret's Bay, 150
St. Martin, 9, 88, 93–94,
    138–140
St. Pierre, 94, 97
St. Thomas, 66, 72–77
St. Vincent, 9, 107–109
Ste. Anne, 91
Ste. Anne's Beach, 97
Sam Lord's Castle, 119
San Andrés, 153–154
San Germán, 66–67
San Juan, 53ff., 60–63
San Juan Gate, 61
San Salvador, 13–14, 33,
    38, 42
Sandy Point, 85
Sans Souci, 44, 52
Santo Domingo, 17, 18
Sauteurs, 113
Savane de Pétrification,
    97
Scarborough, 128
Sea gardens, 41, 128
Senate, Barbados, 118
Ships, 21–22, 24–25. See
    also each island
Shopping, 11, 30–31. See
    also each island
Sint Eustatius, 129, 141,
    143
Sint Maarten, 9, 88,
    93–94, 138–140
Skyline Highway, 125
Slaves, 16–18
Soufrière, 107
Soufrière, Mt.
    (Guadeloupe), 92
Soufrière, Mt. (St.
    Vincent), 109
Spain, 13–18
Spanish Town, 149
Spanish Wells, 42
Special events, 31–32.
    See also each island
Speightstown, 119
Speyside, 128
Sports, 29–30. See also
    each island

Steeple Building, 71
Stevenson, Robert Louis, 11, 80
Store Bay, 128
Sugar, 16–17, 18
Synagogues, 77, 133, 141

Teach, Edward, 41, 77
Telegrams, 32
Telephones, 32
Terre de Haute, 92
The Bottom, 141
Theâtre de Verdure (Port-au-Prince), 50
Tipping, 26
Tobago, 9, 11, 126–128
Tortola, 80–82
Tortuga (Tortue Island), 16, 52
Toussaint L'Ouverture, François, 17, 43–44
Trafalgar Square (Bridgetown), 118

Travel, 21–25, 32. See also each island
Treasure Island, 11, 80
Trinidad, 9, 10, 120–126
Trois Rivières, 92

United States, 18. See also Virgin Islands
University of Puerto Rico, 64

Vaccinations, 20
Vega Baja, 64
Vegie, La, 107
Venezuelan Embassy (Willemstad), 133
Verchilds Mountain, 85
Vigie Beach, 107
Virgin Gorda, 80
Virgin Islands, 9, 30, 31, 66–82
Virgin Islands National Park, 77

Warner, Sir Thomas, 83, 85
Washington, George, 114, 115, 118
Weather. See Climate
West Indies Handicraft Shop, 118
West Point, 133
Wilhelmina, Queen, statue of, 136
Willemstad, 132–133
Windward Islands, 9, 103–113. See also Martinique
Woodford Square (Port of Spain), 124

Yunque, El (mountain), 54, 63

Zion Hill Village, 87